Evi   6973 056302

GREEK

A ROUGH GUIDE DICTIONARY PHRASEBOOK

Compiled by

LEXUS

Credits

Compiled by Lexus with Costas Panayotakis
Lexus Series Editor: Sally Davies
Rough Guides Phrase Book Editor: Jonathan Buckley
Rough Guides Series Editor: Mark Ellingham

First edition published in 1995 by Rough Guides Ltd,
62–70 Shorts Gardens, London WC2H 9AB.
Reprinted in 1996 and 1998.
Revised in 1999.

Distributed by the Penguin Group.

Penguin Books Ltd, 27 Wrights Lane, London W8 5TZ
Penguin Books USA Inc., 375 Hudson Street, New York 10014, USA
Penguin Books Australia Ltd, 487 Maroondah Highway,
PO Box 257, Ringwood, Victoria 3134, Australia
Penguin Books Canada Ltd, Alcorn Avenue,
Toronto, Ontario, Canada M4V 1E4
Penguin Books (NZ) Ltd, 182–190 Wairau Road,
Auckland 10, New Zealand

Typeset in Bembo and Helvetica to an original design by Henry Iles.
Printed in Spain by Graphy Cems.

British Library Cataloguing in Publication Data
A catalogue for this book is available from the British Library.

ISBN 1-85828-643-3

HELP US GET IT RIGHT

Lexus and Rough Guides have made great efforts to be accurate and
informative in this Rough Guide Greek phrasebook. However, if you feel
we have overlooked a useful word or phrase, or have any other
comments to make about the book, please let us know. All contributors
will be acknowledged and the best letters will be rewarded with a free
Rough Guide phrasebook of your choice. Please write to 'Greek
Phrasebook Update', at either Shorts Gardens (London) or Hudson Street
(New York) – for full addresses see above. Alternatively you can email us at
mail@roughguides.co.uk

Online information about Rough Guides can be found at our website
www.roughguides.com

CONTENTS

Introduction

The Rough Guide Greek dictionary phrasebook is a highly practical introduction to the contemporary language. Laid out in clear A-Z style, it uses key-word referencing to lead you straight to the words and phrases you want – so if you need to book a room, just look up 'room'. The Rough Guide gets straight to the point in every situation, in bars and shops, on trains and buses, and in hotels and banks.

The main part of the Rough Guide is a double dictionary: English-Greek then Greek-English. Before that, there's a section called Basics, which sets out the fundamental rules of the language, with plenty of practical examples. You'll also find here other essentials like numbers, dates, telling the time and basic phrases.

Forming the heart of the guide, the English-Greek section gives easy-to-use transliterations of the Greek words wherever pronunciation might be a problem, and to get you involved quickly in two-way communication, the Rough Guide includes dialogues featuring typical responses on key topics – such as renting a car and asking directions. Feature boxes fill you in on cultural pitfalls as well as the simple mechanics of how to make a phone call, what to do in an emergency, where to change money, and more. Throughout this section, cross-references enable you to pinpoint key facts and phrases, while asterisked words indicate where further information can be found in The Basics.

In the Greek-English dictionary, we've given not just the phrases you're likely to hear (starting with a selection of slang and colloquialisms), but also various labels, instructions and other basic words you may come across in print or in public places.

Finally the Rough Guide rounds off with an extensive Menu Reader. Consisting of food and drink sections (each starting with a list of essential terms), it's indispensable whether you're eating out, stopping for a quick drink, or browsing through a local food market.

καλό ταξίδι!
kalo taxithi!
have a good trip!

Basics

AN

The Greek Alphabet

Set out below is the Greek alphabet, the names of the Greek letters, and the system of transliteration used in this book:

A, α	alfa	a as in cat
B, β	vita	v as in vet
Γ, γ	gama	y as in yes, except before consonants and a or o, when it's a throaty version of the g in gap
Δ, δ	thelta	th as in then
E, ε	epsilon	e as in get
Z, ζ	zita	z
H, η	ita	i as in ski
Θ, θ	thita	as the th in theme (represented by th)
I, ι	yota	i as in bit
K, κ	kapa	k
Λ, λ	lamtha	l
M, μ	mi	m
N, ν	ni	n
Ξ, ξ	ksi	x
O, o	omikron	o as in hot
Π, π	pi	p
P, ρ	ro	r
Σ, σ, ς*	sigma	s
T, τ	taf	t
Y, υ	ipsilon	long i, indistinguishable from ita
Φ, φ	fi	f
X, χ	khi	h as in hat or harsh ch in the Scottish word loch (represented by kh)
Ψ, ψ	psi	ps as in lips
Ω, ω	omega	o as in hot, indistinguishable from omikron

* this letter is used only at the end of a word in lower case

Combinations and diphthongs:

AI, αι	e as in g**e**t
AY, αυ	av or af depending on following consonant
EI, ει	long i, exactly like it**a**
OI, οι	long i, exactly like it**a**
EY, ευ	ev or ef depending on following consonant
OY, ου	oo as in m**oo**n
ΓΓ, γγ	ng as in a**ng**le
ΓΚ, γκ	g as in **g**oat at the beginning of a word; ng in the middle
ΜΠ, μπ	b as in **b**ar and sometimes mb as in e**mb**assy in the middle of a word
ΝΤ, ντ	d at the beginning of a word and sometimes nd as in e**nd** in the middle
ΤΣ, τσ	ts as in hi**ts**

ΑΓΓL

Pronunciation

Throughout this book Greek words have been transliterated into romanized form (see The Greek Alphabet page 9) so that they can be read as though they were English, bearing in mind the notes on pronunciation given below:

a	as in cat
e	as in get
eh	represents e at end of a word; should always be pronounced as in get
g	as in goat
i	as in ski
kh	like the ch in the Scottish way of saying loch
o	as in hot
th	as in then
TH	as in theme

Letters given in bold type indicate the part of the word to be stressed. When two vowels (such as 'ea') are next to each other in the pronunciation, both should be pronounced, as for example in the word: amfiTHeatro (amphitheatre).

Abbreviations

acc	accusative case	neut	neuter
adj	adjective	nom	nominative case
fam	familiar	pl	plural
fem	feminine	pol	polite
gen	genitive case	sing	singular
masc	masculine		

Note

An asterisk (*) next to a word in the dictionaries means that you should refer to the Basics section for further information.

Nouns and Articles

Articles

Greek nouns have one of three genders – masculine, feminine or neuter. The indefinite article (a, an) for each gender is:

masc	fem	neut
ένας	μία	ένα
enas	mia	ena

ένας άνδρας	μία γυναίκα	ένα παιδί
enas anthras	mia yineka	ena pethi
a man	a woman	a child

The definite article (the) is:

	masc	fem	neut		masc	fem	neut
sing	ο	η	το	plural	οι	οι	τα
	o	i	to		i	i	ta

ο πατέρας	οι πατεράδες
o pateras	i paterathes
the father	the fathers

το μωρό	τα μωρά
to moro	ta mora
the baby	the babies

η χώρα	οι χώρες
i khora	i khores
the country	the countries

η μητέρα	οι μητέρες
i mitera	i miteres
the mother	the mothers

ο δρόμος	οι δρόμοι
o thromos	i thromi
the street	the streets

το βουνό   τα βουνά
o voono   ta voona
the mountain   the mountains

Cases

There are three main cases in Greek – nominative, genitive and accusative. The forms of articles, nouns, adjectives and most pronouns change according to their gender, number and case. The indefinite article (a, an) declines as follows:

sing	masc	fem	neut
nom	ένας	μία	ένα
	enas	mia	ena
gen	ενός	μιάς	ενός
	enos	mias	enos
acc	ένα(ν)*	μία	ένα
	ena(n)	mia	ena

The definite article (the) declines as follows:

sing	masc	fem	neut
nom	ο	η	το
	o	i	to
gen	του	της	του
	too	tis	too
acc	το(ν)*	τη(ν)*	το
	to(n)	ti(n)	to

*The forms έναν and τον/την should be used before nouns beginning with a vowel.

plural	masc	fem	neut
nom	οι	οι	τα
	i	i	ta
gen	των	των	των
	ton	ton	ton
acc	τους	τις	τα
	toos	tis	ta

Nominative Case

The nominative is used for the subject of sentences:

το δωμάτιό μου είναι μικρό
to thomatio moo ineh mikro
my room is small

ο Γιάννης διαβάζει ένα βιβλίο
o Yanis thiavazi ena vivlio
John is reading a book

Genitive Case

The genitive case is used to indicate possession and to translate 'of':

αυτό είναι το αυτοκίνητο του Γιώργου
afto ineh to aftokinito too Yorgoo
this is George's car

ο σκύλος του γείτονα
o skilos too yitona
the neighbour's dog

Accusative Case

The accusative case is used for direct objects:

μπορείτε να μας φέρετε το λογαριασμό, παρακαλώ;
boriteh na mas fereteh to logariasmo, parakalo?
could you bring us the bill, please?

έχασα το λεωφορείο
ekhasa to leoforio
I missed the bus

The accusative case is also used with some prepositions (to, from, with etc):

αυτή πήγε στην παραλία
afti piyeh stin paralia
she has gone to the beach

αυτός είναι από τη Σκωτία
aftos ineh apo ti Skotia
he comes from Scotland

αυτοί πηγαίνουν με τα πόδια
afti piyenoon meh ta pothia
they are going on foot

προτιμάμε να ταξιδεύουμε με το τρένο
protimameh na taxithevoomeh meh to treno
we prefer to travel by train

Vocative Case

Another case in Greek is the vocative case, which is used to address someone directly. The vocative has the same endings as the nominative case, apart from masculine nouns and names where the final ς is dropped:

Μαρία, πού είναι ο Γιάννης; Γιάννη, πού είναι η Μαρία;
Maria, poo ineh o Yanis? **Yani, poo ineh i Maria?**
Mary, where is John? John, where is Mary?

Noun Endings

The endings of nouns change according to whether they are singular or plural and depending on whether they are in the nominative, genitive or accusative cases.

Masculine Nouns

Masculine nouns usually have one of three endings:

	-ας	-ης	-ος
	ο χειμώνας	ο εργάτης	ο δάσκαλος
	the winter	the workman	the teacher
sing			
nom	ο χειμώνας	ο εργάτης	ο δάσκαλος
	o khimonas	o ergatis	o thaskalos
gen	του χειμώνα	του εργάτη	του δασκάλου
	too khimona	too ergati	too thaskaloo
acc	το χειμώνα	τον εργάτη	τον δάσκαλο
	to khimona	ton ergati	ton thaskalo

15

plural			
nom	οι χειμώνες	οι εργάτες	οι δάσκαλοι
	i khimones	i ergates	i thaskali
gen	των χειμώνων	των εργατών	των δασκάλων
	ton khimonon	ton ergaton	ton thaskalon
acc	τους χειμώνες	τους εργάτες	τους δασκάλους
	toos khimones	toos ergates	toos thaskaloos

A few masculine nouns end in:

> -άς, -ές or -ούς

but for these only the plural differs from the above endings:

ο ψαράς	οι ψαράδες
o psaras	i psarathes
fisherman	fishermen

ο παπάς	οι παπάδες
o papas	i papathes
the priest	the priests

ο καφές	οι καφέδες
o kafes	i kafethes
the coffee	the coffees

ο καναπές	οι καναπέδες
o kanapes	i kanapethes
the couch	the couches

ο παππούς	οι παππούδες
o papoos	i papoothes
the grandfather	the grandfathers

Feminine Nouns

Feminine nouns either end in:

> -α or -η

η γλώσσα	η νίκη
the tongue, the language	the victory

	sing	
nom	η γλώσσα	η νίκη
	i glosa	i niki
gen	της γλώσσας	της νίκης
	tis glosas	tis nikis
acc	τη γλώσσα	τη νίκη
	ti glosa	ti niki
	plural	
nom	οι γλώσσες	οι νίκες
	i gloses	i nikes
gen	των γλωσσών	των νικών
	ton gloson	ton nikon
acc	τις γλώσσες	τις νίκες
	tis gloses	tis nikes

Some irregular feminine nouns ending in -η take the plural ending -εις, for example:

η λέξη	οι λέξεις
i lexi	i lexis
the word	the words

η απόφαση	οι αποφάσεις
i apofasi	i apofasis
the decision	the decisions

Feminine nouns ending in -ος decline like masculine nouns. For example:

η έξοδος	η είσοδος
i exothos	i isothos
the exit	the entrance

Neuter Nouns

Neuter nouns have one of the following endings:

-ο, -ι or -μα

		το δέντρο the tree	το ψωμί the bread, the loaf	το όνομα the name
sing	nom	το δέντρο to thendro	το ψωμί to psomi	το όνομα to **o**noma
	gen	του δέντρου too thendroo	του ψωμιού too psomi-**oo**	του ονόματος too on**o**matos
	acc	το δέντρο to thendro	το ψωμί to psomi	το όνομα to **o**noma
plural	nom	τα δέντρα ta thendra	τα ψωμιά ta psomi**a**	τα ονόματα ta on**o**mata
	gen	των δέντρων ton thendron	των ψωμιών ton psomi**on**	των ονομάτων ton onom**a**ton
	acc	τα δέντρα ta thendra	τα ψωμιά ta psomi**a**	τα ονόματα ta on**o**mata

Several neuter nouns end in -ος:

το είδος to **i**thos the kind	τα είδη ta **i**thi the kinds	το μέγεθος to me**ye**THos the size	τα μεγέθη ta me**ye**THi the sizes

Adjectives and Adverbs

Most adjectives also change as follows according to gender and number:

masc	fem	neut	masc	fem	neut
ακριβός expensive			γλυκός sweet		
ακριβός akriv**os**	ακριβή akriv**i**	ακριβό akriv**o**	γλυκός glik**os**	γλυκιά glik**ia**	γλυκό glik**o**
όμορφος beautiful			ελαφρύς light		
όμορφος **o**morfos	όμορφη **o**morfi	όμορφο **o**morfo	ελαφρύς elafr**is**	ελαφριά elafr**ia**	ελαφρύ elafr**i**

Adjective endings follow the pattern of the corresponding noun endings. Adjectives should agree with their nouns in gender, number, and case:

ο καλός φίλος   έχω μερικούς καλούς φίλους
o kalos filos   **ekho merikoos kaloos filoos**
the good friend   I have some good friends

η όμορφη πόλη   είδαμε ένα ωραίο έργυ
i omorfi poli   **ithameh enah oreo ergo**
the beautiful town   we saw a good film

The most common irregular adjective is:

ο πολύς a lot of, much, many

	sing	plural
masc	ο πολύς **o polis**	οι πολλοί **i poli**
fem	η πολλή **i poli**	οι πολλές **i poles**
neut	το πολύ **to poli**	τα πολλά **ta pola**

Comparatives

The comparative is formed by putting the word πιό [**pio**] 'more' in front of the adjective:

αυτό το ξενοδοχείο είναι πιό/λιγότερο ακριβό από εκείνο
afto to xenothokhio ineh pio/ligotero akrivo apo ekino
this hotel is more/less expensive than that one

είναι πιό ήσυχα εδώ
ineh pio isikha etho
it's quieter here

Superlatives

Superlatives are formed by putting the definite article in front of the comparative:

η Ομόνοια είναι η πιό διάσημη πλατεία στην Αθήνα
i Omoni-a ineh i pio thiasimi plati-a stin ATHina
Omonia Square is the most famous square in Athens

αυτός ο δρόμος είναι ο λιγότερο επικίνδυνος
aftos o thromos ineh o ligotero epikinthinos
this road is the least dangerous

η ταβέρνα Ο Γιάννης είναι η πιο δημοφιλής ταβέρνα στη
Μυτιλήνη
i taverna O Yanis ineh i pio thimofilis taverna sti Mitilini
the O Yanis taverna is the most popular in Mitilini

'As … as' is translated as τόσο … όσο:

αυτό το εστιατόριο είναι τόσο ακριβό όσο και το άλλο
afto to estiatorio ineh toso akrivo oso keh to alo
this restaurant is as expensive as that one

αυτή η πόλη δεν είναι τόσο ενδιαφέρουσα όσο νόμιζα
afti i poli then ineh toso enthiaferoosa oso nomiza
this town is not as interesting as I thought

The following common adjectives have irregular comparatives and superlatives:

κακός	χειρότερος	χείριστος
kakos	khiroteros	khiristos
bad	worse	worst
κακός	χειρότερος	χείριστος
καλός	καλύτερος	κάλλιστος
kalos	kaliteros	kalistos
good	better	best
μικρός	μικρότερος	ελάχιστος
mikros	mikroteros	elakhistos
small	smaller	smallest

μεγάλος	μεγαλύτερος	μέγιστος
megalos	megaliteros	meyistos
big	bigger	biggest

λίγος	λιγότερος	ελάχιστος
ligos	ligoteros	elakhistos
few	fewer	fewest

πολύς	περισσότερος	
polis	perisoteros	
a lot of	a lot more of	

Adverbs

If the adjective ends in -ος, remove this ending and add -α to create the adverb:

adjective	adverb		adjective	adverb
καλός	καλά		ωραίος	ωραία
kalos	kala		oreos	oreh-a
good	well		nice	nicely
κακός	κακά		τυχερός	τυχερά
kakos	kaka		tikheros	tikhera
bad	badly		lucky	luckily

If the adjective ends in -ης, remove this ending and add -ως to create the adverb:

adjective	adverb
συνεχής	συνεχώς
sinekhis	sinekhos
continuous	continuously
ακριβής	ακριβώς
akrivis	akrivos
precise	precisely
διεθνής	διεθνώς
thi-eTHnis	thi-eTHnos
international	internationally

21

Possessive Adjectives

my	μου	moo	its	του	too
your (sing, fam)	σου	soo	our	μας	mas
his	του	too	your (pl, pol)	σας	sas
her	της	tis	their	τους	toos

Possessive adjectives do not change according to case, gender or number. They follow the noun they refer to, but note that the definite article is placed in front of the noun:

το διαβατήριό μου	τα λεφτά τους	το βιβλίο της
to thiavatirio moo	ta lefta toos	to vivlio tis
my passport	their money	her book

Pronouns

Possessive Pronouns

Possessive pronouns (mine, hers etc) are formed by placing the word δικός in front of the possessive. δικός declines like an adjective, agreeing with the object possessed in case, gender and number:

	masc	fem	neut
mine	δικός μου	δική μου	δικό μου
	thikos moo	thiki moo	thiko moo
yours (sing, fam)	δικός σου	δική σου	δικό σου
	thikos soo	thiki soo	thiko soo
his	δικός του	δική του	δικό του
	thikos too	thiki too	thiko too
hers	δικός της	δική της	δικό της
	thikos tis	thiki tis	thiko tis
its	δικός του	δική του	δικό του
	thikos too	thiki too	thiko too
ours	δικός μας	δική μας	δικό μας
	thikos mas	thiki mas	thiko mas
yours (pl, pol)	δικός σας	δική σας	δικό σας
	thikos sas	thiki sas	thiko sas
theirs	δικός τους	δική τους	δικό τους
	thikos toos	thiki toos	thiko toos

Plurals take the usual adjective endings:

αυτές είναι οι δικές μας
aftes ineh i thikes mas
these are ours

Personal Pronouns

nom	gen	acc
εγώ [ego] I	μου [moo] me	με/εμένα [meh/emena] me
εσύ [esi] you★	σου [soo] you	σε/εσένα [seh/esena] you
αυτός [aftos] he	του [too] him	τον [ton] him
αυτή [afti] she	της [tis] her	την [tin] her
αυτό [afto] it	του [too] it	το [to] it
εμείς [emis] we	μας [mas] us	μας/εμάς [mas/emas] us
εσείς [esis] you★★	σας/εσάς [sas/esas] you	σας/εσάς [sas/esas] you
αυτοί [afti] they (**m**)	τους [toos] them	τους/αυτούς [toos/aftoos] them
αυτές [aftes] they (**f**)	τους [toos] them	τις/αυτές [tis/aftes] them
αυτά [afta] they (**n**)	τους [toos] them	τα/αυτά [ta/afta] them

★ εσύ is used when speaking to one person and is the familiar form generally used when speaking to family, friends and children.

★★ εσείς is the polite form which can be used to address one person or several people.

αυτή του έδωσε τα χρήματα
afti too ethoseh ta khrimata
she gave him the money

εγώ τους είδα να το κλέβουν
ego toos itha na to klevoon
I saw them stealing it

Where two forms are given for the accusative, the second is used after prepositions:

θα πάω μαζί με αυτές
тна pao mazi meh aftes
I will go with them

αυτό είναι ένα δώρο γιά εσένα
afto ineh ena thoro ya esena
this is a present for you

In Greek the subject pronoun (nominative) is usually omitted:

έφυγε χθές	θα ήθελα να παραγγείλω
efiyeh khTHes	THa **i**THela na parangilo
he left yesterday	I'd like to order

Although it may be retained for emphasis:

αυτή ήταν πρώτη	εσύ φταίς
afti **i**tan pr**o**ti	esi ftes
SHE was first	YOU are to blame

αυτός έκλεψε το πορτοφόλι μου
aftos **e**klepseh to portof**o**li moo
HE stole my wallet

Examples using pronouns in genitive and accusative:

το πήρε από την τσάντα μου	εσύ τους το έδωσες;
to pireh apo tin ts**a**nda moo	esi toos to **e**thoses?
he took it from my bag	did YOU give it to them?

την πήρα μαζί μου	τα αγόρασε χθες
tin pira maz**i** moo	ta ag**o**raseh khTHes
I took her with me	she bought them yesterday

θα σου τον συστήσω	την είδα
THa soo ton sist**i**so	tin **i**tha
I shall introduce you to him	I saw her

δε σε ακούω καλά
theh seh ak**oo**-o kala
I cannot hear you very well

Verbs

The form of the verb given in dictionaries is usually the first person singular of the present tense. This is the basic form (equivalent to the infinitive) and the endings are either -ω (active verbs) or -μαι (passive verbs).

Although there are two categories of Greek verbs (active and passive), many verbs that are not passive in English are considered passive in Greek.

Present Tense

Present tense endings for verbs ending in -ω depend on whether or not the stress falls on the last syllable:

	stress not on last syllable	stress on last syllable	
	αγοράζω buy	πουλώ sell	μπορώ be able
I	αγοράζ-ω	πουλ-ώ	μπορ-ώ
	agorazo	poolo	boro
you	αγοράζ-εις	πουλ-άς	μπορ-είς
	agorazis	poolas	boris
he/she	αγοράζ-ει	πουλ-ά	μπορ-εί
	agorazi	poola	bori
we	αγοράζ-ουμε	πουλ-άμε	μπορ-ούμε
	agorazoomeh	poolameh	boroomeh
you	αγοράζ-ετε	πουλ-άτε	μπορ-είτε
	agorazeteh	poolateh	boriteh
they	αγοράζ-ουν	πουλ-ούν	μπορ-ούν
	agorazoon	pooloon	boroon

πόσο το πουλάς;
poso to poolas?
how much are you selling it for?

το αγοράζω για χίλιες δραχμές
to agorazo ya khili-es thrakhmes
I am buying it for 1,000 drachmas

δεν μπορεί να περπατήσει
then bori na perpatisi
he can't walk

Passive verbs ending in -μαι take the following endings:

ντώνομαι be dressed, dress (oneself)

I	ντών-ομαι	[dinomeh]
you	ντών-εσαι	[dineseh]
he/she	ντών-εται	[dineteh]
we	ντυν-όμαστε	[dinomasteh]
you	ντών-εστε	[dinesteh]
they	ντών-ονται	[dinondeh]

The verbs 'to be' and 'to have' are irregular:

είμαι I am [imeh]	είμαστε we are [imasteh]
είσαι you are [iseh]	είσαστε/είστε you are [isasteh/isteh]
είναι he/she/it is [ineh]	είναι they are [ineh]

έχω I have [ekho]	έχουμε we have [ekhoomeh]
έχεις you have [ekhis]	έχετε you have [ekheteh]
έχει he/she/it has [ekhi]	έχουν they have [ekhoon]

Past Simple Tense

To describe an action that has taken place in the past, use the past simple tense in Greek. To form this, take the basic form of the verb and add the following endings. Note that in the simple past, the stress moves back one syllable and sometimes changes have to be made to the form of the verb which comes before these endings. For example, where necessary, the letter ε is added to the beginning of the verb so that the stress can move back a syllable:

ακού-ω (I hear)   κάν-ω (I do)

ακού-σ-α I heard [akoosa]	έκαν-α I did [ekana]
ακού-σ-ες you heard [akooses]	έκανες you did [ekanes]
ακού-σ-ε he/she heard [akooseh]	έκανε he/she/it did [ekaneh]
ακού-σ-αμε we heard [akoosameh]	εκάναμε we did [ekanameh]
ακού-σ-ατε you heard [akoosateh]	εκάνατε you did [ekanateh]
ακού-σ-αν they heard [akoosan]	έκαναν they did [ekanan]

The past tense of 'to be' and 'to have' is:

ήμουν I was [**i**moon]   ήμασταν we were [**i**mastan]
ήσουν you were [**i**soon]   ήσασταν you were [**i**sastan]
ήταν he/she/it was [**i**tan]   ήταν they were [**i**tan]

είχα I had [**i**kha]   είχαμε we had [**i**khameh]
είχες you had [**i**khes]   είχατε you had [**i**khateh]
είχε he/she/it had [**i**kheh]   είχαν they had [**i**khan]

πόσα χρήματα είχατε στην τσάντα σας;
p**o**sa khr**i**mata **i**khateh stin ts**a**nda sas?
how much money did you have in your handbag?

επισκεφτήκατε το Αρχαιολογικό Μουσείο;
episkeft**i**kateh to Arkheoloyik**o** Moosio?
did you visit the Archaeological Museum?

οι τιμές ήταν πιό φτηνές πέρυσι
i tim**es i**tan pi**o** ftin**es** perisi
prices were cheaper last year

υπογράψατε στο βιβλίο;
ipogr**a**psateh sto vivl**i**o?
did you sign the book?

The Indefinite

The Greek indefinite form of the verb has no direct equivalent in English although its use often corresponds to the infinitive used after verbs such as 'to want', 'to be able to', 'can', etc, and has the following pattern:

να + basic form of verb + ending of the verb preceding it.

It must agree in person and number with the main verb preceding it:

θα μπορούσα να πληρώσω με επιταγή;
THα bor**oo**sà na plir**o**so meh epitaγ**i**?
could I pay by cheque?

The exception to this is the impersonal verb 'to have to', 'must' which always takes the same form πρέπει:

πρέπει να πηγαίνουμε τώρα
prepi na piyenoomeh tora
we must go now

Here is a list of some useful verbs with their indefinite and past simple in the first person:

present	indefinite	past simple	perfect
βλέπω see	να δω	είδα	έχω δει
vlepo	**na tho**	**itha**	**ekho thi**
βρίσκω find	να βρω	βρήκα	έχω βρει
vrisko	**na vro**	**vrika**	**ekho vri**
δίνω give	να δώσω	έδωσα	έχω δώσει
thino	**na thoso**	**ethosa**	**ekho thosi**
έρχομαι come	να έλθω	ήλθα	έχω έλθει
erkhomeh	**na elTHo**	**ilTHa**	**ekho elTHi**
κάνω do	να κάνω	έκανα	έχω κάνει
kano	**na kano**	**ekana**	**ekho kani**
λέω say	να πω	είπα	έχω πει
le-o	**na po**	**ipa**	**ekho pi**
μένω stay	να μείνω	έμεινα	έχω μείνει
meno	**na mino**	**emina**	**ekho mini**
παίρνω take	να πάρω	πήρα	έχω πάρει
perno	**na paro**	**pira**	**ekho pari**
πηγαίνω go	να πάω	πήγα	έχω πάει
piyeno	**na pao**	**piga**	**ekho pa-i**
πίνω drink	να πιώ	ήπια	έχω πιεί
pino	**na pio**	**ipia**	**ekho pi-i**
στέλνω send	να στείλω	έστειλα	έχω στείλει
stelno	**na stilo**	**estila**	**ekho stili**
τρώω eat	να φάω	έφαγα	έχω φάει
tro-o	**na fa-o**	**efaga**	**ekho fa-i**
ρωτώ ask	να ρωτήσω	ρώτησα	έχω ρωτήσει
roto	**na rotiso**	**rotisa**	**ekho rotisi**

αγοράζω buy agorazo	να αγοράσω na agoraso	αγόρασα agorasa	έχω αγοράσει ekho agorasi
κλείνω close klino	να κλείσω na kliso	έκλεισα eklisa	έχω κλείσει ekho klisi
κοιτάζω look kitazo	να κοιτάξω na kitaxo	κοίταξα kitaxa	έχω κοιτάξει ekho kitaxi
σταματώ stop stamato	να σταματήσω na stamatiso	σταμάτησα stamatisa	έχω σταματήσει ekho stamatisi
νομίζω think nomizo	να νομίσω na nomiso	νόμισα nomisa	έχω νομίσει ekho nomisi
γράφω write grafo	να γράψω na grapso	έγραψα egrapsa	έχω γράψει ekho grapsi

Future Tense

The simplest way to form the continuous future tense in Greek is to take the present tense forms and add the word θα in front of them:

I will be waiting	θα περιμένω	[THa perimeno]
you will ...	θα περιμένεις	[THa perimenis]
he/she will ...	θα περιμένει	[THa perimeni]
we will ...	θα περιμένουμε	[THa perimenoomeh]
you will ...	θα περιμένετε	[THa perimeneteh]
they will ...	θα περιμένουν	[THa perimenoon]

To form the simple future tense you use θα and the appropriate forms of the indefinite (without the να):

I will buy	θα αγοράσω	[THa agoraso]
you will ...	θα αγοράσεις	[THa agorasis]
he/she/it will ...	θα αγοράσει	[THa agorasi]
we will ...	θα αγοράσουμε	[THa agorasoomeh]
you will ...	θα αγοράσετε	[THa agoraseteh]
they will ...	θα αγοράσουν	[THa agorasoon]

θα σε δω το βράδυ
THa seh tho to vrathi
I'll see you tonight

Imperatives

The imperative form of the verb is used to give commands. To create the singular, familiar imperative, take the indefinite form of the verb (without the να) and change the final -ω to -ε:

κοίταξε εκεί!
kitaxeh eki!
look over there!

πρόσεξε!
prosexeh!
watch out!

Polite and plural forms of the imperative are created by changing the final -ω of the indefinite form (without the να) to -ετε or -τε :

ρωτήστε τον αστυνόμο εκεί πέρα
rotisteh ton astinomo eki pera
ask the policeman over there

υπογράψτε εδώ, παρακαλώ
ipograpsteh etho, parakalo
sign here, please

Negative imperatives are formed by placing μη or μην in front of the second person of the indefinite form (without the να) of the verb:

μην πάτε από αυτόν το δρόμο
min pateh apo afton ton thromo
don't go along this street

μην πιείς αυτό το νερό
min pi-is afto to nero
do not drink this water

Some common irregular imperatives are:

familiar	polite/plural
βρες find [vres]	βρείτε [vriteh]
δες see [thes]	δείτε [thiteh] or δέστε [thesteh]
πιές drink [pies]	πιείτε [pi-iteh] or πιέστε [pi-esteh]
πες say [pes]	πείτε [pesteh] or πέστε [pesteh]
ελα come [ela]	ελάτε [elateh]

Negatives

To form the negative, place the word δε or δεν in front of the verb:

δε μου αρέσει αυτό
theh moo aresi afto
I don't like this

δε μιλάω καλά Ελληνικά
theh mila-o kala Elinika
my Greek is not very good

δεν μπορώ να βρώ το ξενοδοχείο
then boro na vro to xenothokhio
I cannot find the hotel

Questions

The word order and intonation for questions in Greek are
the same as in English:

πού είναι το γραφείο του ΕΟΤ, παρακαλώ;
poo ineh to grafio too E-OT, parakalo?
where is the tourist information office, please?

Note that in questions in Greek, a semi-colon is used instead
of a question mark.

Dates

To say the date, take the ordinal number, then the genitive
of the month. The exception is 'the first', when you should
use the ordinal number:

σήμερα είναι εικοσιεφτά Φεβρουαρίου
simera ineh ikosi-efta Fevroo-arioo
today is the 27th of February

αύριο είναι πρώτη Ιουλίου   χθες ήταν τρεις Δεκεμβρίου
avrio ineh proti looli-oo   **khтнes itan tris thekemvrioo**
tomorrow is the 1st of July   yesterday was the 3rd of
                                    December

Πρωταπριλιά   Πρωτομαγιά
protaprilia   **protomaya**
1st of April   1st of May

Instead of saying 'nineteen ninety-five' you literally say 'one
thousand, nine hundred, ninety five:

χίλια ενιακόσια ενενήντα πέντε
khilia eniakosia eneninda pendeh

Time

what time is it? τί ώρα είναι; [ti ora ineh?]
one o'clock μία η ώρα [mia i ora]
two o'clock δύο η ώρα [thio i ora]
it's one o'clock είναι μία η ώρα [ineh mia i ora]
it's two o'clock είναι δύο η ώρα [ineh thio i ora]
it's ten o'clock είναι δέκα η ώρα [ineh theka i ora]
five past one μία και πέντε [mia keh pendeh]
ten past two δύο και δέκα [thio keh theka]
quarter past one μία και τέταρτο [mia keh tetarto]
quarter past two δύο και τέταρτο [thio keh tetarto]
twenty past ten δέκα και είκοσι [theka keh ikosi]
half past ten δέκα και μισή [theka keh misi]
twenty to ten δέκα παρά είκοσι [theka para ikosi]
quarter to two δύο παρά τέταρτο [thio para tetarto]
at half past four στις τέσσερις και μισή [stis teseris keh misi]
at eight o'clock στις οκτώ [stis okto]
14.00 δεκατέσσερις [theka-teseris]
17.30 δεκαεφτά και τριάντα [theka-efta keh trianda]
2 am δύο η ώρα το βράδυ [thio i ora to vrathi]
2 pm δύο η ώρα το μεσημέρι [thio i ora to mesimeri]
6 am έξι η ώρα το πρωί [exi i ora to pro-i]
6 pm έξι η ώρα το απόγευμα [exi i ora to apoyevma]
noon το μεσημέρι [to mesimeri]
midnight τα μεσάνυχτα [ta mesanikhta]

an hour η ώρα [i ora]
a minute το λεπτό [to lepto]
one minute ένα λεπτό [ena lepto]
two minutes δύο λεπτά [thio lepta]
a second το δευτερόλεπτο [to thefterolepto]
a quarter of an hour ένα τέταρτο [ena tetarto]
half an hour μισή ώρα [misi ora]
three quarters of an hour τρία τέταρτα της ώρας [tria tetarta tis oras]

Numbers

0 μηδέν [mithen]
1 ένα [ena]
2 δύο [thio]
3 τρία [tria]
4 τέσσερα [tesera]
5 πέντε [pendeh]
6 έξι [exi]
7 επτά [epta]
8 οχτώ [okhto]
9 εννιά [enia]
10 δέκα [theka]
11 έντεκα [endeka]
12 δώδεκα [thotheka]
13 δεκατρία [theka-tria]
14 δεκατέσσερα [theka-tesera]
15 δεκαπέντε [theka-pendeh]
16 δεκαέξι [theka-exi]
17 δεκαεπτά [theka-epta]
18 δεκαοχτώ [theka-okhto]
19 δεκαεννιά [theka-enia]
20 είκοσι [ikosi]
21 εικοσιένα [ikosi-ena]
22 εικοσιδύο [ikosi-thio]
30 τριάντα [trianda]
31 τριανταένα [trianda-ena]
40 σαράντα [saranda]
50 πενήντα [peninda]
60 εξήντα [exinda]
70 εβδομήντα [evthominda]
80 ογδόντα [ogthonda]
90 ενενήντα [eneninda]
100 εκατό [ekato]
110 εκατό δέκα [ekato theka]

200 διακόσια [thiakosia]
300 τριακόσια [triakosia]
1,000 χίλια [khilia]
2,000 δύο χιλιάδες [thio khiliathes]
5,000 πέντε χιλιάδες [pendeh khiliathes]
10,000 δέκα χιλιάδες [theka khiliathes]
20,000 είκοσι χιλιάδες [ikosi khiliathes]
50,000 πενήντα χιλιάδες [peninda khiliathes]
100,000 εκατό χιλιάδες [ekato khiliathes]
1,000,000 ένα εκατομμύριο [ena ekatomirio]

Ordinals

Ordinal numbers decline like regular adjectives:

1st πρώτος [protos]
2nd δεύτερος [thefteros]
3rd τρίτος [tritos]
4th τέταρτος [tetartos]
5th πέμπτος [pemptos]
6th έκτος [ektos]
7th έβδομος [evthomos]
8th όγδοος [ogtho-os]
9th ένατος [enatos]
10th δέκατος [thekatos]

Basic Phrases

yes
ναί
neh

no
όχι
okhi

OK
εντάξει
endaxi

hello
χαίρετε
khereteh

good morning
καλημέρα
kalimera

good evening
καλησπέρα
kalispera

good night
καληνύχτα
kalinikhta

goodbye
αντίο
andio

hi
γειά
ya

see you
γειά, θα τα πούμε
ya, THa ta poomeh

please
παρακαλώ
parakalo

thank you
ευχαριστώ
efkharisto

yes, please
ναί, παρακαλώ
neh, parakalo

no thank you
όχι, ευχαριστώ
okhi, efkharisto

excuse me, please (to attract
    attention, to get past someone)
συγγνώμη, παρακαλώ
signomi, parakalo

sorry!
συγγνώμη!
signomi!

pardon? (sorry?, what did you
    say?)
ορίστε;
oristeh?

what did you say?
πώς είπατε;
pos ipateh?

I don't understand
δεν καταλαβαίνω
then katalaveno

do you speak English?
μιλάτε Αγγλικά;
milateh Anglika?

I don't speak Greek
δεν μιλάω Ελληνικά
then milo Elinika

please speak more slowly
παρακαλώ, μιλάτε πιό αργά;
parakalo, milateh pio arga?

could you repeat that?
το ξαναλέτε αυτό, σας παρακαλώ;
to xanaleteh afto, sas
  parakalo?

please write it down
μου το γράφετε, παρακαλώ;
moo to grafeteh, parakalo?

I would like ...
θα ήθελα ...
THa iTHela ...

can I have ...?
μπορώ να έχω ...;
boro na ekho ...?

how much is it?
πόσο κάνει;
poso kani?

cheers!
εις υγείαν!
is iyian!

where is/are the ...?
πού είναι ...;
poo ineh ...?

i velona

koh

klosti

Conversion Tables

1 centimetre = 0.39 inches   1 inch = 2.54 cm

1 metre = 39.37 inches = 1.09 yards   1 foot = 30.48 cm

1 kilometre = 0.62 miles = 5/8 mile   1 yard = 0.91 m

1 mile = 1.61 km

km	1	2	3	4	5	10	20	30	40	50	100
miles	0.6	1.2	1.9	2.5	3.1	6.2	12.4	18.6	24.8	31.0	62.1

miles	1	2	3	4	5	10	20	30	40	50	100
km	1.6	3.2	4.8	6.4	8.0	16.1	32.2	48.3	64.4	80.5	161

1 gram = 0.035 ounces   1 kilo = 1000 g = 2.2 pounds

g	100	250	500	1 oz = 28.35 g
oz	3.5	8.75	17.5	1 lb = 0.45 kg

kg	0.5	1	2	3	4	5	6	7	8	9	10
lb	1.1	2.2	4.4	6.6	8.8	11.0	13.2	15.4	17.6	19.8	22.0

kg	20	30	40	50	60	70	80	90	100
lb	44	66	88	110	132	154	176	198	220

lb	0.5	1	2	3	4	5	6	7	8	9	10	20
kg	0.2	0.5	0.9	1.4	1.8	2.3	2.7	3.2	3.6	4.1	4.5	9.0

1 litre = 1.75 UK pints / 2.13 US pints

1 UK pint = 0.57 litre   1 UK gallon = 4.55 litre
1 US pint = 0.47 litre   1 US gallon = 3.79 litre

centigrade / Celsius $°C = (°F - 32) \times 5/9$

°C	-5	0	5	10	15	18	20	25	30	36.8	38
°F	23	32	41	50	59	64	68	77	86	98.4	100.4

Fahrenheit $°F = (°C \times 9/5) + 32$

°F	23	32	40	50	60	65	70	80	85	98.4	101
°C	-5	0	4	10	16	18	21	27	29	36.8	38.3

English

→

Greek

A

a, an* enas, mia, ena
about: about 20 peripoo ikosi
 it's about 5 o'clock ineh yiro
 stis pendeh
 a film about Greece ena ergo
 ya tin Elatha
above pano apo
abroad sto exoteriko
absolutely! (I agree) apolitos!
accelerator to gazi
accept thekhomeh
accident to thistikhima
 there's been an accident
 eyineh ena thistikhima
accommodation i thiamoni
 see room
accurate akrivis
ache o ponos
 my back aches pona-i i plati
 moo
across: across the road
 apenandi sto thromo
adapter to polaplo
 (for voltage change) i briza taf
address i thi-efTHinsi
 what's your address? pia
 ineh i thi-efTHinsi soo?

Addresses are written
with the street number
after the name of the
street, e.g.

Γιάννης Παπαδόπουλος
Ελευθερίου Βενιζέλου 28
Χανιά 73100
Κρήτη

Yiannis Papadopoulos
Eleutheriou Venizelou 28
Khania 73100
Kriti

When sending mail, always use
postcodes; they can be found in
special lists in post offices. You can
write Greek addresses in the Greek
or Roman alphabet.

address book i adzenda ton
 thi-efTHinseon
admission charge timi
 isothoo
adult (man/woman) o enilikos/i
 eniliki
advance: in advance
 prokatavolika
aeroplane to a-eroplano
after meta
 after you meta apo sas
 after lunch meta apo to
 yevma
afternoon apo-yevma
 in the afternoon kata to apo-
 yevma
 this afternoon afto to apo-
 yevma
aftershave i kolonia meta to
 xirisma
aftersun cream to galaktoma
 ya ton ilio
afterwards meta
again xana
against enandion
age i ilikia
ago: a week ago prin apo mia
 evthomatha
 an hour ago prin apo mia ora

agree: I agree simfono
AIDS to AIDS
air o a-eras
 by air a-eroporikos
air-conditioning o klimatismos
airmail: by airmail
 a-eroporikos
airmail envelope o
 a-eroporikos fakelos
airport to a-erothromio
 to the airport, please sto
 a-erothromio, parakalo
airport bus to leoforio
 a-erothromi-oo
aisle seat THesi thipla sto
 thiathromo
alarm clock to xipnitiri
Albania i Alvania
Albanian (adj) Alvanikos
alcohol to alko-ol
alcoholic inopnevmatothis
all: all the boys ola ta agoria
 all the girls ola ta koritsia
 all the men oli i andres
 all the women oles i yinekes
 all of it olokliro
 all of them ola afta
 that's all, thanks afta ineh
 ola, efkharisto
allergic: I'm allergic to ... imeh
 aleryikos meh ...
allowed: is it allowed?
 epitrepeteh?
all right endaxi
 I'm all right imeh endaxi
 are you all right? (adj) iseh
 endaxi?
 (pol) esis endaxi?
almond to amigthalo

almost skhethon
alone monos
alphabet to alfavito
 see page 9
already ithi
also episis
although an keh
altogether sinolika
always panda
am*: I am imeh
am: at seven am stis efta pro
 mesimvrias
amazing (surprising)
 ekpliktikos
 (very good) thavmasios
ambulance to asTHenoforo
 call an ambulance! kalesteh
 ena asTHenoforo!

 Dial 166 for an
 ambulance.

America i Ameriki
American (adj) Amerikanikos
 I'm American (man/woman)
 imeh Amerikanos/
 Amerikana
among anamesa
amount to poso
 (money) ta khrimata
amp: a 13-amp fuse mia
 asfalia thekatria amper
amphitheatre to amfiTHeatro
Ancient Greece i arkhea
 Elatha
Ancient Greek ta arkhea
 Elinika
and keh

angry THimom**e**nos
animal to z**o**-o
ankle o astr**a**galos
anniversary (wedding) i ep**e**tios
 too g**a**moo
annoy: this man's annoying
 me aft**o**s o **a**ndras meh
 enokhl**i**
annoying enokhlitik**o**s
another **a**los, **a**li, **a**lo
 can we have another room?
 bor**oo**meh na **e**khoomeh
 ena **a**lo thom**a**tio?
 another beer, please **a**li m**i**a
 b**i**ra, parakal**o**
antibiotics to andiviotik**o**
antihistamine to andi-
 istaminik**o** f**a**rmako
antique: is it an antique? **i**neh
 ant**i**ka?
antique shop to paleop**o**lio
antiseptic to andisiptik**o**
any: have you got any
 bread/tomatoes? **e**kheteh
 ps**o**mi/dom**a**tes?

dialogue

> do you have any change?
> **e**khis kaTH**o**loo psil**a**?
> sorry, I don't have any
> lip**a**meh, then **e**kho
> kaTH**o**loo

anybody kan**i**s
 does anybody speak
 English? mil**a**-i kan**i**s
 Anglik**a**?
 there wasn't anybody there

then **i**tan kan**i**s ek**i**
anything otith**i**poteh

dialogues

> anything else? t**i**poteh
> al**o**?
> nothing else, thanks
> t**i**poteh, efkharist**o**

> would you like anything to
> drink? THa TH**e**lateh na
> pi-**i**teh kat**i**?
> I don't want anything,
> thanks then TH**e**lo
> t**i**poteh, efkharist**o**

apart from ekt**o**s ap**o**
apartment to thiam**e**risma
appendicitis i skoliko-ith**i**tis
appetizer to pr**o**to pi**a**to
 appetizers ta orektik**a**
aperitif to aperit**i**f
apology i sign**o**mi
apple to m**i**lo
appointment to randev**oo**

dialogue

> good afternoon, sir, how
> can I help you? kalisp**e**ra
> sas, k**i**ri-eh, pos bor**o** na
> sas vo-iTH**i**so?
> I'd like to make an
> appointment THa **i**TH**e**la
> na kl**i**so **e**na randev**oo**
> what time would you like?
> ti **o**ra TH**e**leteh?
> three o'clock tris i **o**ra

I'm afraid that's not possible; is four o'clock all right? fovameh oti afto then yineteh; boriteh stis teseris?

yes, that will be fine neh, poli kala

the name was ...? to onoma sas?

apricot to verikoko

April o Aprilios

archaeology i arkheoloyia

are*: we are imasteh
 you are isteh
 they are ineh

area i periokhi

area code o kothikos ariTHmos

arm to kheri

arrange: will you arrange it for us? THa to kanonisis ya mas?

arrival i afixi

arrive ftano
 when do we arrive? poteh ftanoomeh?
 has my fax arrived yet? eftaseh to fax moo?
 we arrived today ftasameh simera

art i tekhni

art gallery i pinakoTHiki

artist (man/woman) o kalitekhnis/i kalitekhnitha

as: as big as ... megalo san ...
 as soon as possible oso pio grigora yineteh

ashtray to tasaki, to stokhto-thokhio

ask roto
 I didn't ask for this then zitisa afto
 could you ask him to ...? boris na too pis na ...?

asleep: she's asleep kimateh

aspirin i aspirini

asthma to asTHma

astonishing ekpliktikos

at: at the hotel sto xenothokhio
 at the station sto staTHmo
 at six o'clock stis exi i ora
 at Yanni's stoo Yanni

Athens i ATHina

athletics o aTHlitismos

attractive elkistikos

aubergine i melidzana

August o Avgoostos

aunt i THia

Australia i Afstralia

Australian (adj) Afstralezikos
 I'm Australian (man/woman) imeh Afstralos/Afstraleza

automatic (adj) aftomatos
 (car) to aftomato aftokinito

automatic teller i mikhani ya metrita

autumn to fTHinoporo
 in the autumn sto fTHinoporo

avenue i leoforos

average (not good) metrio
 on average kata meson oro

awake: is he awake? ineh xipnios?

away: go away! fiyeh
 is it far away? ineh poli makria?

awful apesios
axle o axonas

B

baby to moro
baby food i pethiki trofi
baby's bottle to bibero
baby-sitter i baby-sitter
back (of body) i plati
 (back part) piso
 at the back sto piso meros
 can I have my money back?
 boro na ekho ta lefta moo
 piso?
 to come/go back epistrefo,
 yirizo piso
backache ponos stin plati
bacon to bacon
bad kakos
 a bad headache enas
 askhimos ponokefalos
badly askhima
bag i tsanda
 (suitcase) i valitsa
baggage i aposkeves
baggage check o khoros
 filaxis aposkevon
baggage claim anazitisi
 aposkevon
bakery o foornaris
balcony to balkoni
 a room with a balcony ena
 thomatio meh balkoni
bald falakros
ball (large) i bala
 (small) to balaki
ballet to baleto

banana i banana
band (musical) to singrotima
bandage o epithesmos
Bandaid® to lefkoplast
bank i trapeza

Banks are usually open
Monday to Thursday from
8 am to 2 pm, and Fridays
from 8 am to 1.30 pm Certain
branches in the major cities and
tourist centres open extra hours in
the evenings and on Saturday
mornings for exchanging money.
Usually you have to queue twice,
once to get the transaction approved
and a second time to pick up the
cash. The best rates for exchanging
money or travellers' cheques are to
be found in banks and post offices
(where there's usually less of a
queue) rather than hotels, tourist
shops etc.

bank account o trapezikos
 logariasmos
bar to bar

Bars, 'barakia' in the
plural, are a recent
transplant confined to big
cities and holiday resorts. They
range from unappealing clones of
Parisian bars to imitation British
pubs and are invariably more
expensive than cafés. They are,
however, most likely to stock a
range of foreign label beers. Some
bars and cafés close in the

afternoon but many remain open from early in the morning until late at night. In summer, the chief socializing time is rarely before 8 pm and can often start around 10 pm It is not offensive to be drunk as long as you don't annoy other people. Driving after drinking any alcohol is strictly forbidden.
see also **café**

a bar of chocolate mia sokolata
barber's to koorio
basket to kalaTHi
basketball to basketball, i kalaTHosferisi
bath to banio
  can I have a bath? boro na kano ena banio?
bathroom to lootro, to banio
  with a private bathroom meh ithiotiko lootro
bath towel i petseta too banioo
battery i bataria
bay o kolpos
be* imeh
beach i paralia
beach mat i psaTHa
beach umbrella i ombrela
beans ta fasolia
  green beans ta fasolakia
  runner beans ta fasolakia freska
  broad beans ta kookia
beard ta yenia
beautiful oreos
because epithi

because of ... exetias ...
bed to krevati
  I'm going to bed now pao ya ipno tora
bed and breakfast thomatio meh pro-ino
bedroom to ipnothomatio
beef to moskhari
beer i bira
  two beers, please thio bires, parakalo

Most bars serve foreign label beers in bottles or cans (Amstel, Heineken, Becks, etc.) You will not often find places which serve draught beer.

before prin
begin arkhizo
  when does it begin? poteh arkhizi?
beginner (man/woman) o arkharios/i arkharia
beginning: at the beginning kat arkhas
behind piso
  behind me apo piso moo
beige bez
believe pistevo
belly-dancing to tsifteteli
below apo kato
belt i zoni
bend (in road) i strofi
berth (on ship) i klini
beside: beside the ... thipla sto ...
best aristos
better kaliteros

better than ... kaliteros apo ...
are you feeling better?
esTHaneseh kalitera?
between metaxi
beyond pera apo
bicycle to pothilato
big megalos
  too big poli megalo
  it's not big enough then ineh
  arketa megalo
bike to pothilato
  (motorbike) to mikhanaki
bikini to bikini
bill o logariasmos
  (US) to khartonomisma
  could I have the bill, please?
  boro na ekho ton
  logariasmo, parakalo?
bin o skoopithotenekes
bin liners i sakoola
  skoopithion
bird to pooli
biro® to stilo
birthday ta yeneTHlia
  happy birthday! khronia
  pola!
biscuit to biskoto
bit: a little bit ligo
  a big bit ena megalo komati
  a bit of ... ligo apo ...
  a bit expensive ligo akrivo,
  akrivootsiko
bite (by insect) to tsibima
  (by dog) i thagonia
bitter (taste etc) pikros
black mavros
blanket i kooverta
bleach (for toilet) to Harpik®
bless you! ya soo!

blind tiflos
blinds ta pantzooria
blister i fooskala
blocked (road, pipe)
  frakarismenos
  (sink) voolomenos
block of flats i polikatikia
blond xanTHos
blood to ema
  high blood pressure ipsili
  pi-esi ematos
blouse i blooza
blow-dry to khtenisma
  I'd like a cut and blow-dry
  THa iTHela kopsimo keh
  khtenisma
blue bleh
  blue eyes galana matia
blusher i poothra
boarding house i pansion
boarding pass i karta
  epivivaseos
boat (small) to ka-iki
  (for passengers) to plio
body to soma
boil (verb) vrazo
boiled egg to vrasto avgo
boiler o vrastiras
bone to kokalo
bonnet (of car) to kapo
book to vivlio
  (verb) klino
  can I book a seat? boro na
  kliso mia THesi?

dialogue

  **I'd like to book a table for
  two** THa iTHela na kliso

ena trapezi ya thio atoma
**what time would you like it
booked for?** ti ora to
THeleteh?
half past seven stis efta
keh misi
that's fine endaxi
and your name? to onoma
sas, parakalo?

bookshop to vivliopolio
bookstore to vivliopolio
boot (footwear) i bota
(of car) to port-bagaz
border (of country) ta sinora
bored: I'm bored vari-emeh
boring varetos
**born: I was born in
Manchester** yeniTHika sto
Manchester
I was born in 1960 yeniTHika
to 1960 (khilia eniakosia
exinda)
borrow thanizomeh
may I borrow ...? boro na
thanisto ...?
both keh i thio
bother: sorry to bother you
signomi poo sas enokhlo
bottle to bookali
a bottle of house red ena
bookali kokino spitiko krasi
bottle-opener to anikhtiri
bottom (of person) o kolos
at the bottom of the hill sto
vaTHos too lofoo
at the bottom of the road sto
telos too thromoo
box to kooti

box office to tamio
boy to agori
boyfriend o filos
bra to sooti-en
bracelet to vrakhioli
brake to freno
(verb) frenaro
brandy to koniak
bread to psomi
white bread to aspro psomi
brown bread to mavro
psomi
wholemeal bread to starenio
psomi
break (verb) spao
I've broken the ... espasa to ...
I think I've broken my wrist
nomizo oti espasa ton karpo
moo
break down (car) paTHeno
vlavi
I've broken down khalaseh to
aftokinito moo
breakdown (car) i vlavi

The place where you hire
a car should give you the
telephone number for the
local Express Service in case of
breakdowns. Tourists driving their
own car with proof of AA/RAC or
similar membership are given free
road assistance from the ELPA, the
Greek equivalent, which runs
breakdown services based in
Athens, Patra, Larissa, Volos,
Ioannina, Corfu, Tripoli, Crete and
Thessaloniki. The information
number is 174. In an emergency ring

their road assistance service on 104, anywhere in the country.

breakdown service i vlaves aftokiniton
breakfast to pro-ino
break-in: I've had a break-in meh listepsan
breast to stiTHos
breathe anapneo
breeze to aeraki
bridge (over river) i yefira
brief sindomos
briefcase o khartofilakas
bright (light etc) fotinos
  bright red khtipitos kokinos
brilliant (idea, person) katapliktikos
bring ferno
  I'll bring it back later THa to fero piso argotera
Britain i Vretania
British Vretanikos
brochure to prospektoos
broken spasmenos
  it's broken ineh spasmeno
bronchitis i vronkhititha
brooch i karfitsa
broom i skoopa
brother o athelfos
brother-in-law o gambros
brown kafeh
  brown hair kastana malia
  brown eyes kastana matia
bruise i melania
brush i voortsa
  (for hair) i voortsa ya ta malia
  (artist's) to pinelo
bucket o koovas

buffet car to boofeh
buggy (for child) to pethiko amaxaki
building to ktirio
bulb (light bulb) i lamba
Bulgaria i Voolgaria
Bulgarian (adj) Voolgarikos
bumper o profilaktiras
bunk i kooketa
bureau de change Sinalagma
  see **bank**
burglary i thiarixi
burn (noun) to kapsimo
  (verb) keo
burnt: this is burnt afto ineh kameno
burst: a burst pipe mia spasmeni solina
bus to leoforio
  what number bus is it to ...? ti ariTHmo ekhi to leoforio ya ...?
  when is the next bus to ...? poteh ineh to epomeno leoforio ya ...?
  what time is the last bus? ti ora ineh to telefteo leoforio?
  could you let me know when we get there? boriteh na moo to piteh, otan ftasoomeh eki?

For city buses, tickets should be bought in advance from newspaper or cigarette kiosks. You can use the same type of tickets for buses and trolleybuses in Athens. When you get on, always validate your ticket by inserting it into the machine on the bus/trolleybus. Buses have their destination written on the front; check this carefully, rather than the number, to make sure you are not on the wrong bus. For the major inter-city lines, ticketing is now computerized, with assigned seating and sold-out vehicles common. On smaller rural/island routes, it's generally first-come, first-served with some standing allowed and tickets dispensed on the spot by a conductor.

dialogue

does this bus go to ...? piyeni afto to leoforio sto ...?

no, you need a number ... okhi, prepi na pareteh to leoforio ariTHmos ...

business i thooli-es
bus station to praktorio leoforion, o staTHmos leoforion
bus stop i stasi leoforioo
bust (sculpture) i protomi (measurement) to stiTHos
busy (restaurant etc) polisikhnastos
I'm busy tomorrow imeh apaskholimenos avrio
but ala
butcher's o khasapis
butter to vootiro
button to koobi

buy agorazo
where can I buy ...? poo boro na agoraso ...?
by: by bus/car meh to leoforio/aftokinito
written by ... grameno apo ...
by the window thipla sto paraTHiro
by the sea konda sti THalasa
by Thursday prin apo tin Pempti
bye yasoo

C

cabbage to lakhano
cabin (on ship) i kabina
cable car to teleferik
café i kafeteria, to kafenio

The 'kafenio' is the traditional Greek coffee shop or café. Although its main business is Greek coffee it also serves spirits, beer, tea and soft drinks. A 'zakharoplastio' is a cross between café and patisserie and it serves coffee, alcohol, yoghurt and honey, sticky cakes etc, both to eat in and take away. A 'galaktopolio' is a type of take-away café, specializing more in dairy products (yoghurt, ice cream, custard desserts etc). These last two types of café are usually more family-oriented than a 'kafenio' and many also serve a basic continental breakfast. Usually the only edibles

sold in cafés are very sweet cakes
and preserves, although some city
cafés serve savoury snacks and
sandwiches.
See also **bar**

cagoule to athiavrokho
cake to cake
cake shop to zakharoplastio
call fonazo
(to phone) tilefono
what's it called? pos to
leneh?
he/she is called ... ton/tin
leneh ...
please call a doctor seh
parakalo, tilefoniseh seh ena
yatro
**please give me a call at
7.30 am tomorrow** seh
parakalo, tilefoniseh moo
avrio to pro-i stis efta keh
misi
please ask him to call me seh
parakalo, pes too na moo
tilefonisi
call back: I'll call back later
THa xanarTHo argotera
(phone back) THa seh paro
piso
**call round: I'll call round
tomorrow** THa peraso avrio
camcorder i mikhani lipseos
camera i fotografiki mikhani
camera shop to katastima
fotografikon ithon
camp (verb) kataskinono
can we camp here?
boroomeh na

kataskinosoomeh etho?
camping gas to igra-erio

Camping gas canisters
can be bought either from
a hardware store,
supermarkets or from campsite
shops; you can't carry canisters on
planes.

campsite to kambing

Official campsites range
from ramshackle
compounds on the islands
to highly organized sites run by EOT
(Greek Tourist Organization).
Freelance camping is officially
illegal and police crack down on
people camping rough in popular
tourist resorts. However, in quiet
rural inland areas you may find that
nobody is very bothered about it. It
is always best to ask permission
first in the village taverna or café
before pitching a tent.

can to kooti, i konserva
a can of beer mia bira seh
kooti
can: can you ...? boriteh
na ...?
can I have ...? boro na
ekho ...?
I can't ... then boro ...
Canada o Kanathas
Canadian Kanathezikos
I'm Canadian (man/woman)
imeh Kanathos/Kanatheza

canal to kanali
cancel akirono
candies i karameles
candle to keri
canoe to kano
canoeing kano kano
can-opener to anikhtiri
cap (hat) to kapelo
 (of bottle) to kapaki
car to aftokinito
 by car meh to aftokinito
carafe i karafa
 a carafe of house white,
 please mia karafa aspro
 spitiko krasi, parakalo
caravan to trokhospito
caravan site topoTHesia ya
 trokhospita
carburettor to karbirater
card (birthday etc) i karta
 here's my (business) card
 oristeh, i karta moo
cardigan i zaketa
cardphone i tilekarta
 see phone
careful prosektikos
 be careful! prosekheh!
caretaker o/i epistatis
car ferry to feri-bot
car hire enikiasis aftokiniton
 see rent
car park to parking
carpet to khali
 (fitted) i moketa
carriage (of train) to vagoni
carrier bag i sakoola
carrot to karoto
carry metafero
carry-cot to port-beh-beh

carton i koota
carwash to plindirio
 aftokiniton
case (suitcase) i valitsa
cash ta metrita
 will you cash this for me?
 THa moo to exaryiroseteh?
cash desk to tamio
cash dispenser i mikhani ya
 metrita
cashier o/i tamias
cassette i kaseta
cassette recorder to
 kasetofono
castle to kastro
casualty department Protes
 Vo-iTHi-es
cat i gata
catch piano
 where do we catch the bus
 to ...? apo poo THa
 paroomeh to leoforio?
cathedral o kaTHethrikos
 naos
Catholic (adj) kaTHolikos
cauliflower to koonoopithi
cave i spilia
ceiling to tavani
celery to selino
cellar (for wine) to kelari
cemetery to nekrotafio
Centigrade* Kelsioo
centimetre* ena ekatosto
central kendrikos
central heating i kendriki
 THermansi
centre to kendro
 how do we get to the city
 centre? pos THa pameh sto

kendro?
cereal ta cornflakes
certainly sigoora
 certainly not fisika okhi
chair i karekla
champagne i sampania
change (money) ta resta
 (verb: money, trains) alazo
 can I change this for ...? boro na alaxo afto ya ...?
 I don't have any change then ekho psila
 can you give me change for a 5,000 drachma note? boriteh na moo khalaseteh pendeh khiliathes thrakhmes?

Kiosks may sometimes refuse to change a 1,000 or 5,000 drachma note for you, unless you buy something from them.

dialogue

 do we have to change (trains)? prepi na alaxoomeh treno?
 yes, change at Corinth/no, it's a direct train neh, alaxteh stin KorinTHo/okhi, piyeni katefTHian

changed: to get changed alazo rookha
chapel to eklisaki
charge i timi, i thapani
 (verb) khreono

charge card i pistotiki karta
 see credit card
cheap ftinos
 do you have anything cheaper? ekheteh tipoteh ftinotero?
check (verb) epaliTHevo
 (US: cheque) i epitayi
 see cheque
 (US: bill) o logariasmos
 see bill
 could you check the ..., please? boriteh na elenxeteh to ..., parakalo?
checkbook to karneh epitagon
check-in to check-in
check in kano check-in
 where do we have to check in? poo prepi na kanoomeh check-in?
cheek (on face) to magoolo
cheerio! yasoo!
cheers! (toast) stin iya sas!, is iyian!
cheese to tiri
chemist's to farmakio

Greek chemists are well-qualified to give you advice on minor ailments; there's generally an all-night chemist's in bigger towns and cities; they work on a rota system and you generally find the address of the one currently open on the door of any chemist's.

cheque i epitayi

do you take cheques?
perneteh epitayes?
see **credit card**
cheque book to karneh
epitagon
cheque card i karta
epitagon
cherry to kerasi
chess to skaki
chest to stiTHos
chewing gum i tsikhla
chicken to kotopoolo
chickenpox i anemovloyia
child to pethi
 children ta pethia
child minder i dada
children's pool i pisina ton
 pethion
children's portion i pethiki
 meritha
chin to pigooni
china i porselani
Chinese (adj) Kinezikos
chips i tiganites patates
chocolate i sokolata
 milk chocolate i sokolata
 galaktos
 plain chocolate sokolata sketi
 a hot chocolate i zesti
 sokolata, mia sokolata rofima
choose thialego
Christian name to mikro
 onoma
Christmas ta khristooyena
 Christmas Eve i paramoni
 ton khristooyenon
 merry Christmas! kala
 khristooyena!
church i eklisia

cicada o tzitzikas
cider cider
cigar to pooro
cigarette to tsigaro
cigarette lighter o anaptiras
cinema o kinimatografos, to
 sinema
circle o kiklos
 (in theatre) o exostis
city i poli
city centre to kendro tis
 polis
clean (adj) kaTHaros
 can you clean these for me?
moo pleneteh afta?
cleaning solution (for contact
lenses) to kaTHaristiko
thialima
cleansing lotion to galaktoma
kaTHarismoo
clear kaTHaros
 (obvious) profanis
clever exipnos
cliff o apotomos vrakhos
climbing i orivasia
cling film to na-ilon
clinic i kliniki
cloakroom i gardaroba
clock to rolo-i
close klino

dialogue

what time do you close? ti
ora klineteh?
we close at 8 pm on
weekdays and 6 pm on
Saturdays klinoomeh stis
okto to vrathi tis

kaTHimerines keh stis exi
to apoyevma ta Savata
do you close for lunch?
klineteh ya mesimeriano
fayito?
yes, between 1 and 3.30 pm
neh, apo ti mia mekhri tis
tris keh misi

closed klistos
cloth (fabric) to ifasma
 (for cleaning etc) to pani
clothes ta rookha
clothes line i aplostra
clothes peg to mandalaki
cloud to sinefo
cloudy sinefiasmenos
clutch to debrayaz, o
 siblektis
coach (bus) to poolman
 (on train) to vagoni
coach station o staTHmos
 iperastikon leoforion
coach trip to taxithi meh
 poolman
coast i akti
 on the coast stin akti
coat (long coat) to palto
 (jacket) to sakaki
coathanger i kremastra
cockroach i katsaritha
cocoa to kakao
coconut i karitha
code (for phoning) o kothikos
 what's the (dialling) code for
 Athens? pios ineh o kothikos
 ya tin ATHina?
 see dialling code
coffee o kafes

two Greek coffees, please
thio Elinikoos kafethes,
parakalo

When you ask for a
coffee, say what kind you
want:

Eliniko	Greek/Turkish coffee
galliko	filter coffee
Nescafeh	zesto/pagomeno
	hot/iced instant coffee

Other useful terms are:

sketo	unsweetened
metrio	medium-sweet
gliko	very sweet

coin to kerma
Coke® i koka-kola
cold krios
 I'm cold kriono
 I have a cold imeh
 kriomenos
collapse: he's collapsed
 katarefseh
collar o yakas
collect paralamvano
 I've come to collect ... ilTHa
 ya na paro ...
collect call tilefono collect
college to koleyio
colour to khroma
 do you have this in other
 colours? to ekheteh seh ala
 khromata?
colour film to enkhromo
 film
comb i khtena
come erkhomeh

dialogue

where do you come from?
apo poo iseh?
I come from Edinburgh
imeh apo to Ethimvoorgo

come back epistrefo
 I'll come back tomorrow THa
 epistrepso avrio
come in beno mesa
comfortable (chair) anapaftikos
 (clothes) anetos
 (room, hotel) volikos
compact disc to compact
 disc
company (business) i eteria
compartment (on train) to
 koopeh
compass i pixitha
complain paraponoomeh
complaint to parapono
 I have a complaint ekho ena
 parapono
completely telios
computer o ipolo-yistis
concert i sinavlia
concussion i thiasisi
 engefaloo
conditioner (for hair) to
 kondisioner
condom to profilaktiko
conference to sinethrio
confirm epieveono
congratulations! sinkharitiria!
connecting flight sinthesi
 ptisis
connection (travel) i sinthesi
conscious sinesTHanomenos

constipation i thiskiliotis
consulate to proxenio
contact erkhomeh seh epafi
contact lenses i faki epafis
contraceptive (pill) to
 andisiliptiko
 (condom) to profilaktiko
convenient volikos
 that's not convenient then
 meh volevi
convent to monastiri
cook (verb) ma-yirevo
 not cooked misopsimeno
cooker i koozina
cookie to biskoto
cooking utensils ta ma-yirika
 skevi
cool throseros
Corfu i Kerkira
cork o felos
corkscrew to anikhtiri
corner: on the corner sti
 gonia
 in the corner sti gonia
cornflakes ta cornflakes
correct (right) sostos
corridor o thiathromos
cosmetics ta kalindika
cost (verb) stikhizo
 how much does it cost? poso
 kani?
cot i koonia
cotton to vamvaki
cotton wool to vamvaki
couch o kanapes
couchette i kooketa
cough o vikhas
cough medicine to farmako
 ya ton vikha

could: could you ...? boriteh na ...?
  could I have ...? boro na ekho ...?
  I couldn't ... then boroosa na ...

country (nation) i khora
  (countryside) i exokhi

countryside i exokhi

couple (man and woman) to zevgari
  a couple of ... thio apo ...

courgette to kolokiTHaki

courier o/i sinothos

course (main course etc) to piato
  of course veveh-a
  of course not fisika okhi

cousin (male/female) o xathelfos/i xathelfi

cow i a-yelatha

crab to kavoori

cracker to krakeraki

craft shop to ergastiri

crash i sigroosi
  I've had a crash trakara

crazy trelos

cream (on milk, in cake) i krema
  (lotion) i krema thermatos
  (colour) krem

creche o pethikos staTHmos

credit card i pistotiki karta

Credit/charge cards are useful – indeed almost essential – for renting cars. However, most hotels, restaurants and shops prefer cash, rather than cheques or cards, so check in advance if they are accepted.

dialogue

> **can I pay by credit card?** boro na pliroso meh pistotiki karta?
> **which card do you want to use?** ti karta THeleteh na khrisimopi-iseteh?
> **yes, sir** endaxi, kiri-eh
> **what's the number?** ti ariTHmo ekhi?
> **and the expiry date?** keh poteh ineh i imerominia lixeos?

Crete i Kriti

crisps ta tsips

crockery ta piatika

crossing (by sea) to THalasio taxithi

crossroads to stavrothromi

crowd o kosmos

crowded yematos kosmo

crown (on tooth) i korona

cruise i krooazi-era

crutches i pateritses

cry (weep) kleo
  (shout) fonazo

cucumber to agoori

cup to flidzani
  a cup of ..., please ena flidzani ..., parakalo

cupboard to doolapi

cure i THerapia

curly sgooros, katsaros

current to revma
curtains i koortines
cushion to maxilaraki
custom to eTHimo
Customs to Telonio
cut to kopsimo
(verb) kovo
I've cut myself kopika
cutlery ta makheropiroona
cycling i pothilasia
cyclist o/i pothilatis
Cyprus i Kipros

D

dad o babas
daily kaTHimerina
damage (verb) katastrefo
damaged katastrafikeh
I'm sorry, I've damaged this
lipameh, to khalasa
damn! na pari i oryi!
damp (adj) igros
dance o khoros
(verb) khorevo
would you like to dance?
THelis na khorepsoomeh?
dangerous epikinthinos
Danish thanos
dark (adj: colour) skotinos
(hair) mavros
it's getting dark skotiniazi
date*: what's the date today?
poso ekhi o minas simera?
let's make a date for next
Monday as sinandiTHoomeh
tin epomeni theftera
dates (fruit) i khoormathes

daughter i kori
daughter-in-law i nifi
dawn i avyi
at dawn tin avyi
day i mera
the day after tin epomeni
mera
the day after tomorrow
meTHavrio
the day before tin pro-
igoomeni mera
the day before yesterday
prokhtes
every day kaTHeh mera
all day oli tin imera
in two days' time meta apo
thio meres
day trip to taxithi
afTHimeron
dead peTHamenos, nekros
deaf koofos
deal (business) i simfonia
it's a deal simfonisameh,
endaxi
death o THanatos
decaffeinated coffee o kafes
khoris kafe-ini
December o thekemvrios
decide apofasizo
we haven't decided yet then
ekhoomeh apofasisi akoma
decision i apofasi
deck (on ship) to katastroma
deckchair i poliTHrona, i sez
long
deduct afero
deep vaTHis
definitely oposthipoteh
definitely not seh kamia

periptosi
degree (qualification) to ptikhio
delay i kaTHisterisi
deliberately epitithes
delicatessen ta delicatessen
delicious nostimotatos
deliver thianemo
delivery (of mail) i thianomi, i
  parathosi
demotic i dimotiki
Denmark i thania
dental floss to othondiko
  nima
dentist o/i othondiatros

dialogue

it's this one here afto etho
ineh
this one? afto?
no, that one okhi, ekino
here? etho?
yes neh

dentures i masela
deodorant to aposmitiko
department to tmima
department store to megalo
  katastima
departure i anakhorisi
departure lounge i eTHoosa
  anakhoriseos
depend: it depends exartateh
  it depends on ... exartateh
  apo ...
deposit (as security) i
  kataTHesi
  (as part payment) i prokatavoli
description i perigrafi

dessert to glikisma
destination o pro-orismos
develop anaptiso
  (a film) emfanizo

dialogue

could you develop these
films? boriteh na
emfaniseteh afta ta film?
when will they be ready?
poteh THa ineh etima?
tomorrow afternoon avrio
to apoyevma
how much is the four-hour
service? poso kani i
emfanisi seh teseris ores?

diabetic (man/woman) o
  thiavitikos/i thiavitiki
  diabetic foods i thiavitiki
  trofi
dial (verb) kalo, perno
  ariTHmo
dialling code o kothikos
  ariTHmos

For direct international
calls from Greece, dial the
country code (given
below), the area code (minus the
first 0), and finally the subscriber
number:

UK: 0044	Australia: 0061
Ireland: 00353	New Zealand: 0064
US & Canada: 001	

diamond to thiamandi
diaper i pana

diarrhoea i thiaria
diary to imerolo-yio
dictionary to lexiko
didn't
 see not
die peTHeno
diesel i dizel
diet i thi-eta
 I'm on a diet kano thi-eta
 I have to follow a special diet
 prepi na kano ithiki thi-eta
difference i thiafora
 what's the difference? pia
 ineh i thiafora?
different thiaforetikos
 this one is different afto etho
 ineh thiaforetiko
 a different table ena alo
 trapezi
difficult thiskolos
difficulty i thiskolia
dinghy to zodiak®
dining room i trapezaria
dinner (evening meal) to
 thipno
 to have dinner tro-o
 vrathino
direct (adj) kat-efTHian
 is there a direct train?
 iparkhi kat-efTHian treno
 ya ...?
direction i katefTHinsi
 which direction is it? pros ta
 poo ineh?
 is it in this direction? ineh
 pros afti tin katefTHinsi?
directory enquiries i
 plirofori-es

The number for directory
enquiries is 131 for
Athens numbers, 132 for
other numbers in Greece and 161 for
international numbers.

dirt i vroma
dirty vromikos
disabled anapiros
 is there access for the
 disabled? iparkhi prosvasi ya
 toos anapiroos?
disappear exafanizomeh
 it's disappeared
 exafanistikeh
disappointed apogo-
 itevmenos
disappointing apogo-iteftiko
disaster i katastrofi
disco i diskotek
discount i ekptosi
 is there a discount? kaneteh
 ekptosi?
disease i arostia
disgusting a-ithiastikos
dish (meal) to piato
 (bowl) to bol
dishcloth i patsavoora
disinfectant to apolimandiko
disk (for computer) i thisketa
disposable diapers i
 khartines panes
disposable nappies i
 khartines panes
distance i apostasi
 in the distance eki kato
distilled water apestagmeno
 nero
district i sinikia

disturb enokhlo

diversion (detour) i parakampsi

diving board i santiha vootias

divorced: I'm divorced (man/woman) khorismenos/khorismeni

dizzy: I feel dizzy zalizomeh

do kano

what shall we do? ti THa kanoomeh?

how do you do it? pos to kaneteh?

will you do it for me? boriteh na moo to kaneteh?

dialogues

how do you do? ti kaneteh?

nice to meet you kharika ya ti gnorimia

what do you do? ti thoolia kaneteh?

I'm a teacher, and you? imeh thaskalos, ki esis?

I'm a student imeh fititis

what are you doing this evening? ti THa kaneteh apopseh?

we're going out for a drink; do you want to join us? THa pameh ya ena poto – THeleteh na elTHeteh mazi mas?

do you want cream? THeleteh krema?

I do, but she doesn't ego neh, ekini, omos, okhi

doctor o/i yatros

we need a doctor khriazomasteh enan yatro

please call a doctor seh parakalo, kaleseh enan yatro

Any chemist's will have a list of the nearest doctor's surgeries; if you're a citizen of an EU country, take the form E111 (obtainable from post offices in the UK) with you – this should enable you to get free treatment and pay for prescriptions at the local rate. In practice, hospital staff often meet the E111 with uncomprehending looks and you may have to request reimbursement from the NHS on your return. Some form of travel insurance is therefore advisable and is essential for non-EU citizens. In tourist areas, it should be easy to find an English-speaking doctor and the tourist police (phone 171) may be able to help with some names if you have any difficulty.

dialogue

where does it hurt? poo ponateh?

right here akrivos etho

does that hurt more? sas pona-i afto pio poli?

yes neh

take this to a chemist thosteh afto seh ena farmaki-o

document to engrafo
dog o skilos
doll i kookla
domestic flight ptisi esoterikoo
donkey o ga-itharos
don't! mi!
  don't do that! min to kanis afto!
  (stop) stamata!
  see **not**
door i porta
doorman o THiroros
double thiplo
double bed to thiplo krevati
double room to thiplo thomatio
doughnut to donat
down kato
  down here etho kato
  put it down over there valeh to eki kato
  it's down there on the right vrisketeh eki kato sta thexia
  it's further down the road ineh ligo parakato
downmarket (restaurant etc) ftinos
downstairs kato
dozen mia doozina
  half a dozen misi doozina
drain o okhetos
draught beer varelisia bira
draughty: it's draughty kani revma
drawer to sirtari
drawing to skhethio
dreadful friktos
dream to oniro

dress to forema
dressed: to get dressed dinomeh
dressing (for cut) i gaza
  (for salad) to lathoxitho
dressing gown i roba
drink to poto
  (verb) pino
  a cold drink to anapsiktiko
  can I get you a drink? boro na seh keraso kanena poto?
  what would you like (to drink)? ti THa THelateh na pi-iteh?
  no thanks, I don't drink okhi, efkharisto, then pino
  I'll just have a drink of water THa paro monon ena potiri nero
drinking water to posimo nero
  is this drinking water? ineh posimo afto to nero?

Although water in villages is pure (and tastes wonderful) because it comes from the mountains, mineral water is preferable to tap water in big towns or on some of the drier and more remote islands.

drive othiga-o
  we drove here othiyisameh etho
  I'll drive you home THa seh pao spiti

Cars have obvious advantages for getting to the more inaccessible parts of mainland Greece, but this is one of the more expensive countries in Europe to rent a car. If you drive your own vehicle to and through Greece, you'll need international third party insurance, the so-called Green Card, as well as an International Driving Licence and the registration documents. Upon arrival your passport will get a carnet stamp; this normally allows you to keep a vehicle in Greece for up to six months, exempt from road tax. Greece has the highest accident rate in Europe after Portugal, and many of the roads can be quite perilous – asphalt can turn into a dirt track without warning on the smaller routes, and railway crossings are rarely guarded. Uphill drivers insist on their right of way, as do those first to approach a one-lane bridge – headlights flashed at you mean the opposite of what they mean in the UK or North America and signify that the driver is coming through. Wearing a seatbelt is compulsory and children under 10 are not allowed to sit in the front seats. If you are involved in any kind of accident it's illegal to drive away, and you can be held at a police station for up to 24 hours. If this happens, ring your consulate immediately, in order to get a lawyer (you have this right). Don't make a statement to anyone who doesn't speak, and write, very good English. There are a limited number of express highways between Pátra, Athens, Vólos and Thessaloniki, on which tolls are levied – currently between 400dr and 700dr at each sporadically placed gate. They're nearly twice as quick as the old roads, and well worth using.

driver o/i othigos
driving licence i athia othiyiseos, to thiploma othiyiseos
drop: just a drop, please
(of drink) poli ligo, parakalo
drug to farmako
drugs (narcotics) ta narkotika
drunk (adj) meTHismenos
drunken driving methismeno othiyima

The legal limit is 0.5% but don't drink and drive.

dry (adj) stegnos
(wine) xiros
dry-cleaner to stegno-kaTHaristirio
duck i papia
due: he was due to arrive yesterday eprokito na ftasi khtes
when is the train due? poteh ftani to treno?
dull (pain) exasTHenimenos
(weather) moondos

(boring) varetos
dummy (baby's) i pipila
during kata ti thiarkia
dust i skoni
dusty skonismeno
dustbin o skoopithodenekes
duty-free (goods) ta aforoloyita
duty-free shop to katastima
aforolo-yiton
duvet to paploma

E

each kaTHeh
how much are they each?
poso ekhi to kaTHena?
ear to afti
earache: I have earache ekho
pono sto afti
early noris
early in the morning noris to
pro-i
I called by earlier perasa pro-
igoomenos
earrings ta skoolarikia
east i anatoli
in the east stin anatoli
Easter to Paskha
Easter Sunday i Kiriaki too
Paskha

Easter is by far the most
important festival of the
Greek year and taken
much more seriously than it is
anywhere in western Europe. From
Wednesday of Holy Week the state

radio and TV networks are given
over solely to religious programmes
until the following Monday. The
festival is an excellent time to be in
Greece, both for the beautiful and
moving religious ceremonies and for
the days of feasting that follow. In
the week leading up to Easter
Sunday you should wish people a
Happy Easter 'kalo paskha'.

easy efkolos
eat tro-o
we've already eaten, thanks
fagameh ithi, efkharisto

eating habits
Greeks don't generally eat
breakfast; however, you
can get a continental-style breakfast
of bread, jam, yoghurt and coffee at
most cafés. Greeks usually have a
late lunch – between 2-3 pm The
evening meal is also eaten late –
between 9 and 11 pm, although it is
possible to eat earlier in some more
touristic establishments. Greek
cuisine and restaurants are simple
and straightforward. There's no
snobbery about eating out.

eau de toilette i kolonia
EC i eok
economy class tooristiki
THesi
egg to avgo
hard-boiled egg avgo
sfikhto
fried egg tiganito avgo

eggplant i melidzana
either: either ... or ... i ... i ...
  either of them opio naneh
elastic to lastikho
elastic band to lastikhaki
elbow o angonas
electric ilektrikos
electrical appliances
  ilektrikes siskeves
electric fire i ilektriki somba
electrician o ilektrologos
electricity to ilektriko revma

 The supply is 220V, though
anything requiring 240V
will work. Most plugs are
two round pins: a travel plug is useful.

elevator to asanser
else: something else kati alo
  somewhere else kapoo aloo

dialogue

would you like anything
else? THa THelateh
tipoteh alo?
no, nothing else, thanks
okhi, tipoteh alo,
efkharisto

e-mail to e-mail
embassy i presvia
emergency i ektakti anangi
  this is an emergency! ineh
  epigon!
emergency exit i exothos
  kinthinoo
empty (adj) athios

end to telos
  (verb) teliono
  at the end of the street sto
  telos too thromoo
  when does it end? poteh
  telioni?
engaged (toilet, telephone)
  katilimenos
  (to be married: man/woman)
  aravoniasmenos/
  aravoniasmeni
engine (car) i mikhani too
  aftokinitoo
England i Anglia
English ta Anglika
  I'm English (man/woman) imeh
  Anglos/Anglitha
  do you speak English?
  milateh anglika?
enjoy: to enjoy oneself
  thiaskethazo

dialogue

how did you like the film?
pos soo fanikeh to ergo?
I enjoyed it very much; did
you enjoy it? moo areseh
para poli; esena soo
areseh?

enjoyable efkharistos
enlargement (of photo) i
  me-yenTHisi
enormous terastios
enough arketa
  there's not enough then
  iparkhi arketo
  it's not big enough then ineh

arketa megalo
that's enough ftani, arki
entrance i isothos
envelope o fakelos
epileptic (man/woman) o epiliptikos/i epiliptiki
equipment o exoplismos
error to laTHos
especially ithika
essential vasikos, aparetitos
it is essential that ... ineh aparetito na ...
EU Evropa-iki Enosi
euro to evro
Eurocheque to Eurocheque
Eurocheque card i karta Eurocheque
Europe i Evropi
European (adj) Evropa-ikos
European Union Evropa-iki Enosi
even: even the Greeks akoma keh i Elines
even if ... akoma ki an ...
evening to vrathi
this evening simera to vrathi
in the evening to vrathi
evening meal to thipno
eventually telika
ever poteh

dialogue

have you ever been to Crete? ekheteh pa-i poteh stin Kriti?
yes, I was there two years ago neh, imoon eki prin apo thio khronia

every kaTHeh
every day kaTHeh mera
everyone oli
everything kaTHeh ti
everywhere pandoo
exactly! akrivos!
exam to thiagonisma
example to parathigma
for example parathigmatos kharin
excellent exohos
excellent! exokha!
except ektos
excess baggage to ipervaro
exchange rate sinalagmatiki isotimia
exciting sinarpastikos
excuse me (to get past) signomi
(to get attention) parakalo
(to say sorry) meh sinkhoriteh
exhaust (pipe) i exatmisi
exhausted (tired) exandlimenos
exhibition i ekTHesi
exit i exothos
where's the nearest exit? poo ineh i plisi-esteri exothos?
expect perimeno
expensive akrivos
experienced embiros
explain exigo
can you explain that? boris na moo to exiyisis?
express mail to katepigon
express train to treno express
extension (telephone) i sinthesi tilefonoo
could you get me extension 221, please? meh sintheh-

eteh meh to 221 (thiak**o**sia ik**o**si **e**na), parakal**o**?
extension lead i pro-**e**ktasi
extra: can we have an extra chair? bor**oo**meh na ekh**oo**meh mia kar**e**kla ak**o**ma?
 do you charge extra for that? khre**o**neteh epipl**e**on ya af**to**?
extraordinary asin**i**THistos
extremely ipervolik**a**
eye to m**a**ti
 will you keep an eye on my suitcase for me? THa moo to pros**e**kheteh?
eyebrow pencil to mol**i**vi ya ta fr**i**thia
eye drops i stag**o**nes ya ta m**a**tia
eyeglasses (US) ta yial**i**a
eyeliner to eyeliner
eye make-up remover to gal**a**ktoma kaTHarism**oo**
eye shadow i ski**a** mati**o**n

F

face to pr**o**sopo
factory to ergost**a**sio
Fahrenheit* vaTHm**i** Faren**a**-it
faint (verb) lipoTH**i**mao
 she's fainted lipoTH**i**miseh
 I feel faint esTH**a**nomeh lipoTH**i**mia
fair (funfair) to pan**i**yiri
 (trade) i ek**THe**si
 (adj) th**i**keos
fairly ark**e**ta

fake i apom**i**misi
Fall to fTHin**o**poro
 see autumn
fall (verb) p**e**fto
 she's had a fall **e**peseh
false pseftik**o**s
family i iko-y**e**nia
famous thi**a**simos
fan (electrical) o anemist**i**ras
 (hand held) i vent**a**lia
 (sports) o/i opath**o**s
fan belt to vendil**a**ter
fantastic fandastik**o**s
far makri**a**

dialogue

> **is it far from here?** ineh makri**a** ap**o** eth**o**?
> **no, not very far** **o**khi, **o**khi keh pol**i** makri**a**
> **well how far?** p**o**so makri**a**, thilath**i**?
> **it's about 20 kilometres** ineh peri**poo** ik**o**si khili**o**metra

fare i tim**i** too isitir**i**oo
farm to agr**o**ktima
fashionable tis m**o**thas
fast grig**o**ros
fat (person) pakh**i**s
 (on meat) to l**i**pos
father o pat**e**ras
father-in-law o peTH**e**ros
faucet i vr**i**si
fault to el**a**toma
 sorry, it was my fault sign**o**mi, **i**tan sf**a**lma moo

it's not my fault then fteo ego
faulty elatomatikos
favourite agapimenos
fax to fax
(verb: person) stelno fax seh ...
(document) stelno seh fax
February o Fevrooarios
feel esTHanomeh
I feel hot zestenomeh
I feel unwell then
esTHanomeh kala
I feel like going for a walk
ekho orexi na pao mia volta
how are you feeling? pos
esTHaneseh?
I'm feeling better
esTHanomeh kalitera
felt-tip pen o markathoros
fence o fraktis
fender o profilaktiras
ferry to feri bot

There are three different
varieties of vessel:
medium-sized to large
ordinary ferries (which operate the
main services), hydrofoils (run by
the **Ceres "Flying Dolphins"** and
Dodecanese Hydrofoils, among
other companies), and local 'kaikia'
(small boats which in season cover
short island hops and excursions).
Costs are very reasonable on longer
journeys, though proportionately
more expensive for shorter, inter-
island connections. The most
reliable, up-to-date information is
available from the local port police
('limenarkhio'), which maintains

offices at Piraeus and on virtually all
fair-sized islands.

festival to festival
fetch pa-o na fero
I'll fetch him THa pa-o na
ton fero
will you come and fetch me
later? THa elTHis na meh
paris argotera?
feverish empiretos
few: a few liyi, liyes, liga
a few days liyes meres
fiancé o aravoniastikos
fiancée i aravoniastikia
field to khorafi
fight o agonas
figs ta sika
fill yemizo
fill in yemizo
do I have to fill this in? prepi
na to yemiso?
fill up yemizo telios
fill it up, please yemisteh tin,
parakalo
filling (in cake, sandwich) i
yemisi
(in tooth) to sfra-yisma
film to film

dialogue

do you have this kind of
film? ekheteh tetio film?
yes – how many
exposures? neh – meh
poses stasis?
36 trianda-exi

film processing i emfanisi too film

filter coffee o kafes filtroo

filter papers ta filtra ya kafeh

filthy vromeros

find vrisko
  I can't find it then to vrisko
  I've found it to vrika

find out anakalipto
  could you find out for me? boris na maTHis?

fine (weather) oreos
  (punishment) to prostimo

dialogues

how are you? ti kanis?
I'm fine thanks mia khara, efkharisto

is that OK? afto ineh endaxi?
that's fine thanks ineh mia khara, efkharisto

finger to thakhtilo

finish teliono
  I haven't finished yet then ekho teliosi akomi
  when does it finish? poteh telioni?

fire: fire! pirkaya!
  can we light a fire here? boroomeh na anapsoomeh fotia etho?

it's on fire pireh fotia

fire alarm o sinayermos pirkayas

fire brigade i pirosvestiki ipiresia

 In the event of a fire, phone 199.

fire escape i exothos pirkayas

fire extinguisher o pirosvestiras

first protos
  I was first imoon protos
  at first stin arkhi
  the first time i proti fora
  first on the left protos sta aristera

first aid i protes vo-iTHi-es

first aid kit to kooti proton vo-iTHi-on

first class (travel etc) proti THesi

first floor to proto patoma
  (US) to iso-yio

first name to onoma

fish to psari

fisherman o psaras

fishing village to psarokhori

fishmonger's to psarathiko

fit (attack) i prosvoli
  it doesn't fit me then moo khora-i

fitting room to thokimastirio

fix ftiakhno
  (arrange) kanonizo
  can you fix this? boris na to ftiaxis?

fizzy meh anTHrakiko

flag i simea

flannel to sfoogari

flash (for camera) to flas
flat (apartment) to thiamerisma
  (adj) epipethos
  I've got a flat tyre me epiaseh lastikho
flavour i gefsi
flea o psilos
flight i ptisi
flight number ariTHmos ptisis
flippers ta vatrakhopethila
flood i plimira
floor (of room) to patoma
  (of building) o orofos
  on the floor sto patoma
florist o anTHopolis
flour to alevri
flower to looloothi
flu i gripi
fluent: he speaks fluent Greek
  mila-i aptesta elinika
fly i miga
  (verb) peto
  can we fly there? boroomeh na pameh eki a-eroporikos?
fly in peta-o pros
fly out peta-o apo
fog i omikhli
foggy: it's foggy ekhi omikhli
folk dancing i thimotiki khori
folk music i thimotiki moosiki
follow akolooTHo
  follow me akolootha meh
food to fa-yito
food poisoning trofiki thilitiriasi
food shop/store to bakaliko
foot* to pothi
  on foot meh ta pothia
football (game) to pothosfero

  (ball) i bala
football match o pothosferikos agonas
for ya
  do you have something for ...? (headache/diarrhoea etc)
  ekheteh kati ya ...?

dialogues

who's the moussaka for?
ya pion ineh o moosakas?
that's for me ya mena
and this one? ki afto etho?
that's for her afto ineh ya ekini

where do I get the bus for Akropolis? apo poo THa paro to leoforio ya tin Akropoli?
the bus for Acropolis leaves from Stathiou Street to leoforio ya tin Akropoli fevyi apo tin Otho Stathioo

how long have you been here for? poso kero iseh etho pera?
I've been here for two days, how about you? vriskomeh etho pera etho keh thio meres, esi?
I've been here for a week vriskomeh etho pera etho keh mia vthomatha

forehead to metopo

foreign xenos
foreigner (man/woman) o
   xenos/i xeni
forest to thasos
forget xekhno
   I forget xekhno
   I've forgotten xekhasa
fork (for eating) to pirooni
   (in road) i thiaklathosi
form (document) i etisi
formal (dress) episimos
fortnight to theka-
   penTHimero
fortunately eftikhos
forward: could you forward my
   mail? boriteh na moo
   stileteh ta gramata moo?
forwarding address i thi-
   efTHinsi apostolis
foundation cream krema
   prosopoo ya makiyaz
fountain i piyi
foyer to foyer
fracture to katagma
free elefTHeros
   (no charge) thorean
   is it free of charge? ineh
   thorean?
freeway i eTHniki othos
freezer i katapsixi
French (adj) galikos
   (language) ta galika
French fries i tiganites patates
frequent sikhnos
   how frequent is the bus to
   Corinth? kaTHeh poteh ekhi
   leoforio ya tin KorinTHo?
fresh (weather, breeze) throseros
   (fruit etc) freskos

fresh orange o freskos khimos
   portokali
Friday i Paraskevi
fridge to psiyio
fried tiganismenos
fried egg to tiganito avgo
friend (male/female) o filos/i fili
friendly filikos
from apo
   when does the next train
   from Patras arrive? poteh
   ftani to epomeno treno apo
   tin Patra?
   from Monday to Friday apo
   theftera os Paraskevi
   from next Thursday apo tin
   ali Pempti

dialogue

where are you from? apo
   poo iseh?
I'm from Slough imeh apo
   to Sla-oo

front to mbrostino meros
   in front mbrosta
   in front of the hotel mbrosta
   apo to xenothokhio
   at the front sto mbrostino
   meros
frost i pagonia, o pa-yetos
frozen pagomenos
frozen food i katepsiymeni
   trofi
fruit ta froota
fruit juice o khimos frooton
fry tiganizo
frying pan to tigani

full yematos
  it's full of ... ineh yemato
  meh ...
  I'm full khortasa
full board fool pansion
fun: it was fun kala itan,
  kanameh kefi
funeral i kithia
funny (strange) paraxenos
  (amusing) astios
furniture ta epipla
further parapera
  it's further down the road
  ineh akoma parakato

dialogue

how much further is it to
Piraeus? poso ineh akomi
mekhri ton Pirea?
about 5 kilometres yiro sta
pendeh khiliometra

fuse i asfalia
  the lights have fused
  ka-ikaneh ta fota
fuse box to kooti meh tis
  asfali-es
fuse wire to sirma asfalias
future to melon
  in future sto melon

G

gallon* ena galoni
game (cards etc) to pekhnithi
  (match) o agonas
  (meat) to kiniyi

garage (for fuel) to
  venzinathiko
  (for repairs) to sineryio
  (for parking) to garaz

Greek garages are usually
open from approx. 8 am
to 8 pm; the address of
those which are open at night and at
weekends is usually on the door of
the garage office. There will always
be at least one petrol pump per
district open at the weekend, but it's
best to carry a full petrol can at all
times.
see petrol

garden o kipos
garlic to skortho
gas to gazi
gas cylinder (camping gas) i fiali
  gazi
gasoline i venzini
  see petrol
gas permeable lenses i
  imiskliri faki epafis
gas station to venzinathiko
gate i avloporta
  (at airport) i exothos
gay (adj) omofilofilos
gay bar to gay bar
gears i takhitita
gearbox to kivotio takhititon
gear lever o levi-es takhititon
general yenikos
gents (toilet) i too-aleta ton
  anthron
genuine (antique etc)
  afTHendikos

German (adj) Yermanikos
(language) ta Yermanika
German measles i eriTHra
Germany i Yermania
get (fetch) perno
will you get me another one,
please? THa moo paris alo
ena, parakalo?
how do I get to ...? pos boro
na pao sto ...?
do you know where I can get
them? mipos xereteh poo
boro na vro tetia?

dialogue

can I get you a drink? na
seh keraso kanena poto?
no, I'll get this one, what
would you like? okhi, ego
kernao afti ti fora; ti THa
iTHeles?
a glass of red wine ena
potiri kokino krasi

get back (return) epistrefo
get in (arrive) ftano
get off kateveno
where do I get off? poo THa
katevo?
get on (to train etc) aneveno
get out (of car etc) vyeno
get up (in the morning)
sikonomeh
gift to thoro

It is customary to give
gifts to people on their
name days, birthdays, at

Christmas and on New Year's Eve,
and when you want to thank
someone for a favour.

gift shop katastima thoron,
ithi thoron
gin to tzin
a gin and tonic, please ena
tzin meh tonik, parakalo
girl to koritsi
girlfriend i filenatha
give thino
can you give me some
change? boriteh na moo
thoseteh psila?
I gave it to him to ethosa seh
afton
will you give this to ...? to
thinis afto ston ...?

dialogue

how much do you want for
this? posa THelis ya afto?
10,000 drachmas theka
khiliathes thrakhmes
I'll give you 7,000 drachmas
soo thino efta khiliathes

give back epistrefo, thino piso
glad efkharistimenos
glass (material) to yali
(tumbler, wine glass) to potiri
a glass of wine ena potiri
krasi
glasses ta yalia
gloves ta gandia
glue i kola
go pao

we'd like to go to the ...
theloomeh na pameh sto ...
where are you going? poo
pateh?
where does this bus go? poo
pa-i afto to leoforio?
let's go! pameh
she's gone (left) efiyeh
where has he gone? poo
piyeh aftos?
I went there last week piga
eki tin perasmeni
evthomatha
hamburger to go
khamboorger ya to spiti
go away fevgo
go away! fiyeh!
go back (return) epistrefo
go down (the stairs etc)
kateveno
go in beno
go out (in the evening) v-yeno
**do you want to go out
tonight?** theleteh na pateh
exo apopseh?
go through thiaskhizo, pao
thia mesoo
go up (the stairs etc) aneveno
goat i katsika
goat's cheese to katsikisio tiri
God o THeos
goggles i maska
gold o khrisos
golf to golf
golf course to yipetho golf
good kalos
good! kala!
it's no good (product etc) afto
then ineh kalo

(not worth trying) then ofeli
goodbye ya khara, adio
good evening kalispera
Good Friday i Megali
Paraskevi

Good Friday is a public
holiday in Greece. Post
offices, banks and some
shops close at noon, but
supermarkets and public transport
are not greatly affected.

good morning kalimera
good night kalinikhta
goose i khina
got: we've got to ... prepi
na ...
have you got any ...? ekheteh
kaTHoloo ...?
government i kivernisi
gradually siga-siga
grammar i gramatiki
gram(me) ena gramario
granddaughter i egoni
grandfather o papoos
grandmother i ya-ya
grandson o egonos
grapefruit to grapefruit
grapefruit juice o khimos
grapefruit
grapes ta stafilia
grass to khortari, to grasithi
grateful evgnomon
gravy o zomos too kreatos
great (excellent) poli kalo
that's great! iperokha!
it's a great success ineh
megali epitikhia

Great Britain i Megali Vretania
Greece i Elatha
greedy akhortagos
Greek (adj) Elinikos
  (language) ta Elinika
  (man) o Elinas
  (woman) i Elinitha
  the Greeks i Elines
Greek coffee Elinikos kafes
Greek-Cypriot (adj) Elinokiprios
Greek Orthodox Elinikos OrTHothoxos
green prasinos
green card (car insurance) i asfalia ya othiyisi sto exoteriko
greengrocer's o manavis
grey grizos
grill i psistaria
grilled psitos sti skhara
grocer's to bakaliko
ground to ethafos
  on the ground sto ethafos
ground floor to iso-yio
group to groop
guarantee i engi-isi
  is it guaranteed? ineh engiimeno?
guest (man/woman) o filoxenoomenos/i filoxenoomeni
  see **hospitality**
guesthouse i pansion

It is difficult to find guesthouses in less touristy areas of Greece, but local people may offer you private rooms (thomatia) and food. Between November and early April, private rooms are closed to keep hotels in business.

guide o/i xenagos
guidebook o tooristikos othigos
guided tour i xenayisi
guitar i kiTHara
gum (in mouth) to oolo
gun (pistol) to pistoli
  (rifle) to oplo
gym to yimnastirio

H

hair ta malia
hairbrush i voortsa ya malia, i khtena
haircut (man's) to koorema
  (woman's) to kopsimo
hairdresser's to komotirio
  (men's) to koorio
hairdryer to pistolaki
hair gel o afros malion
hairgrips ta piastrakia malion
hair spray to spray ya ta malia
half misos
  half an hour misi ora
  half a litre miso litro
  about half that peripoo to miso apo afto
half board demi-pansion
half-bottle miso bookali
half fare miso isitirio
half price misotimis

ham to zambon
hamburger to khamboorger
hammer to sfiri
hand to kheri
handbag i tsanda
handbrake to khirofreno
handkerchief to mandili
  (paper) to khartomandilo
handle to kherooli
hand luggage to sakvooa-yaz
hang-gliding i anemoporia
hangover o ponokefalos
  I've got a hangover ekho
  ponokefalo
happen simveni
  what's happening? ti
  simveni?
  what has happened? ti
  sinevi?
happy eftikhismenos
  I'm not happy about this then
  imeh efkharistimenos meh
  afto
harbour to limani
hard skliros
  (difficult) thiskolos
hard-boiled egg to sfikhto
  avgo
hard lenses i skliri faki
hardly meta vias
  hardly ever s-khethon poteh
hardware shop ta ithi
  kingalerias
hat to kapelo
hate miso
have* ekho
  can I have a ...? boro na
  ekho ena ...?
  do you have ...? ekheteh ...?

what'll you have? ti THa
piiteh?
I have to leave now prepi na
piyeno tora
do I have to ...? prepi na ...?
can we have some ...?
boroomeh na ekhoomeh
merika ...?
hayfever aler-yia sti yiri
hazelnuts to foondooki
he* aftos
  is he here? ineh etho?
head to kefali
headache o ponokefalos
headlights i provolis
headphones ta akoostika
health food shop katastima
  iyi-inon trofon
healthy iyi-is
hear akoo-o

dialogue

> can you hear me? meh
> akoos?
> I can't hear you, could you
> repeat that? then seh
> akoo-o, boris na to
> epanalavis?

hearing aid ta akoostika
heart i karthia
heart attack i karthiaki
  prosvoli
heat i zesti
heater i THermansi
  (radiator) to kalorifer
heating i THermansi
heavy varis

heel (of foot) i fterna
(of shoe) to tak**oo**ni
could you heel these?
bor**i**teh na moo valeteh
ken**oo**ryia tak**oo**nia saft**a**?
heelbar o tsag**a**ris
height to **i**psos
helicopter to elik**o**ptero
hello ya sas
(familiar) ya soo
(answer on phone) embr**o**s
helmet (for motorcycle) to
kr**a**nos
help i vo-**i**THia
(verb) vo-**i**TH**o**
help! vo-**i**THia!
can you help me? bor**i**teh na
meh vo-**i**THiseteh?
**thank you very much for your
help** efkharist**o** ya ti vo-
iTHia sas
helpful exipiretik**o**s
hepatitis i ipat**i**titha
her*: I haven't seen her then
tin **e**kho thi
to her saft**i**n
with her maz**i** tis
for her yaft**i**n
that's her aft**i** **i**neh
that's her towel aft**i** **i**neh i
pets**e**ta tis
herbal tea tsa-i too voon**oo**
herbs ta v**o**tana
here eth**o**
here is/are ... na ...
here you are (offering) orist**e**h
hers* thik**o** tis
that's hers aft**o** **i**neh thik**o** tis
hey! eh!

hi! (hello) ya soo
hide (something) kr**i**vo
(oneself) kriv**o**meh
high psil**o**s
highchair to karekl**a**ki
mor**oo**
highway i eTHnik**i** oth**o**s
hill o l**o**fos
him*: I haven't seen him then
ton **e**kho thi
to him saft**o**n
with him maz**i** too
for him yaft**o**n
that's him aft**o**s **i**neh
hip o gof**o**s
hire nik**i**-azo
for hire enik**i**-azondeh
where can I hire a bike? poo
bor**o** na nik**i**-aso **e**na
poth**i**lato?
see **rent**
his*: it's his car **i**neh to
aftok**i**nito too
that's his **i**neh thik**o** too
hit khtip**a**o
hitch-hike k**a**no otost**o**p
hobby to kh**o**bi
hold krat**a**o
hole i tr**i**pa
holiday i thiak**o**pes
on holiday seh thiak**o**pes
Holy Week i Meg**a**li
Evthom**a**tha
home to sp**i**ti
at home (in my house etc) sto
sp**i**ti
(in my country) stin patr**i**tha
moo
we go home tomorrow

piyeno stin patritha moo
avrio
honest timios
honey to meli
honeymoon o minas too
melitos
hood (US) to kapo
hope elpizo
  I hope so etsi elpizo
  I hope not elpizo pos okhi
hopefully meh kali tikhi
horn (of car) to klaxon
horrible friktos
horse to alogo
horse riding i ipasia
hospital to nosokomio
hospitality i filoxenia
  thank you for your hospitality
  sas efkharisto ya ti filoxenia
  sas

If you are invited for a
meal, it is customary to
bring a present of sweets
or flowers for your host. You will be
treated very courteously – in some
places (especially small villages)
hospitality is still a matter of honour.
For this reason avoid offending your
hosts by being unfriendly and
unwilling to eat what you are
served. As few Greeks are
vegetarians, it is wise to warn your
host in advance if you cannot eat
certain foods.

hot zestos
  (spicy) kafteros, kaftos
  I'm hot zestenomeh

it's hot today kani poli zesti
simera
hotel to xenothokhio

There are five hotel
categories: classes A to E,
A allegedly being the best
and E the most basic. All except the
highest category have to keep
within set price limits. Categories
assigned to establishments should
not be regarded as absolutely rigid:
some of the low-ranking places will
also have more expensive rooms
including en suite facilities, and vice
versa. You need your passport or ID
for registration.

hotel room: in my hotel room
  sto thomatio too
  xenothokhioo
hour i ora
house to spiti
house wine to krasi too
  magazioo
  see **wine**
hovercraft to hovercraft, o
  a-erolisTHitiras
how pos
  how many? posi?
  how do you do? khero poli

dialogues

  how are you? pos iseh?
  fine, thanks, and you? poli
  kala, efkharisto; ki esi?

  how much is it? poso kani

afto?
5000 drachmas pendeh
khiliathes thrakhmes
I'll take it THa to paro

humid igros
humour to khioomor

Avoid jokes about
politicians and political
parties, Macedonia and
the relationship between Greece and
Turkey. It's not a good idea to joke or
flirt with women you meet in
villages as this could cause offence.

hungry pinasmenos
  are you hungry? pinas?
hurry (verb) viazomeh
  I'm in a hurry viazomeh
  there's no hurry then iparkhi
  via
  hurry up! viasoo!
hurt travmatizomeh
  it really hurts pona-i poli
husband o sizigos
hydrofoil to iptameno thelfini

I

I ego
ice o pagos
  with ice meh pago
  no ice, thanks khoris pago,
  efkharisto
ice cream to pagoto
ice-cream cone to pagoto
  khonaki

iced coffee to frapeh
ice lolly to pagoto xilaki
idea i ithea
idiot o vlakas
if an
ignition i miza
ill arostos
  I feel ill imeh arostos
illness i arostia
imitation (leather etc) i
  apomimisi
immediately amesos
important spootheos
  it's very important ineh poli
  simandiko
  it's not important then ineh
  spootheo
impossible athinaton
impressive endiposiakos
improve veltiono
  I want to improve my Greek
  THelo na kaliterepso ta
  Elinika moo
in: it's in the centre ineh sto
  kendro
  in my car mesa sto aftokinito
  moo
  in Athens stin ATHina
  in two days from now seh
  thio meres apo tora
  in May sto Ma-io
  in English sta Anglika
  in Greek sta Elinika
  is he in? ineh eki?
  in five minutes seh pendeh
  lepta
inch* i intsa
include perilamvano
  does that include meals? afto

perilamvani keh fayito?
is that included in the price?
perilamvaneteh stin timi?
inconvenient akatalilos, avolos
incredible apiTHanos
Indian (adj) Inthikos
indicator to flas, o thiktis
indigestion i thispepsia
indoor pool i esoteriki pisina
indoors mesa
inexpensive ftinos
  see cheap
inner tube (for tyre) i sabrela
infection i molinsi
infectious kolitikos
inflammation i anaflexi
informal anepisimos
information i plirofori-es
  do you have any
  information about ...?
  ekheteh tipoteh plirofori-es
  skhetika meh ...?
information desk i plirofori-es
injection i enesi
injured travmatismenos
  she's been injured khtipiseh
in-laws ta peTHerika
innocent aTHo-os
insect to endomo
insect bite to tsibima
  endomoo
  do you have anything for
  insect bites? ekheteh
  tipoteh ya tsibimata apo
  endoma?
insect repellent to AUTAN®
inside mesa
  inside the hotel mesa sto
  xenothokhio

let's sit inside as katsoomeh
mesa
insist epimeno
  I insist epimeno
insomnia i a-ipnia
instant coffee to neskafeh
instead andi
  give me that one instead
  thosteh moo afto sti THesi
  too aloo
  instead of ... sti THesi too ...
insulin i insoolini
insurance i asfalia
intelligent exipnos
interested: I'm interested in ...
  enthiaferomeh poli ya ...
interesting enthiaferon
  that's very interesting ineh
  poli enthiaferon
international thi-ethnis
internet to Internet
interpret thi-erminevo
interpreter o/i thi-ermineas
intersection to stavrothromi
interval (at theatre) to thi-alima
into mesa
  I'm not into ... then moo
  aresi ...
introduce sistino
  may I introduce ...? boro na
  sas sistiso ton ...?
invitation i prosklisi
invite proskalo
Ionian Sea to I-onio pelagos
Ireland i Irlanthia
Irish Irlanthos
  I'm Irish (man/woman) imeh
  Irlanthos/Irlantheza
iron (for ironing) to ilektriko

sithero
can you iron these for me?
boriteh na moo ta
sitheroseteh?
is* ineh
island to nisi
it afto
  it is ... ineh ...
  is it ...? ineh ...?
  where is it? poo ineh?
  it's him ineh aftos
  it was ... itan ...
Italian (adj) Italos
  (language) ta Italika
Italy i Italia
itch: it itches meh tro-i

J

jack (for car) o grilos
jacket to sakaki
jar to vazaki
jam i marmelatha
jammed: it's jammed ineh
  frakarismeno
January o I-anooarios
jaw to sagoni
jazz i tzaz
jealous ziliaris
jeans ta tzins
jellyfish i tsookhtra
jersey to fanelaki
jetty o molos
Jewish Evra-ikos
jeweller's to khrisokho-io
jewellery ta kosmimata
job i thoolia
jogging to jogging

to go jogging pao ya jogging
joke to astio
journey to taxithi
  have a good journey! kalo
  taxithi!
jug i kanata
  a jug of water mia kanata
  nero
juice o khimos
July o I-oolios
jump pithao
jumper to poolover
jump leads ta kalothia batarias
junction i thiastavrosi
June o I-oonios
just (only) monon
  just two mono thio
  just for me mono ya mena
  just here akrivos etho
  not just now okhi tora
  we've just arrived molis
  ftasameh

K

keep krato
  keep the change krata ta
  resta
  can I keep it? boro na to
  kratiso?
  please keep it kratisteh to,
  sas parakalo
ketchup to ketsap
kettle i booyota, o vrastiras
key to klithi
  the key for room 201, please
  to klithi ya to 201 (thiakosia
  ena), parakalo

key ring to brelok
kidneys ta nefra
kill skotono
kilo* ena kilo
kilometre* ena khiliometro
 how many kilometres is it
 to ...? posa khiliometra ineh
 mekhri to ...?
kind (generous) evyenikos
 that's very kind ineh poli
 evyeniko

dialogue

> which kind do you want? ti
> ithos THeleteh?
> I want this/that kind THelo
> afto/ekino to ithos

king o vasilias
kiosk to periptero
kiss to fili
 (verb) filao

It is customary to greet
friends and relatives by
kissing them on both
cheeks. The exception to this is
when men greet each other when
they generally shake hands instead.
Foreign visitors are expected to
accept the same kind of greeting,
although you wouldn't necessarily
be expected to reciprocate – in fact
it could cause offence if a foreign
visitor were to kiss someone's wife
in greeting.

kitchen i koozina

kitchenette i koozinoola
Kleenex® ta khartomandila
knee to gonato
knickers i kilota
knife to makheri
knitwear plekta rookha
knock khtipo
knock down khtipo
 he's been knocked down
 khtipiTHikeh
knock over (object) anapotho-
 yirizo
 (pedestrian) khtipo
know (somebody) gnorizo
 (something, a place) xero
 I don't know then xero
 I didn't know that then to
 ixera
 do you know where I can
 find ...? mipos xereteh poo
 boro na vro ...?

L

label i etiketa
ladies' (toilets) i too-aleta ton
 yinekon
ladies' wear yinekia ithi
lady i kiria
lager i bira
 see beer
lake i limni
lamb (meat) to arni
lamp i lamba
lane (on motorway) i loritha
 (small road) i parothos
language i glosa
language course maTHimata

xenis glosas
large megalos
last telefteos
last week i perasmeni
evthomatha
last Friday tin perasmeni
Paraskevi
last night kh-THes vrathi
what time is the last train to
Salonika? ti ora ineh to
telefteo treno ya tin
THesaloniki?
late arga
sorry I'm late meh
sinkhoriteh poo aryisa
the train was late to treno
ikheh kaTHisterisi
we must go – we'll be late
prepi na piyenoomeh – THa
aryisoomeh
it's getting late nikhtoni
later argotera
I'll come back later THa
yiriso argotera
see you later adio, THa ta
xanapoomeh
later on argotera
latest o pi-o prosfatos
by Wednesday at the latest
tin Tetarti to argotero
laugh yelo
launderette to plindirio
rookhon
laundromat to plindirio
rookhon
laundry (clothes) i boogatha, ta
aplita
(place) to kaTHaristirio
lavatory i too-aleta

law o nomos
lawn to grasithi
lawyer o/i thikigoros
laxative to kaTHartiko
lazy tebelis
lead (electrical) o agogos
(verb) othigo
where does this lead to? poo
othiyi afto?
leaf to filo
leaflet to thiafimistiko
leak i thiaro-i
(verb) stazo
the roof leaks i steyi stazi
learn maTHeno
least: not in the least katholoo
at least toolakhiston
leather to therma
leave (bag etc) afino
(go away) fevgo
(forget) xekhnao
I am leaving tomorrow fevgo
avrio
he left yesterday efiyeh
kh-THes
may I leave this here? boro
nafiso afto etho?
I left my coat in the bar afisa
tin tsanda moo sto bar
when does the bus for
Athens leave? poteh fevyi to
leoforio ya tin ATHina?
leeks ta prasa
left aristera
on the left pros ta aristera
to the left pros ta aristera
turn left stripseh aristera
there's none left then
emineh tipoteh

left-handed aristerokhiras
left luggage (office) o khoros
 filaxis aposkevon
leg to pothi
lemon to lemoni
lemonade i lemonatha
lemon tea tsai meh lemoni
lend thanizo
 will you lend me your ... ?
 THa moo thanisis to thiko
 soo ...?
lens (of camera) o fakos
lesbian i lesvia
less ligotero
 less than ligotero apo
 less expensive ligotero
 akrivo
lesson to maTHima
let (allow) epitrepo
 will you let me know? THa
 moo to pis?
 I'll let you know THa soo po
 let's go for something to eat
 pameh na fameh kati
let off katevazo
 will you let me off at ...? THa
 meh katevaseteh sto ...?
letter to grama
 do you have any letters for
 me? ekho kanena grama?
letterbox to gramatokivotio

Letterboxes in Greece are
usually bright yellow. If
you are confronted with
two slots, 'esoteriko' is for domestic
mail and 'exoteriko' is for overseas.

lettuce to marooli

lever o levi-es
library i vivlioTHiki
licence i athi-a
lid to kapaki
lie (tell untruth) leo psemata
lie down xaplono
life i zo-i
lifebelt i zoni asfalias
lifeguard o navagosostis
life jacket to sosivio
lift (in building) to asanser
 could you give me a lift?
 boriteh na meh pateh?
 would you like a lift?
 THeleteh na sas pao?
light to fos
 (not heavy) elafros
 do you have a light? (for
 cigarette) ekhis fotia?
 light green anikhto prasino
 light bulb i lamba, o glombos
 I need a new light bulb
 khriazomeh mia kenoorya
 lamba
lighter (cigarette) o anaptiras
lightning i astrapi
like (verb) moo aresi
 I like it moo aresi afto
 I like going for walks moo
 aresi na piyeno peripato
 I like you moo aresis
 I don't like it then moo aresi
 afto
 do you like it? soo aresi afto?
 I'd like to go swimming THa
 iTHela na pao ya kolimbi
 I'd like a beer THa iTHela
 mia bira
 would you like a drink? THa

iTHeles ena poto?
would you like to go for a walk? THa iTHeles na pameh mia volta?
what's it like? meh ti miazi?
I want one like this THelo ena san ki afto
lime to moskholemono
lime cordial to lime
line (on paper) i grami
(phone) i tilefoniki grami
could you give me an outside line? THa moo thoseteh grami?
lips ta khilia
lip salve to vootiro kakao
lipstick to krayon
liqueur to liker
listen akoo-o
litre* ena litro
a litre of white wine ena litro aspro krasi
little mikros
just a little, thanks ligo mono, efkharisto
a little milk ligo gala
a little bit more ligo akomi
live zo
we live together sizoomeh

dialogue

where do you live? poo menis?
I live in London meno sto Lonthino

lively thrastirios
liver to sikoti

loaf i fradzola
lobby (in hotel) to saloni
lobster o astakos
local dopios
can you recommend a local wine/restaurant? boriteh na mas sistiseteh ena dopio krasi/estiatorio?
see **wine**
lock i klitharia
(verb) klithono
it's locked ineh klithomeno
lock in klithono mesa
lock out klithono apo exo
I've locked myself out klithoTHika apexo
locker (for luggage etc) i THiritha
lollipop to glifidzoori
London to LonTHino
long makris
how long will it take to fix it? poso kero THa pari ya na to ftiaxeteh?
how long does it take? posi ora kani?
a long time polis keros, poli ora
one day/two days longer mia mera/thio meres parapano
long-distance call to iperastiko tilefonima
look: I'm just looking, thanks efkharisto, vlepo mono
you don't look well then feneseh kala
look out! prosexe!
can I have a look? boro na tho?

look after prosekho, frondizo
look at kitazo
look for psakhno
  I'm looking for ... psakhno
  ya ...
look forward to perimeno
  meh khara
  I'm looking forward to it to
  perimeno pos keh pos
loose (handle etc) khalaros
lorry to fortigo
lose khano
  I've lost my way ekho
  khaTHi
  I'm lost, I want to get to ...
  ekho khaTHi, THelo na pao
  sto ...
  I've lost my (hand)bag ekhasa
  tin tsanda moo
lost property (office) to grafio
  apolesTHendon
lot: a lot, lots pola
  not a lot okhi pola
  a lot of people poli anTHropi
  a lot bigger poli megalitero
  I like it a lot moo aresi poli
lotion i losion
loud thinatos
lounge to saloni
love i agapi
  (verb) agapo
  I love Greece latrevo tin
  Elatha
lovely oreos
low khamilos
luck i tikhi
  good luck! kali tikhi!
luggage i aposkeves
luggage trolley to karotsaki ya

tis aposkeves
lump (on body) to priximo
lunch to yevma
lungs o pnevmonas
luxurious (hotel, furnishings)
  politelis
luxury politelias

M

Macedonia i Makethonia
machine i mikhani
mad (insane) trelos
  (angry) trelos apo THimo
magazine to periothiko
maid (in hotel) i servitora
maiden name to patronimo
mail ta gramata, to
  takhithromio
  (verb) takhithromo
  is there any mail for me?
  ekho kanena grama?
  see **post**
mailbox to gramatokivotio
  see **letterbox**
main kirios
main course to kirio piato
Mainland Greece i Ipirotiki
  Elatha
main post office kendriko
  takhithromio
main road (in town) o
  kendrikos thromos
  (in country) o aftokinito-
  thromos
main switch o kendrikos
  thiakoptis
make (brand name) i marka

(verb) kano
I make it 500 drachmas
ipoloyizo oti kani pedakosi-
es thrakhmes
what is it made of? apo ti
ineh ftiagmeno?
make-up to make-up
man o andras
manager o thi-efTHindis, o
manager
can I see the manager? boro
na tho ton thi-efTHindi?
manageress i thi-efTHindria

manners
It is bad manners to
refuse someone else's
offer to pay for your share in a meal,
or their offer to pay for the wine; the
equivalent of the two-finger gesture
is a five-finger or a raised middle
finger gesture; avoid these, unless
you want to get in trouble.

manual to aftokinito meh
kanonikes takhitites
many pola
not many liga, okhi pola
map o khartis
March o Martios
margarine i margarini
market i agora
marmalade i marmelatha
married: I'm married (said by a
man/woman) imeh
pandremenos/pandremeni
are you married? (said to a
man/woman) isteh
pandremenos/pandremeni?

mascara i maskara
match (football etc) to mats, o
agonas
matches ta spirta
material (fabric) to ifasma
matter: it doesn't matter then
pirazi
what's the matter? ti
simveni?
mattress to stroma
May o Ma-ios
may: may I have another one?
THa iTHela ki alo ena?
may I come in? boro na bo?
may I see it? boro na to
tho?
may I sit here? boro na
kaTHiso etho?
maybe isos
mayonnaise i ma-yoneza
me* emena
that's for me afto ineh ya
mena
send it to me stilteh to seh
mena
me too ki ego episis
meal to fa-yito

dialogue

did you enjoy your meal?
sas areseh to fayito?
it was excellent, thank you
itan poli nostimo,
efkharisto

mean: what do you mean? ti
eno-iteh?

dialogue

what does this word
mean? ti simeni afti i lexi?
it means ... in English
simeni ...sta Anglika

measles i ilara
meat to kreas
mechanic o mikhanikos
medicine to farmako
Mediterranean i Meso-yios
medium (adj: size) metrios
medium-dry imixiro krasi
medium-rare misopsimeno
medium-sized metrio
 meyeTHos
meet sinandao
 nice to meet you kharika
 poo sas gnorisa
 where shall I meet you? poo
 THa sas sinandiso?
meeting i sinandisi
meeting place to meros
 sinandisis
melon to peponi
men i anthres
mend thiorTHono
 could you mend this for me?
 boriteh na moo to
 ftiaxeteh?
menswear ta anthrika ithi
mention anafero
 don't mention it parakalo
menu to menoo
 may I see the menu, please?
 boro na tho to menoo,
 parakalo?
 see Menu Reader

message to minima
 are there any messages for
 me? iparkhi kanena minima
 ya mena?
 I want to leave a message
 for ... thelo nafiso ena
 minima ya ...
metal to metalo
metre* to metro
microwave (oven) o foornos
 mikrokimaton, to
 microwave
midday to mesimeri
 at midday to mesimeri
middle: in the middle sti
 mesi
 in the middle of the night
 arga ti nikhta
 the middle one to meseo
midnight ta mesanikhta
 at midnight ta mesanikhta
might: I might THa boroosa
 I might not then THa
 boroosa
 I might want to stay another
 day bori na THelo na mino
 akomi mia mera
migraine i imikrania
mild (weather) eTHrios
 (taste) elafros
mile* ena mili
milk to gala
milkshake to milkshake
millimetre* ena khiliosto
minced meat o kimas
mind: never mind then pirazi
 I've changed my mind alaxa
 gnomi

dialogue

do you mind if I open the window? seh pirazi an anixo to paraTHiro?
no, I don't mind okhi, then meh pirazi

mine*: it's mine ineh thiko moo
mineral water to emfialomeno nero
mint (sweet) i menda
minute to lepto
in a minute seh ena lepto
just a minute ena lepto
mirror o kaTHreftis
Miss thespinis
miss khano
I missed the bus ekhasa to leoforio
missing lipi
one of my ... is missing lipi ena ...
there's a suitcase missing lipi mia valitsa
mist i katakhnia
mistake to laTHos
I think there's a mistake nomizo oti iparkhi ena laTHos etho
sorry, I've made a mistake meh sinkhoriteh, ekana laTHos
misunderstanding i parexiyisi
mix-up: sorry, there's been a mix-up meh sinkhoriteh, iparkhi ena berthema
modern modernos

modern art gallery i galeri modernas tekhnis
Modern Greek ta Nea Elinika
moisturizer i ithatiki krema
moment: I won't be a moment mia stigmi parakalo
monastery to monastiri
Monday i theftera
money ta lefta
month o minas
monument to mnimio
moon to fengari
moped to mikhanaki
more* perisoteros
can I have some more water, please? akomi ligo nero, parakalo
more expensive/interesting pio akrivo/enthiaferon
more than 50 perisotero apo peninda
more than that pio poli ap afto
a lot more poli perisotero

dialogue

would you like some more? THa THelateh ligo akomi?
no, no more for me, thanks okhi, okhi alo ya mena, efkharisto
how about you? ki esis?
I don't want any more, thanks then THelo alo, efkharisto

morning to pro-i

this morning simera to pro-i

in the morning to pro-i

mosquito to koonoopi

mosquito repellent to fithaki ya ta koonoopia

most: I like this one most of all afto moo aresi pio poli apo ola

most of the time siniTHos

most tourists i perisoteri tooristes

mostly kirios

mother i mitera

motorbike i motosikleta

motorboat i varka meh mikhani

motorway i eTHniki othos

mountain to voono

in the mountains pano sta voona

mountaineering i orivasia

mouse to pondiki

moustache to moostaki

mouth to stoma

mouth ulcer pliyi sto stoma

move metakino

he's moved to another room piyeh seh alo thomatio

could you move your car? boriteh na metakiniseteh to aftokinito sas?

could you move up a little? boriteh na metakiniTHiteh ligo?

where has it moved to? poo metaferTHikeh?

movie to film

movie theater o kinimato-grafos, to sinema

Mr kiri-eh

Mrs kiria

Ms thespinis

much poli

much better/worse poli kalitera/khirotera

much hotter poli pio zesta

not much okhi poli

not very much okhi para poli

I don't want very much then THelo para poli

mud i laspi

mug (for drinking) i koopa

I've been mugged meh listepsan

mum i mama

mumps i parotititha

museum to moosio

There is usually an admission charge for both state-run and private museums, archaeological sites and art galleries. Entrance to all state-run sites and museums is free to everyone on Sundays and public holidays. Opening hours vary considerably (and often change) and you should find these out before you go in order to avoid disappointment. Some small museums and sites may close for a long lunch. Churches and monasteries are usually open to visitors when there is no service. Visitors are requested to be properly dressed (long trousers for men; long sleeves, long skirt and no trousers for women).

mushrooms ta manitaria
music i moosiki
musician o/i moosikos
Muslim (adj) Moosoolmanikos
mussels ta mithia
must: I must ... prepi na ...
 I mustn't drink alcohol then
 prepi na pio alko-ol
mustard i moostartha
my* o/i/to ... moo
myself: I'll do it myself THa to
 kano o ithios
 by myself apo monos moo

N

nail (finger) to nikhi
 (metal) to karfi
nailbrush i voortsa ya ta
 nikhia
nail varnish to mano
name to onoma
 my name's John meh leneh
 John
 what's your name? pos seh
 leneh?
 what is the name of this
 street? pos leneh afto to
 thromo?

It is not uncommon to
hear Greeks address or
greet each other formally
by their profession: 'kalimera yatreh'
('good morning doctor'). First names
are only used between friends and
relatives. In formal situations 'kirios'
(Mr) 'kiri-eh' (Mr) or 'kiria' (Mrs/

Miss/Ms) + surname are used. It is
possible, however, to use 'kiri-eh/
kiria' + first name in semi-formal
relationships, e.g. to a neighbour
who is older than you, or a
shopkeeper you know well.

napkin i petseta
nappy i pana
narrow (street) stenos
nasty (person) apesios
 (weather, accident) askhimos
national eTHnikos
nationality i eTHnikotita
natural fisikos
nausea i naftia
navy (blue) ble maren
near konda
 is it near the city centre?
 ineh konda sto kendro tis
 polis?
 do you go near the
 Acropolis? pernateh apo tin
 Akropoli?
 where is the nearest ...? poo
 ineh to plisi-estero ...?
nearby etho konda
nearly skhethon
necessary aparetitos,
 anangeos
neck o lemos
necklace to koli-e
necktie i gravata
need: I need ...
 khriazomeh ...
 do I need to pay? khriazeteh
 na pliroso?
needle i velona
negative (film) to arnitiko

neither: neither (one) of them
kanenas apo aftoos
neither ... nor ... ooteh ...
ooteh ...
nephew o anipsios
net (in sport) to thikhti
network map o khartis
othikoo thiktioo
never poteh

dialogue

have you ever been to
Athens? ekheteh pa-i
poteh stin ATHina?
no, never, I've never been
there okhi, poteh, then
ekho pa-i poteh eki

new neos, kenooryos
news (radio, TV etc) ta nea
newsagent's to praktorio
efimerithon
newspaper i efimeritha
newspaper kiosk to periptero
meh efimerithes
New Year to neo etos

New Year's Eve and Day
are traditionally family
celebrations, although
nowadays many Greeks celebrate
both by going out to expensive
dinner dances. It is traditional to
have fireworks at midnight and cut
the cake with the lucky coin in it.

Happy New Year!
eftikhismenos o kenooryos

khronos!
New Year's Eve i
protokhronia
New Zealand i Nea Zilanthia
New Zealander: I'm a New
Zealander (man/woman) imeh
Neozilanthos/Neozilantheza
next epomenos
the next turning on the left i
epomeni strofi sta aristera
the next street on the left o
epomenos thromos sta
aristera
at the next stop stin epomeni
stasi
next week tin ali evtho-
matha
next to thipla apo
nice (food) nostimos
(looks, view etc) oreos
(person) kalos
niece i anipsia
night i nikhta
at night to vrathi
good night kalinikhta

dialogue

do you have a single room
for one night? ekheteh ena
mono thomatio ya mia
nikhta?
yes, madam malista, kiria
moo
how much is it per night?
poso kani ti mia nikhta?
it's 5000 drachmas for one
night ineh pendeh
khiliathes thrakhmes ya

mia nikhta
thank you, I'll take it
efkharisto, THa to kliso

nightclub to nait-klab
nightdress to nikhtiko
night porter o nikhterinos
THiroros
no okhi
 I've no change then ekho
 psila
 there's no ... left then
 emineh kaTHoloo ...
 no way! apokli-eteh!
 oh no! (upset) okh!, o okhi!
nobody kanenas
 there's nobody there then
 ineh kanis eki
noise i fasaria
noisy: it's too noisy ekhi poli
 fasaria
non-alcoholic khoris alko-ol
none kanis
non-smoking compartment o
 khoros ya mi kapnizondes
noon to mesimeri
no-one kanenas
nor: nor do I ooteh kego
normal fisiolo-yikos
north o voras
 in the north sta vori-a
 north of Athens vori-a tis
 ATHinas
northeast o vorio-anatolikos
northwest o vorio-thitikos
northern vorios
Northern Ireland i Vorios
 Irlanthia
Norway i Norviyia

Norwegian (adj) Norviyikos
nose i miti
nosebleed i emorayia sti miti
not* then
 no, I'm not hungry okhi, then
 pina-o
 I don't want any, thank you
 efkharisto, then THelo
 it's not necessary then ineh
 aparetito
 I didn't know that then to
 ixera
 not that one – this one okhi
 afto – to alo
note (banknote) to khartonomisma
notebook to blokaki, to
 simiomatario
notepaper (for letters) to kharti
 alilografias
nothing tipoteh
 nothing for me, thanks
 tipoteh ya mena, efkharisto
 nothing else tipoteh alo
novel to miTHistorima
November o No-emvrios
now tora
number* o ariTHmos
 I've got the wrong number
 pira laTHos noomero
 what is your phone number?
 pio ineh to tilefono soo?
number plate i pinakitha
nurse (man/woman) o
 nosokomos/i nosokoma
nursery slope i pista
 ekmaTHisis
nut (for bolt) to paximathi
nuts to karithi

O

o'clock* i ora
occupied (toilet) katilimenos
October o Oktovrios
odd (strange) paraxenos
of* too
off (lights) klisto
  it's just off Omonia Square
  ligo pio eki apo tin Omoni-a
  we're off tomorrow
  fevgoomeh avrio
offensive (language, behaviour)
  prosvlitikos
office (place of work) to grafio
officer (said to policeman)
  astinomeh
often sikhna
  not often okhi sikhna
  how often are the buses?
  kaTHeh poteh ekhi leoforia?
oil (for car) ta lathia
  (for salad) to lathi
ointment i alifi
OK endaxi
  are you OK? iseh kala?
  is that OK with you? iseh
  efkharistimenos etsi?
  is it OK to ...? pirazi na ...?
  that's OK thanks (it doesn't
  matter) ineh endaxi,
  efkharisto
  I'm OK (nothing for me) tipoteh
  ya mena
  (I feel OK) imeh mia khara
  is this train OK for ...? afto
  ineh to treno ya ...?
  I said I'm sorry, OK? soo ipa

signomi, endaxi?
old (person) yeros
  (thing) palios

dialogue

how old are you? poso
khronon iseh?
I'm twenty-five imeh
ikosi-pendeh khronon
and you? ki esi?

old-fashioned demodeh
old town (old part of town) i palia
  poli
  in the old town stin palia poli
olive oil to eleolatho
olives i eli-es
omelette i omeleta
on pano
  (lights) anikhto
  on the street/beach sto
  thromo/stin paralia
  is it on this road? ineh safto
  to thromo?
  on the plane mesa sto
  a-eroplano
  on Saturday to Savato
  on television stin tileorasi
  I haven't got it on me then to
  ekho mazi moo
  this one's on me (drink) ego
  kernao afti ti fora
  the light wasn't on to fos
  then itan anikhto
  what's on tonight? ti pezi
  simera?
once (one time) mia fora
  at once (immediately) amesos

one* enas, mia, ena
  the white one to aspro
one-way ticket: a one-way
  ticket to ... ena aplo ya ...
onion to kremithi
only mono
  only one mono ena
  it's only 6 o'clock ineh mono
  exi i ora
  I've only just got here molis
  eftasa
on/off switch o thiakoptis
open (adj) aniktos
  (verb: door, shop) anigo
  when do you open? poteh
  aniyeteh?
  I can't get it open then boro
  na to anixo
  in the open air stin ipeTHro
opening times ores litooryias
open ticket isitirio meh
  anikhti epistrofi
opera i opera
operation (medical) i enkhirisi
operator (telephone: man/woman)
  o tilefonitis/i tilefonitria

The number for the
international operator is
161.

opposite: the opposite
  direction stin andiTHeti
  katefTHinsi
  the bar opposite to bar
  apenandi
  opposite my hotel apenandi
  apo to xenothokhio moo
optician o optikos

or i
orange (fruit) to portokali
  (colour) portokali
orange juice i portokalatha
orchestra i orkhistra
order: can we order now? (in
  restaurant) boroomeh na
  paragiloomeh tora?
  I've already ordered, thanks
  ekho ithi paragili, efkharisto
  I didn't order this then
  paragila afto
  out of order then litooryi
ordinary kanonikos
other alos, ali, alo
  the other one to alo
  the other day tis pro-ales
  I'm waiting for the others
  perimeno toos aloos
  do you have any others?
  ekheteh tipoteh ala?
otherwise thiaforetika
our* o/i/to ... mas
ours* thikos mas
out: he's out then ineh etho
  three kilometres out of town
  tria khiliometra exo apo tin
  poli
outdoors exo
outside ... exo ...
  can we sit outside?
  borroomeh na
  kaTHisoomeh exo?
oven o foornos
over: over here etho
  over there eki, eki pera
  over 500 pano apo
  pendakosia
  it's over teliosa

overcharge: you've
  overcharged me meh
  khreosateh parapano
overcoat to palto
overlook: I'd like a room
  overlooking the courtyard
  THa iTHela ena thomatio
  meh THea stin avli
overnight (travel) oloniktio
overtake prosperno
owe: how much do I owe you?
  poso sas khrostao?
own: my own ... thiko
  moo ...
  are you on your own? iseh
  monos soo?
  I'm on my own imeh monos
  moo
owner (man/woman) o
  ithioktitis/i ithioktitria

P

pack (verb) ftiakhno tis
  valitses
  a pack of ... ena paketo ...
package (parcel) to paketo
package holiday i
  organomeni ekthromi
packed lunch to etimo
  mesimeriano
packet: a packet of cigarettes
  ena paketo tsigara
padlock to looketo, i klitharia
page (of book) i selitha
  could you page Mr ...?
  boriteh na fonaxeteh ton
  kirio ...?

pain o ponos
  I have a pain here
  esTHanomeh ena pono etho
painful othiniros
painkillers to pafsipono
paint i boya
painting o pinakas zografikis
pair: a pair of ... ena
  zevgari ...
Pakistani (adj) Pakistanikos
palace to palati
pale khlomos
  pale blue galazios
pan to tapsi
panties to slip, i kilotes
pants (underwear: men's) to
  sovrako
  (women's) to slip, i kilotes
  (US: trousers) to pandaloni
pantyhose to kalson
paper to kharti
  (newspaper) i efimeriTHa
  a piece of paper ena komati
  kharti
paper handkerchiefs ta
  khartomandila
parcel to thema
pardon (me)? (didn't
  understand/hear) signomi?
parents: my parents i gonis
  moo
parents-in-law ta peTHerika
park to parko
  (verb) parkaro
  can I park here? boro na
  parkaro etho?
parking lot to parking
part to meros
partner (boyfriend, girlfriend) o

fílos, i fíli
party (group) i omatha
  (celebration) to parti
pass (in mountains) to perasma
passenger o/i epivatis
passport to thiavatirio
past: in the past sto
  parelTHon
  just past the information
  office amesos meta to grafio
  pliroforion
path to monopati
pattern to s-khethio
pavement to pezothromio
  on the pavement sto
  pezothromio
pavement café kafenio sto
  thromo
pay plirono
  can I pay, please? boro na
  pliroso, parakalo?
  it's already paid for ineh ithi
  pliromeno

dialogue

payphone to tilefono meh
  kermata
peaceful irinikos
peach to rothakino
peanuts fistikia arapika

pear to akhlathi
peas ta bizelia
peculiar (taste, custom)
  paraxenos
pedestrian crossing i thiavasi
  pezon
pedestrian precinct o pezo-
  thromos
peg (for washing) to mandalaki
  (for tent) to palooki
pen to stilo
pencil to molivi
penfriend (male/female) o fílos
  thi' alilografías/i fíli thi'
  alilografías
penicillin i penikilini
penknife o soo-yias
pensioner o/i sindaxiookhos
people i anTHropi
  the other people in the hotel i
  ali anTHropi sto xeno-
  thokhio
  too many people ipervolika
  poli anTHropi
pepper (spice) to piperi
  (vegetable) i piperia
peppermint (sweet) i menda
per: per night tin vrathia
  how much per day? poso tin
  imera?
per cent tis ekato
perfect telios
perfume to aroma
perhaps isos
  perhaps not isos okhi
period (time, menstruation) i
  periothos
perm i permanand
permit i athia

person to atomo
personal stereo to walkman®
petrol i venzini

Petrol is either 3-star 'apli' (regular), 4-star 'sooper' (super) or unleaded 'amolivthi'. Most petrol stations are staffed, not self-service. see **garage**

petrol can ena thokhio venzinis
petrol station to venzinathiko
pharmacy to farmakio
   see **chemist's**
phone to tilefono
   (verb) perno tilefono, tilefono

Phone, telegraph, fax, and telex facilities are provided by OTE (Greek Telecommunications). In the largest towns, there is sometimes an OTE branch which opens 24 hours, but most are likely to be open from 7 am to 10 or 11 pm Local calls are relatively straightforward – in many hotel lobbies or cafés you'll find red payphones which presently take a 10-drachma coin. Long-distance and international calls can be made from local branches of the OTE and from street kiosks (periptero) which have a telephone meter (o metritis) – you pay after having made the call. It is, however, preferable to make international calls from an OTE branch as a periptero can be

unreliable and the line may be bad. Reverse charge calls can only be made from branches of the OTE. Phone-cards are sold from newspaper or tobacco kiosks. All public phones in Athens now take phonecards instead of coins. see **speak**

phone book o tilefonikos katalogos
phonecard i tilekarta
phone number o ariTHmos tilefonoo
photo i fotografia
   excuse me, could you take a photo of us? meh sinkhoriteh, THa boroosateh na mas pareteh mia fotografia?
phrase book to vivlio thialogon
piano to piano
pickpocket o portofolas
pick up: will you be there to pick me up? THa iseh eki na meh paris?
picnic to piknik
picture i ikona
pie i pita
   (meat) i kreatopita
   (fruit) i frootopita
piece to komati
   a piece of ... ena komati ...
pill to khapi
   I'm on the pill perno antisiliptika khapia
pillow to maxilari
pillow case i maxilaroTHiki

pin i karfitsa

pineapple o ananas

pineapple juice o khimos anana

pink roz

pipe (for smoking) i pipa, to tsibooki

(for water) o solinas

pipe cleaners kaTHaristis pipas

Piraeus o Pireas

pistachio nuts fistiki-a Eyinis

pity: it's a pity ineh krima

pizza i pitsa

place to meros

is this place taken? ineh piasmeni afti i THesi?

at your place sti THesi soo

at his place sti THesi too

plain (not patterned) monokhromo

plane to a-eroplano

by plane meh to a-eroplano

plant to fito

plaster cast o yipsos

plasters to lefkoplast

plastic plastikos

(credit cards) i pistotiki karta

plastic bag i plastiki sakoola

plate to piato

plate-smashing spasimo pi-aton

platform i platforma

which platform is for Patras, please? pia platforma ya tin Patra, parakalo?

play (in theatre) to THeatriko ergo

(verb) pezo

playground to yipetho

pleasant efkharistos

please parakalo

yes please neh, parakalo

could you please ...? THa boroosateh, parakalo, na ...?

please don't stamata, seh parakalo

pleased to meet you kharika poli

pleasure: i efkharistisi

my pleasure efkharistisi moo

plenty: plenty of ... poli/ pola ...

there's plenty of time iparkhi arketi ora

that's plenty, thanks efkharisto, arki

pliers i pensa

plug (electrical) i briza

(for car) to boozi

(in sink) i tapa

plumber o ithravlikos

pm* meta mesimvrias

poached egg to avgo poseh

pocket i tsepi

point: two point five thio koma pendeh

there's no point then iparkhi logos

points (in car) i platines

poisonous thilitiriothis

police i astinomia

call the police! kalesteh tin astinomia!

There is a separate tourist police force called 'Tooristiki Astinomia' which should be able to deal with any problems you may have. You should phone 171 for the tourist police.

policeman o astifilakas
police station to astinomiko tmima
policewoman i astinomikos
polish to verniki
polite evgenikos
polluted molismenos
pony to poni
pool (for swimming) i pisina
poor (not rich) ftokhos
 (quality) kakos
pop music i moosiki pop
pop singer o tragoothistis pop, i tragoothistria pop
population o pliTHismos
pork to khirino
port (for boats) to limani
 (drink) i mavrothafni
porter (in hotel) o akh-THoforos
portrait to portreto
posh (restaurant) akrivos
 (people) kiriles
possible thinatos
 is it possible to ...? ineh thinaton na ...?
 as ... as possible oso to thinaton ...
post (mail) ta gramata
 (verb) takhithromo
 could you post this for me?

boriteh na moo to takhithromiseteh?
postbox to gramatokivotio
postcard i kartpostal
postcode o takhithromikos kothikos
poster (for room) to poster
 (in street) i afisa
post office to takhithromio

Post office hours are approximately 8 am to 2.30 pm Monday to Friday. Some post offices in the larger cities may be open until 9 pm from Monday to Friday for postal services only. You may be asked to open a heavy envelope or registered letter in order to show its contents. Stamps can also be bought from street kiosks, but the proprietors are entitled to a 10 per cent commission and never seem to know the current international rates.

poste restante post restand
pots and pans (cooking implements) katsaroles keh tigania
potato i patata
potato chips ta tsips
pottery ta keramika
pound* (money) i lira
 (weight) i libra
power cut i thiakopi revmatos
power point o revmatothotis
practise: I want to practise my Greek THelo na exaskiso ta

Elinika moo
prawns i garithes
(larger) i karavitha
prefer: I prefer ... protimo ...
pregnant engios
prescription (for chemist) i sindayi
present (gift) to thoro
president (of country) o pro-ethros
pretty (beautiful) omorfos, oreos
(quite) arketa
it's pretty expensive ineh arketa akrivo
price i timi
priest o papas
prime minister o proTHi-poorgos
printed matter ta endipa
priority (in driving) i protereotita
prison i filaki
private ithiotikos
private bathroom to ithiotiko banio
probably piTHanon
problem to provlima
no problem! kanena provlima!
program(me) to programa
promise: I promise iposkhomeh
pronounce: how is this pronounced? pos to proferis afto?
properly (repaired, locked etc) opos prepi
protection factor (of suntan lotion) o vaTHmos prostasias

Protestant o thiamartiromenos
public convenience i kinokhristi tooaleta
public holiday i thimosia aryia
pudding (dessert) to glikisma
pull travao
pullover to poolover
puncture to foo-it
purple mov
purse (for money) to portofoli
(US: handbag) i tsanda
push sprokhno
pushchair to karotsaki
put vazo
where can I put ...? poo boro na valo ...?
could you put us up for the night? boriteh na mas filoxeniseteh ya ena vrathi?
pyjamas i pitzames

Q

quality i piotita
quarantine i karantina
quarter to tetarto
quayside: on the quayside stin provlita
question i erotisi
queue i oora
quick grigora
that was quick afto itan grigoro
what's the quickest way there? pios ineh o pio grigoros thromos?
fancy a quick drink? ekhis

orexi ya ena poto sta grigora?
quickly grigora
quiet (place, hotel) isikhos
quiet! siopi!
quince to kithoni
quite (fairly) arketa
(very) telios
that's quite right poli sosta
quite a lot arketa

R

rabbit o lagos
race (for runners, cars) i koorsa
racket i raketa
radiator (in room) to kalorifer
(of car) to psiyio aftokinitoo
radio to rathiofono
on the radio sto rathiofono
rail: by rail sithirothromikos
railway o sithirothromos
rain i vrokhi
in the rain mes tin vrokhi
it's raining vrekhi
raincoat i kabardina, to athiavrokho
rape o viasmos
rare (steak) okhi poli psimeno
rash (on skin) to exanTHima
raspberry to vatomooro
rat o arooreos
rate (for changing money) i timi sinalagmatos
rather: it's rather good ineh malon kalo
I'd rather ... THa protimoosa na ...

razor (dry) to xirafaki
(electric) i xiristiki mikhani
razor blades to xirafaki
read thiavazo
ready etimos
are you ready? (to man/woman) iseh etimos/etimi?
I'm not ready yet then imeh etimos akomi

dialogue

when will it be ready?
poteh THa ineh etimo?
it should be ready in a couple of days THa prepi na ineh etimo seh mia-thio meres

real pragmatikos
really pragmatika
(very) poli
really! (surprise, doubt) psemata!
really? (interest) aliTHia?
rearview mirror o kaTHreftis aftokinitoo
reasonable (prices etc) loyikos
receipt i apothixi
recently prosfata
reception (in hotel) i resepsion
(for guests) i thexiosi
at reception stin paralavi
reception desk to grafio ipothokhis
receptionist i/o resepsionist
recognize anagnorizo
recommend: could you recommend ...? boriteh na moo sistiseteh ...?

record (music) o thiskos
red kokinos
red wine to kokino krasi
refund i epistrofi khrimaton
 can I have a refund? moo
 epistrefondeh khrimata?
region i periokhi
registered: by registered mail
 sistimeno
registration number o
 ariTHmos kikloforias
relative o/i singenis
religion i THriskia
remember: I don't remember
 then THimameh
 I remember THimameh
 do you remember?
 THimaseh?
rent (for apartment etc) to enikio
 (verb) niki-azo
 to/for rent eniki-azonteh

dialogue

I'd like to rent a car THa
iTHela na nikiaso ena
aftokinito
for how long? ya poso
kero?
two days ya thio meres
this is our range afti ineh i
lista mas
I'll take the ... THa paro
to ...
is that with unlimited
mileage? ineh meh
aperioristo ariTHmo
khiliometron?
it is neh, ineh

can I see your licence
please? boro na tho tin
athi-a sas, parakalo?
and your passport keh to
thiavatirio sas
is insurance included?
simperilamvaneteh i
asfalia?
yes, but you pay the first
3,000 drachmas neh, ala
esis THa pliroseteh tis
protes tris khiliathes
thrakhmes
can you leave a deposit of
1,000 drachmas? boriteh
na afiseteh ya engi-isi
khili-es thrakhmes?

rented car to enikiasmeno
 aftokinito
repair i episkevi
 can you repair it? boriteh na
 to episkevaseteh?
repeat epanalamvano
 could you repeat that?
 boriteh na to
 epanalaveteh?
reservation (train, bus) to
 klisimo THesis

dialogue

I have a reservation ekho
kani mia kratisi
yes sir, what name please?
malista, kiri-eh; seh ti
onoma, parakalo?

reserve krato

dialogue

can I reserve a table for tonight? boro na kliso ena trapezi ya apopseh?
yes madam, for how many people? malista, kiria moo; ya posa atoma?
for two ya thio
and for what time? keh ya ti ora?
for eight o'clock ya tis okhto
and could I have your name please? to onoma sas, parakalo?
see alphabet page 9 for spelling

rest: I need a rest khriazomeh xekoorasi
the rest of the group to ipolipo groop
restaurant to estiatorio

There are two basic types of restaurants: the 'estiatorio' and the taverna. Distinctions between the two are slight but restaurants can be more formal and more expensive than tavernas. The latter may be found more often in the old parts of towns – they may have a more limited choice of dishes and may not display a menu. The best strategy is to go where the Greeks go.

rest room i too-aleta
  see toilet
retired: I'm retired imeh seh sindaxi
return: a return to ... ena isitirio met epistrofis ya to ...
reverse charge call to tilefonima kolekt
reverse gear i opisTHen
revolting apesios
Rhodes i Rothos
rib to plevro
rice to rizi
rich (person) ploosios
  (food) varis
ridiculous yelios
right (correct) sostos
  (not left) thexia
you were right ikhes thikio
that's right sosta
this can't be right afto then bori na ineh sosto
right! endaxi!
is this the right road for ...? ineh aftos o sostos thromos ya ...?
on the right sta thexia
turn right stripseh thexia
right-hand drive meh thexio timoni
ring (on finger) to thaktilithi
I'll ring you THa soo tilefoniso
ring back THa seh paro piso
ripe (fruit) orimos
rip-off: it's a rip-off ineh listia
rip-off prices astronomikes times
risky ripsokinthinos

river to potami
road (country) o thromos
  (in town) i othos
  is this the road for ...? ineh
  aftos o thromos ya ...?
  down the road parakato
road accident to
  aftokinitistiko thistikhima
road map o othikos khartis
roadsign i pinakitha
rob: I've been robbed meh
  listepsan
rock o vrakhos
  (music) i rok moosiki
  on the rocks (with ice) meh
  pagakia
roll (bread) to psomaki
roof i orofi, i steyi
  (flat) i taratsa
roof rack i s-khara
  aftokinitoo
room to thomatio
  (space) to meros
  in my room sto thomatio
  moo

dialogue

do you have any rooms?
ekheteh kaTHoloo
thomatia?
for how many people? ya
posa atoma?
for one/for two ya ena/ya
thio
yes, we have some
vacancies neh, ekhoomeh
elefTHera thomatia
for how many nights will it

be? ya posa vrathia to
THeleteh?
just for one night mono ya
ena vrathi
how much is it? poso
kani?
... drachmas with
bathroom and ... drachmas
without bathroom ...
thrakhmes meh mbanio
keh ... thrakhmes khoris
mbanio
can I see a room with
bathroom? boro na tho
ena thomatio meh
mbanio?
OK, I'll take it endaxi, THa
to paro

room service to servis
  thomatioo
rope to skhini
rosé (wine) to rozeh
roughly (approximately) pano-
  kato
round: it's my round ineh i sira
  moo
roundabout (for traffic) o
  kikloforiakos komvos, i
  platia
round trip ticket: a round trip
  ticket to ... ena isitirio met
  epistrofis ya to ...
route i poria
  what's the best route for ...?
  pios ineh o kaliteros thromos
  ya ...?
rubber (material) lastikho
  (eraser) i svistra, i goma

rubber band to lastikhaki
rubbish (waste) ta skoopithia
(poor quality goods) kaki piotita
rubbish! (nonsense) trikhes!
rucksack to sakithio
rude a-yenis
ruins ta eripia, i arkheotites
rum to roomi
rum and coke ena roomi
meh koka kola
run (person) trekho
how often do the buses run?
poso sikh-na pernoon ta
leoforia?
I've run out of money moo
teliosan ta khrimata
rush hour ora ekhmis

S

sad lipimenos
saddle i sela
safe (not in danger) asfalis
(not dangerous) akinthinos,
avlavis
safety pin i paramana
sail to pani
sailboard to windsurf
sailboarding to windsurf
salad i salata
salad dressing to lathoxitho
sale: for sale politeh
salmon o solomos
Salonika i THesaloniki
salt to alati
same: the same o ithios
the same as this to ithio
opos afto

the same again, please to
ithio xana, parakalo
it's all the same to me to
ithio moo kani
sand i amos
sandals ta santhalia
sandwich to sandwich
sanitary napkins i servi-etes
sanitary towels i servi-etes
sardines i sartheles
Saturday to Savato
sauce i saltsa
saucepan i katsarola
saucer to piataki
sauna i sa-oona
sausage to lookaniko
say: how do you say ... in
Greek? pos to leneh ... sta
Elinika?
what did he say? ti ipeh?
I said ... ipa ...
he said ... ipeh ...
could you say that again?
boriteh na to xanapiteh?,
boriteh na to epanalaveteh?
scarf (for neck) to kaskol
(for head) to mandili
scenery to topio
schedule (US) to programa
scheduled flight i
programatismeni ptisi
school to skholio
scissors: a pair of scissors to
psalithi
scotch to skots whisky
Scotch tape® to sellotape®
Scotland i Skotia
Scottish Skotsezikos
I'm Scottish (man/woman)

imeh Skotsezos/Skotseza
scrambled eggs ta khtipita
avga
scratch i gratzoonia
screw i vitha
screwdriver to katsavithi
scuba diving i anapnefstiki
siskevi katathiti
sea i THalasa
by the sea konda sti THalasa
seafood ta THalasina
seafood restaurant i psaro-
taverna
seafront i paralia
on the seafront stin paralia
seagull o glaros
search psakh-no
seashell i akhivaTHa
seasick: I feel seasick
esthanomeh naftia
I get seasick meh piani i
THalasa
seaside: by the seaside konda
stin paralia
seat i THesi
is this anyone's seat? ineh
kanenos afti i THesi?
seat belt i zoni asfalias
sea urchin o akhinos
seaweed ta fikia
secluded apomeros
second (of time) to theftero-
lepto
(adj) thefteros
just a second! mia stigmi!
second class (travel) thefteri
THesi
second floor o thefteros
orofos

(US) o tritos orofos
second-hand apo theftero
kheri
see vlepo, kitazo
can I see? boro na tho?
have you seen ...? ekhis
thi ...?
see you! ta xanalemeh!
I see (I understand) katalava
I saw him this morning ton
itha simera to pro-i
self-catering apartment to
anexartito thiamerisma
self-service self-servis
sell poolo
do you sell ...? poolateh ...?
Sellotape® to sellotape®
send stelno
I want to send this to England
thelo na stilo afto stin Anglia
senior citizen o/i sindaxiookhos
separate (adj) khoristos
separated: I'm separated
(man/woman) imeh
khorismenos/khorismeni
separately (pay, travel)
xekhorista
September o Septemvrios
septic siptikos
serious sovaros
service charge (in restaurant) to
filothorima
service station to
venzinathiko
serviette i hartopetseta, i
petseta
set menu to tabl-dot
several arketi

sew ravo
could you sew this back on?
boriteh na to rapseteh pali
sti THesi too?
sex to sex
shade: in the shade sti skia
shake: let's shake hands as
thosoomeh ta kheria
shallow (water) rikha nera
shame: what a shame! ti
krima!
shampoo to samboo-an
a shampoo and set ena
loosimo meh mizampli
share (verb: room, table etc)
mirazomeh
sharp (knife etc) kofteros
(taste, pain) thinatos
shattered (very tired)
exandlimenos
shaver i xiristiki mikhani
shaving foam o afros
xirismatos
shaving point i priza xiristikis
mikhanis
she* afti
is she here? ineh etho?
sheet (for bed) to sendoni
shelf to rafi
shellfish ta ostraka
sherry to seri
ship to plio
by ship meh plio
shirt to pookamiso
shit! skata!
shock to sok
I got an electric shock from
the ... ilektristika meh ...
shock-absorber to amortiser

shocking (behaviour, prices)
exofrenikos
shoe to papootsi
a pair of shoes ena zevgari
papootsia
shoelaces ta korthonia
papootsion
shoe polish to verniki
papootsion
shoe repairer o tsangaris
shop to magazi

Shops are usually open
Monday to Friday from
8 am to 1.30 pm and from
5 pm to 8.30 pm (on Saturdays they
open only in the morning); however,
some may open all day, especially in
tourist areas.

shopping: I'm going shopping
pao ya psonia
shopping centre to emboriko
kendro
shop window i vitrina
shore i akti
short (person) kondos
(time) ligos
(journey) sindomos
shortcut o sindomos thromos
shorts to sorts
should: what should I do? ti
prepi na kano?
he shouldn't be long then
prepi na aryisi
you should have told me
eprepeh na moo to ikhes pi
shoulder o omos
shout (verb) fonazo

show (in theatre) to ergo
  could you show me? boriteh na moo thixeteh?
shower (in bathroom) to doos (rain) i bora
  with shower meh doos
shower gel to afrolootro
shut (verb) klino
  when do you shut? poteh klineteh?
  when do they shut? poteh klinoon?
  they're shut ineh klista
  I've shut myself out klistika apexo
  shut up! skaseh!
shutter (on camera) to thiafragma (on window) to exofilo, to pandzoori
shy dropalos
sick (ill) arostos
  I'm going to be sick (vomit) ekho tasi pros emeto
  see ill
side i plevra
  the other side of town i ali akri tis polis
side lights ta khamila fota
side salad i salata ya garnitoora
side street to thromaki
sidewalk to pezothromio
sight: the sights of ... ta axioTHeata too ...
sightseeing: we're going sightseeing pameh na thoomeh ta axioTHeata
sightseeing tour i xenayisi sta

axioTHeata
sign (roadsign etc) to sima
signal: he didn't give a signal then ekaneh sima
signature i ipografi
signpost i pinakitha, i tabela
silence i siopi
silk to metaxi
silly ano-itos
silver to asimi
silver foil to aloominokharto
similar omios
simple (easy) aplos
since: since yesterday apo kh-THes
  since I got here apo toteh poo irTHa etho
sing tragootho
singer (man/woman) o tragoo-thistis/i tragoothistria
single (man/woman) monos
  a single to ... ena aplo ya ...
  I'm single imeh elefTHeros/ elefTHeri
single bed to mono krevati
single room to mono thomatio
sink (in kitchen) o nerokhitis
sister i athelfi
sister-in-law (brother's wife) i nifi
  (wife's sister) i kooniatha
sit: can I sit here? boro na kaTHiso etho?
  is anyone sitting here? kaTHeteh kanis etho?
sit down kaTHomeh
  sit down! katseh kato!
site to axioTHeato

(archaeological) arkheoloyikos khoros

size to meh-yeTHos

skin to therma

skindiving i katathisis

skinny kokaliaris

skirt i foosta

sky o ooranos

sleep (verb) kimameh
 did you sleep well? kimi-THikes kala?
 I need a good sleep khriazomeh ena kalo ipno

sleeper (on train) i kooketa

sleeping bag to sleeping bag

sleeping car i klinamaxa, i kooketa

sleeping pill to ipnotiko khapi

sleepy: I'm feeling sleepy nistazo

sleeve to maniki

slide (photographic) to slide

slip (under dress) to misofori

slippery glisteros

slow argos
 slow down! pio arga

slowly siga-siga
 could you say it slowly? boriteh na to piteh arga-arga?
 very slowly poli arga

small mikros

smell: it smells (smells bad) vroma-i

smile (verb) khamo-yelo

smoke o kapnos
 do you mind if I smoke? sas pirazi an kapniso?

I don't smoke then kapnizo

do you smoke? kapnizeteh?

snack: I'd just like a snack THa iTHela na fao kati prokhiyo

snake to fithi

sneeze to ftarnisma

snorkel o anapnefstiras

snow to khioni

so: it's so good ineh poli kalo
 not so fast okhi toso grigora
 so am I keh ego to ithio
 so do I keh ego epísis
 so-so etsi ki etsi

soaking solution (for contact lenses) igro sindirisis fakon epafis

soap to sapooni

soap powder to aporipandiko

sober xemeTHistos

socks i kaltses

socket (electrical) i priza

soda (water) i sotha

sofa o kanapes

soft (material etc) apalos

soft-boiled egg to melato avgo

soft drink to anapsiktiko

soft lenses i malaki faki

sole i sola
 could you put new soles on these? boriteh na moo valeteh kenooryi-es soles safta?

some: can I have some water/rolls? moo thineteh ligo nero?/liga psomakia?
 can I have some? boro na paro ligo?

somebody, someone kapios
something kati
something to drink kati na pi-iteh
sometimes merikes fores
somewhere kapoo
son o yos
song to tragoothi
son-in-law o gambros
soon sindoma
  I'll be back soon THa yiriso sindoma
  as soon as possible oso to thinaton grigorotera
sore: it's sore ineh ereTHismeno
sore throat pona-i o lemos moo
sorry: (I'm) sorry signomi
  sorry? (didn't understand/hear) pardon?, signomi?
sort: what sort of ...? ti ithos ...?
soup i soopa
sour (taste) xinos
south notos
  south of noti-a
  in the south sto noto
  to the south noti-a
South Africa i Noti-os Afriki
South African (adj) Notio-afrikanos
  I'm South African (man/woman) imeh Notio-afrikanos/Notio-afrikana
southeast notio-anatolikos
southwest notio-thitikos
souvenir to enTHimio
Spain i Ispania

Spanish (adj) ispanikos
  (language) ta ispanika
spanner to klithi
spare part ta andalaktika
spare tyre i rezerva
spark plug to boozi
speak: do you speak English? milateh Anglika?
  I don't speak ... then milo ...

dialogue

can I speak to Costas? boro na miliso ston Kosta, parakalo?
who's calling? pios ton zita-i?
it's Patricia i Patricia
I'm sorry, he's not in, can I take a message? lipameh, then ineh etho, boro na too thoso kapio minima?
no thanks, I'll call back later okhi, efkharisto, THa xanaparo argotera
please tell him I called parakalo, piteh too pos tilefonisa

speciality i spesialiteh
spectacles ta yali-a
speed i takhitita
speed limit to orio takhititas
speedometer to konder
spell: how do you spell it? pos to grafeteh?
  see alphabet page 9
spend xothevo
spider i arakhni

spin-dryer to stegnotirio
splinter i agitha
spoke (in wheel) i aktina
spoon to kootali
sport to spor
sprain: I've sprained my ...
straboolixa to ...
spring (season) i anixi
(in seat etc) to elatirio
square (in town) i platia
stairs ta skalopatia, i skales
stale (bread, taste) bayatikos
stall: the engine keeps stalling
i mikhani sinekhos stamata
stamp to gramatosimo
see post office

dialogue

a stamp for England,
please ena gramatosimo
ya Anglia, parakalo
what are you sending? ti
THa stileteh?
this postcard afti tin karta

star to asteri
(in film) o/i star
start i arkhi, to xekinima
(verb) arkhizo
when does it start? poteh
arkhizi?
the car won't start to
aftokinito then xekina
starter (of car) i miza
(food) to proto piato
starters ta orektika
starving: I'm starving
peTHeno tis pinas

state (in country) i politia
the States (USA) i Inomenes
Politi-es
station o staTHmos
statue to agalma
stay: where are you staying?
poo meneteh?
I'm staying at ... meno sto ...
I'd like to stay another two
nights THa iTHela na mino
ales thio nikhtes
steak i brizola
steal klevo
my bag has been stolen
klepsaneh tin tsanda moo
steep (hill) apotomos
steering to timoni
step: on the steps sta
skalopati-a
stereo to stereofoniko
singrotima
sterling i lira sterlina
steward (on plane) o
a-erosinothos
stewardess i a-erosinothos
sticking plaster to lefkoplast
still: I'm still waiting akoma
perimeno
is he still there? ineh akoma
eki?
keep still! stasoo akinitos!
sting: I've been stung by ...
meh tsibiseh ...
stockings i na-ilon kaltses
stomach to stomakhi
stomach ache o ponos sto
stomakhi, o stomakhoponos
stone (rock) i petra
stop stamatao

please, stop here (to taxi driver etc) parakalo, stamatisteh etho

do you stop near ...? stamatateh konda ...?

stop doing that! stamata na to kanis afto!

stopover i stasi

storm i THi-ela

straight: it's straight ahead ineh olo efTHia

a straight whisky ena sketo whisky

straightaway amesos

strange (odd) paraxenos

stranger (man/woman) o xenos/i xeni

I'm a stranger here imeh xenos etho

strap to loori

strawberry i fraoola

stream to rema, to potamaki

street o thromos

on the street sto thromo

streetmap o othikos khartis

string (cord) o spangos
(guitar etc) i khorthi

strong thinatos

stuck frakarismenos

the key's stuck koliseh to klithi

student o fititis, i fititria

stupid vlakas

suburb ta pro-astia

subway (US: railway) o ipo-yios

suddenly xafnika

suede to kastori

sugar i zakhari

suit (man's) to koostoomi

(woman's) to ta-yer

it doesn't suit me (jacket etc) then moo pa-i

it suits you soo pa-i

suitcase i valitsa

summer to kalokeri

in the summer to kalokeri

sun o ilios

in the sun ston ilio

out of the sun sti skia

sunbathe kano ilioTHerapia

sunblock (cream) to andiliako

sunburn to kapsimo apo ton ilio

sunburnt kamenos apo ton ilio

Sunday i Kiriaki

sunglasses ta yalia ilioo

sun lounger i shez long

sunny: it's sunny ekhi liakatha

sun roof (in car) i tzamenia skepi

sunset i thisi too ilioo

sunshade i ombrela ilioo

sunshine i liakatha

sunstroke i ili-asi

suntan to mavrisma

suntan lotion to lathi mavrismatos

suntanned iliokamenos

suntan oil to lathi mavrismatos

super katapliktikos

supermarket to supermarket

supper to thipno

supplement (extra charge) epipleon, to prosTHeto

sure: are you sure? iseh sigooros?

sure! veveos!

surname to epiTHeto

swearword i vrisia

sweater to poolover

sweatshirt i fanela

Sweden i Soo-ithia

Swedish (adj) Soo-ithikos

sweet (taste) glikos
 (dessert) to gliko

sweets i karameles

swelling to priximo

swim kolimbao
 I'm going for a swim pao ya kolibi
 let's go for a swim pameh ya kolibi

swimming costume to ma-yo

swimming pool i pisina

swimming trunks to ma-yo

switch o thiakoptis

switch off (engine) svino
 (TV, lights) klino

switch on (engine) anavo
 (TV, lights) anigo

swollen prismenos

T

table to trapezi
 a table for two ena trapezi ya thio

tablecloth to trapezomandilo

table tennis to ping-pong

table wine to epitrapezio krasi

tailback (of traffic) i oora

tailor o raftis

take (lead) perno
 (accept) thekhomeh

can you take me to the airport? boriteh na meh pateh sto a-erothromio?

do you take credit cards? thekhesteh pistotikes kartes?

fine, I'll take it endaxi THa to paro

can I take this? (leaflet etc) boro na paro afto?

how long does it take? posi ora THa pari?

it takes three hours perni tris ores

is this seat taken? ineh piasmeni i THesi?

hamburger to take away khamboorger ya to spiti

can you take a little off here? (to hairdresser) boriteh na pareteh ligo apo etho?

talcum powder i poothra talk

talk (verb) milo

tall psilos

tampons ta tampax®, ta tabon

tan to mavrisma
 to get a tan mavrizo

tank (of car) to depozito

tap i vrisi

tape (cassette) i kaseta
 (sticky) i tenia

tape measure to metro

tape recorder to magnitofono

taste i yefsi
 can I taste it? boro na to thokimaso?

taxi to taxi
 will you get me a taxi? THa moo kaleseteh ena taxi?

where can I find a taxi? poo
boro na vro ena taxi?

dialogue

**to the airport/to the Hilton
Hotel please** sto a-
erothromio/sto
xenothokhio Khilton,
parakalo
how much will it be? poso
THa stikhisi?
1,500 drachmas khili-es
pendakosi-es thrakmes
**that's fine, right here,
thanks** endaxi, etho pera
ineh, efkharisto

taxi-driver o taxidzis

Greek taxis, especially
Athenian ones, are among
the least expensive in
Western Europe. Within city or town
limits, use of the meter is mandatory
if one is fitted. Double tariff applies
between 1 and 6 am, and outside
city or town limits at any time of the
day, and there are also surcharges
for entering a ferry harbour or
airport and for large items of
luggage. In rural areas, taxis
sometimes have no meters and you
have to agree a price. Taxi-drivers
very often charge you much more
than they should. It's a good idea to
check the official price list usually
displayed in airports for the fare
from an airport to a city centre. You
should be wary of unlicenced taxi-
drivers outside major railway
stations.

taxi rank o staTHmos taxi
tea to tsa-i
  tea for one/two please tsa-i
  ya enan/thio parakalo
teabags ta fakelakia tsa-i
teach: could you teach me?
  boris na meh maTHis?
teacher (man/woman) o
  thaskalos/i thaskala
team i omatha
teaspoon to kootalaki
tea towel i petseta koozinas
teenager o neos, i nea
telegram to tilegrafima
telephone to tilefono
  see phone
television i tileorasi
tell: could you tell him ...?
  boriteh na too piteh ...?
temperature (weather) i
  THermokrasia
  (fever) o piretos
temple (church) o na-os
tennis to tennis
tennis ball i bala too tennis
tennis court to yipetho tennis
tennis racket i raketa tennis
tent i skini
term (at university, school) i
  s-kholiki periothos
terminus (rail) to terma
terrible foveros
terrific exeretikos
than* apo
  smaller than mikroteros apo

thanks, thank you efkharisto
thank you very much
efkharisto para poli
thanks for the lift efkharisto
poo meh pirateh
no thanks okhi efkharisto

dialogue

> thanks efkharisto
> that's OK, don't mention it
> parakalo, then kani
> tipoteh

that ekinos, ekini, ekino
  that one ekino
  I hope that ... elpizo oti ...
  that's nice ti orea!
  is that ...? afto ineh ...?
  that's it (that's right) akrivos
the* o, i, to; (pl) i, i, ta
theatre to THeatro
their* o/i/to ... toos
theirs* thiki toos
them* toos, tis, ta
  for them ya ekinoos
  with them maftoos
  I gave it to them to ethosa
  saftoos
  who? – them pi-i? – afti
then (at that time) toteh
  (after that) katopin
there eki
  over there eki pera
  up there eki pano
  is there ...? iparkhi ...?
  are there ...? iparkhoon ...?
  there is ... iparkhi ...
  there are ... iparkhoon ...

there you are (giving something)
  oristeh
thermometer to
  THermometro
Thermos flask® to THermos
these afti, aftes, afta
  can I have these? boro na
  ekho afta?
Thessaly i THesalia
they* afti, aftes, afta
thick pakhis
  (stupid) khazos
thief (man/woman) o kleftis/i
  kleftra
thigh to booti
thin leptos
  (person) athinatos
thing to pragma
  my things ta pragmata moo
think skeptomeh
  (believe) nomizo
  I think so etsi nomizo
  I don't think so then nomizo
  I'll think about it THa to
  skepto
third party insurance asfalia ya
  khrisi apo tritoos
thirsty: I'm thirsty thipso
this aftos, afti, afto
  this one afto etho
  this is my wife apo etho i
  yineka moo
  is this ...? ineh ...?
those ekini, ekines, ekina
  which ones? – those pi-a? –
  afta
Thrace i THraki
thread i klosti
throat o lemos

throat pastilles pastili-es
lemoo
through thiamesoo
  does it go through ...? (train,
  bus) perna-i apo to ...?
throw (verb) rikhno
throw away (verb) peto
thumb o andikhiras
thunderstorm i kateyitha, i
  THi-ela
Thursday i Pempti
ticket to isitirio

dialogue

a return to Athens ena
isitirio epistrofis ya tin
ATHina
coming back when? poteh
ineh i epistrofi?
today/next Tuesday
simera/tin epomeni Triti
that will be 2,000
drachmas thio khiliathes
thrakhmes, parakalo

ticket office (bus, rail) i
  THiritha
tide i paliri-a
tie (necktie) i gravata
tight (clothes etc) stenos
  it's too tight ineh poli steno
tights to kalson
till mekhri
time* o khronos
  (occasion) i fora
  what's the time? ti ora ineh?
  this time afti ti fora
  last time tin perasmeni fora

next time tin epomeni fora
four times teseris fores
timetable to programa
tin (can) i konserva
tinfoil to asimokharto
tin-opener to anikhtiri
tiny mikroskopikos
tip (to waiter etc) to filothorima

There are no specific
rules on how large a tip
you should leave in a
restaurant, and tipping is not
regarded as essential. In most
restaurants and tavernas a
service charge is included. Look
for the word 'to filothorima' το
φιλοδώρημα on the menu which
indicates whether the service
charge is included. You are expected
to tip cinema- or theatre-attendants.
It is not usual to tip taxi-drivers; they
usually round up the fare if the
amount of change is small and often
claim that they have no change!

tired koorasmenos
  I'm tired imeh koorasmenos
tissues ta khartomandila
to: to Salonica/London ya tin
  THesaloniki/to Lonthino
  to Greece/England ya tin
  Elatha/Anglia
  to the post office sto
  takhithromio
toast (bread) to tost
today simera
toe to thakhtilo too pothioo
together mazi

we're together (in shop etc) imasteh mazi
can we pay together? boroomeh na plirosoomeh mazi?
toilet i too-aleta
where is the toilet? poo ineh i too-aleta?
I have to go to the toilet prepi na pao stin too-aleta

Public toilets are rare in Greece, especially in less touristy places, but are sometimes found in parks or squares. You will have to take advantage of toilets in restaurants and bars or toilets at railway/bus stations and in museums etc. Throughout Greece you place used paper in the adjacent wastebaskets, not in the bowl.

toilet paper kharti iyias
tomato i domata
tomato juice to domatozoomo, o domatokhimos
tomato ketchup to ketsap
tomorrow avrio
tomorrow morning avrio to pro-i
the day after tomorrow methavrio
toner (cosmetic) to tonotiko
tongue i glosa
tonic (water) to tonik
tonight apopseh
tonsillitis i amigthalititha

too (excessively) poli
(also) episis
too hot poli kafto
too much para poli
me too kego episis
tooth to thondi
toothache o ponothondos
toothbrush i othondovoortsa
toothpaste i othondokrema
top: on top of ... pano apo ...
at the top stin korifi
top floor to retire
topless yimnostiTHi
torch o fakos
total to sinolo
tour i peri-iyisi, i xenayisi
is there a tour of ...? iparkhi peri-iyisi ya ...?
tour guide o/i xenagos
tourist (man/woman) o tooristas/i tooristria
tourist information office Grafio Pliroforion E-OT
tour operator to taxithiotiko grafio
towards pros
towel i petseta
town i poli
in town stin poli
just out of town akrivos exo apo tin poli
town centre to kendro tis polis
town hall to thimarkhio
toy to pekh-nithi
track (US) i platforma
see **platform**
tracksuit i aTHlitiki forma
traditional parathosiakos

traffic i kikloforia
traffic jam i kikloforiaki
  simforisi
traffic lights ta fanaria tis
  trokheas
trailer (for carrying tent etc) i
  rimoolka
  (US: caravan) to trokhospito
trailer park topoTHesia ya
  trokhospita
train to treno
  by train meh treno

dialogue

  is this the train for ...? afto
  ineh to treno ya ...?
  sure neh
  **no, you want that platform
  there** okhi, THa pateh seh
  ekini tin platforma eki

trainers (shoes) ta aTHlitika
  papootsia
train station o sithirothromikos staTHmos
tram to tram
translate metafrazo
  could you translate that?
  boriteh na metafraseteh afto?
translation i metafrasi
translator o/i metafrastis
trashcan o skoopithodenekes
travel taxithevo
  we're travelling around
  taxithevoomeh triyiro
travel agent's to taxithiotiko
  grafio
traveller's cheque i

taxithiotiki epitayi
tray o thiskos
tree to thendro
tremendous tromeros
trendy modernos
trim: just a trim please (to
  hairdresser) ligo konditera,
  parakalo
trip (excursion) to taxithi
  I'd like to go on a trip to ...
  THa iTHela na pao ena
  taxithi stin ...
trolley to trolley, to karotsaki
trolleybus to trolley
  see bus
trouble o belas
  I'm having trouble with ...
  ekho provlimata meh ...
  sorry to trouble you meh
  sinkhoriteh poo sas vazo seh
  mbela
trousers to pandaloni
true aliTHinos
  that's not true then ineh
  aliTHia
trunk (US: of car) to port-bagaz
trunks (swimming) to mayo
try prospaTHo, thokimazo
  can I have a try? boro na
  thokimaso?
try on provaro
  can I try it on? boro na to
  thokimaso pano moo?
T-shirt to bloozaki
Tuesday i Triti
tuna o tonos
tunnel i siraga
Turkey i Toorkia
Turkish (adj) Toorkikos

Turkish coffee Toorkikos kafes, Elinikos kafes
see coffee

Turkish-Cypriot (adj) Toorkiko-Kipriakos

turn: turn left/right stripseh aristera/thexia
where do I turn off? poo strivo?

turn off: can you turn the heating off? boris na klisis ti THermansi/to kalorifer?

turn on: can you turn the heating on? boris na anixis ti THermansi/to kalorifer?

turning (in road) i strofi

TV i tileorasi

tweezers to tsimbithaki

twice thio fores
twice as much ta thipla

twin beds thio krevatia

twin room to thomatio meh thio krevatia

twist: I've twisted my ankle stramboolixa ton astragalo moo

type to ithos
a different type of ... ena alo ithos apo ...

typical kharaktiristikos

tyre to lastikho

U

ugly askhimos

UK to Inomeno Vasili-o

ulcer to elkos

umbrella i ombrela

uncle o THios

unconscious anesTHitos

under apo kato
(less than) ligotero apo

underdone (meat) misop-simenos

underground (railway) o ipo-yios

underpants to sovrako, to slip

understand: I understand katalaveno
I don't understand then katalaveno
do you understand? katalavenis?

unemployed anergos

United States i Inomenes Politi-es

university to panepistimio

unleaded petrol i amolivthi venzini

unlimited mileage aperiorista khiliometra

unlock xeklithono

unpack anigo tis valitses

until mekhri

unusual asiniTHistos

up pano
(upwards) pros ta pano
up there eki pano
he's not up yet (not out of bed) then sikoTHikeh akomi
what's up? (what's wrong?) ti yineteh?

upmarket (restaurant etc) akrivos

upset stomach o stomakhoponos

upside down ta pano kato

upstairs pano
urgent epigon
us* mas
  with us meh mas
  for us ya mas
use khrisimopi-o
  may I use ...? boro na
  khrisimopi-iso ...?
useful khrisimos
usual siniTHismenos
  the usual (drink etc) to
  siniTHismeno

V

vacancy: do you have any
  vacancies? (hotel) ekheteh
  elefTHera thomatia?
vacation i thiakopes
  see holiday
vaccination o emvoliasmos
vacuum cleaner i ilektriki
  skoopa
valid (ticket etc) engiros
  how long is it valid for? ya
  poso is-khi-i?
valley i kilatha
valuable (adj) politimos
  can I leave my valuables
  here? boro na afiso ta timalfi
  moo etho?
value i axia
van to trokhospito
vanilla i vanilia
  a vanilla ice cream ena
  pagoto vanilia
vary: it varies metavaleteh
vase to vazo

veal to moskhari
vegetables ta lakhanika
vegetarian o/i khortofagos
vending machine o aftomatos
  politis
very poli
  very little for me poli ligo ya
  mena
  I like it very much moo aresi
  para poli
vest (under shirt) to fanelaki
via thia mesoo
video (film) i video-tenia
  (video recorder) to video
view i THea
villa i vila
village to khorio
vinegar to xithi
vineyard to ambeli
visa i viza
visit (verb) episkeptomeh
  I'd like to visit ... THa iTHela
  na episkefto ...
vital: it's vital that ... ineh
  vasiko na ...
vodka i votka
voice i foni
volleyball to volley-ball, i
  khirosferisi
voltage i tasis
  see electricity
vomit (verb) kano emeto

W

waist i mesi
waistcoat to yileko
wait perimeno

wait for me perimeneh meh!
don't wait for me mi meh perimenis
can I wait until my wife gets here? boro na paragilo otan elTHi i yineka moo?
can you do it while I wait? na perimeno na to kaneteh?
could you wait here for me? boriteh na meh perimeneteh na yiriso?
waiter o servitoros
waiter! garson!
waitress i garsona, i servitora
waitress! sas parakalo!
wake: can you wake me up at 5.30? boriteh na meh xipniseteh stis pendeh keh misi?
wake-up call tilefonima ya xipnima
Wales i Oo-alia
walk: is it a long walk? ineh poli perpatima?
it's only a short walk ekhi ligo perpatima
I'll walk THa perpatiso
I'm going for a walk pao ena peripato
Walkman® to walkman®
wall o tikhos
wallet to portofoli
wander: I like just wandering around moo aresi na khazevo triyiro
want: I want a ... THelo ena ...
I don't want any ... then THelo ...
I want to go home THelo na

pao spiti moo
I don't want to then THelo
he wants to ... THeli na ...
what do you want? ti THelis?
ward (in hospital) o THalamos
warm zestos
I'm so warm zestenomeh arketa
was*: I was ... imoon ...
he/she/it was ... itan ...
wash (verb) pleno
(oneself) plenomeh
can you wash these? boriteh na plineteh afta?
washer (for bolt etc) i rothela
washhand basin o niptiras
washing (clothes) i boogatha
washing machine to plindirio
washing powder i skoni plindirioo, to aporipandiko
washing-up liquid to sapooni piaton
wasp i sfinga
watch (wristwatch) to rolo-i
will you watch my things for me? boriteh na prosekheteh ta pragmata moo?
watch out! prosekheh!
watch strap to looraki roloyioo
water to nero
may I have some water? moo thineteh ligo nero?
waterproof (adj) athi-avrokhos
waterskiing to THalasio ski
wave (in sea) to kima
way: could you tell me the way

to ...? boriteh na moo piteh
pos THa pa-o sto ..?
it's this way apo etho ineh
it's that way apo eki ineh
is it a long way to ...? ineh
makri-a ya to ...?
no way! apokli-eteh!

dialogue

> **could you tell me the way
> to ...?** boriteh na moo
> thixeteh to thromo ya ...?
> **go straight on until you
> reach the traffic lights**
> piyeneteh olo isia mekhri
> na ftaseteh sta fanaria
> **turn left** stripsteh aristera
> **take the first on the right**
> parteh ton proto thromo
> sta thexia
> see **where**

we* emis
weak athinatos
weather o keros

dialogue

> **what's the weather
> forecast?** ti ipeh to theltio
> keroo?
> **it's going to be fine** THa
> ineh kalos keros
> **it's going to rain** THa vrexi
> **it'll brighten up later** THa
> anixi o keros argotera

wedding o gamos

wedding ring i vera
Wednesday i Tetarti
week i evthomatha
a week (from) today seh mia
evthomatha apo simera
a week (from) tomorrow
seh mia evthomatha apo
avrio
weekend to Savatokiriako
at the weekend to
Savatokiriako
weight to varos
weird paraxenos
weirdo o trelaras
welcome: welcome to ... kalos
ilTHateh sto ...
you're welcome (don't mention
it) parakalo
well: I don't feel well then
esTHanomeh kala
she's not well ekini then
ineh kala
you speak English very well
milateh poli kala Anglika
well done! bravo
this one as well ki afto
episis
well well! (surprise) ya thes!

dialogue

> **how are you?** ti kanis?
> **very well, thanks** poli kala,
> efkharisto
> **and you?** ki esi?

well-done (meat)
kalopsimenos
Welsh Oo-alos

I'm Welsh (man/woman) imeh
Oo-alos/Oo-ali
were*: we were imasteh
you were isasteh/isteh
they were itan
west thitikos
in the west sta thitika
West Indian (adj) apo tis
thitikes Inthi-es
wet vregmenos
what? ti?
what's that? ti ineh ekino?
what should I do? ti prepi na
kano?
what a view! ti THea!
what bus do I take? ti
leoforio prepi na paro?
wheel i rotha
wheelchair i anapiriki
poliTHrona
when? poteh?
when we get back otan
yirisoomeh
when's the train/ferry? poteh
fevyi to treno/to karavi?
where? poo?
I don't know where it is then
xero poo ineh

dialogue

where is the cathedral?
poo ineh o kaTHethrikos
naos?
it's over there ineh eki
pera
could you show me where
it is on the map? boriteh
na moo thixeteh sto

kharti poo ineh?
it's just here ineh akrivos
etho
see way

which: which bus? pio
leoforio?

dialogue

which one? pio?
that one ekino
this one? afto?
no, that one okhi, ekino

while: while I'm here oso imeh
etho
whisky to whisky
white aspros
white wine to aspro krasi
who? pios?
who is it? pios ineh?
the man who ... o anTHropos
poo ...
whole: the whole week oli tin
evthomatha
the whole lot ola
whose: whose is this? pianoo
ineh afto?
why? yati?
why not? yati okhi?
wide platis
wife: my wife i sizigos moo
will: will you do it for me? THa
moo to kanis afto?
wind o anemos
window to paraTHiro
near the window konda sto
paraTHiro

in the window (of shop) sti vitrina
window seat i THesi sto paraTHiro
windscreen to parbriz
windscreen wiper o ialokaTHaristiras
windsurfing to windsurfing
windy: it's so windy ekhi poli a-era
wine to krasi
can we have some more wine? boroomeh na ekhoomeh ligo krasi akoma?

Both estatoria and tavernas will usually offer you a choice of bottled wines, and some (mainly tavernas) may have their own house variety, kept in barrels and served out in metal jugs. If you want house wine, ask for 'khima krasi/retsina'. Retsina – pine-resinated wine, a slightly acquired taste – is invariably better straight from the barrel. Not as many tavernas keep wine from the barrel these days, but always ask whether they have wine 'varelisio' or 'khima' – both mean, in effect, 'from the barrel'.

wine list o katalogos ton krasion
winter o khimonas
in the winter ton khimona
winter holiday i khimerines thiakopes
wire to sirma

(electric) to ilektriko kalothio
wish: best wishes poles efkhes
with meh
I'm staying with ... meno meh ...
without khoris
witness o/i martiras
will you be a witness for me? THa iseh martiras moo?
woman i yineka

women
Many women travel by themselves about Greece without being harassed or feeling intimidated. Most of the hassle you are likely to get is from a small minority of Greeks who migrate to the main resorts and towns in summer in pursuit of 'fun-loving' tourists. In remote mountains and inland areas, you may feel more uncomfortable travelling alone. The intensely traditional Greeks may have trouble understanding why you are unaccompanied, and might not welcome your presence in their exclusively male 'kafenia' – often the only place where you can get a drink. Because of the machismo of the majority of Greek men, foreign women should be careful when dealing with approaches; flirting can often lead to unpleasant misunderstandings.

wonderful THavmasios

won't: it won't start then THa xekinisi

wood (material) to xilo

woods (forest) to thasos

wool to mali

word i lexi

work i thoolia

it's not working then thoolevi

I work in ... ergazomeh seh ...

world o kosmos

worry: I'm worried stenokhori-emeh

worry beads to kombolo-i

worse: it's worse ineh khirotera

worst o khiroteros

worth: is it worth a visit? axizi mia episkepsi?

would: would you give this to ...? boriteh na thoseteh afto ston ...?

wrap: could you wrap it up? boriteh na to tilixeteh?

wrapping paper to kharti peritiligmatos

(for presents) kharti ya thora

wrist o karpos

write grafo

could you write it down? boriteh na moo to grapseteh?

how do you write it? pos to grafeteh?

writing paper to kharti alilografias

wrong: it's the wrong key afto ineh laTHos klithi

the bill's wrong o logariasmos ineh laTHos

sorry, wrong number signomi, laTHos noomero

sorry, wrong room signomi, laTHos thomatio

there's something wrong with ... iparkhi kapio laTHos meh ...

what's wrong? ti simveni?

X

X-ray i aktinografia

Y

yacht to yot

yard* i yartha

(courtyard, backyard) i avli

year o khronos

yellow kitrinos

yes neh

yesterday kh-THes

yesterday morning kh-THes to pro-i

the day before yesterday prokh-THes

yet akomi

dialogue

has it arrived yet? akomi then eftaseh?

no, not yet okhi, okhi akomi

you'll have to wait a little

124

longer yet THa prepi na perimeneteh akomi ligo

yoghurt to ya-**oo**rti
you* (fam) esi
  (pl or polite) esis
  I'll see you later THa seh tho argotera
  this is for you afto ineh ya sas
with you mazi sas
young neos
your* (fam) o/i/to ... soo
  (pl or polite) o/i/to ... sas
  your camera i fotografiki mikhani soo/sas
yours (fam) thiko soo
  (pl or polite) thiko sas
youth hostel o xenonas neon

Z

zero mithen
zip to fermoo-ar
  could you put a new zip in? boriteh na valeteh ena kenoor-yio fermoo-ar?
zip code o takhithromikos kothikos
zoo o zo-oloyikos kipos

Greek

→

English

Colloquial Greek

The following are words or expressions you might well hear. You shouldn't be tempted to use any of the stronger ones unless you are sure of your audience.

άντε γαμήσου [**andeh gamisoo**] fuck off!

βλάκα [**vlaka**] idiot, blockhead

βρωμο... [**vromo**] bloody ...

γαμώ το! [**gamo to**] fuck!

γκόμενα [**gomena**] bird, chick

γουστάρω [**goostaro**] I feel like it

δεν πειράζει [**den pirazi**] it doesn't matter

είσαι; [**iseh**] do you want to?

έλα [**ela**] come on!, move!

θαυμάσια! [**THavmasia**] great!

in [**in**] fashionable

καμάκι [**kamaki**] stud, Don Juan

κερατάς [**keratas**] bastard

μαλάκα [**malaka**] wanker

μου τα'πρηξες [**moo taprixes**] you're getting on my tits, you're getting up my nose

μπάτσος [**batsos**] cop

Παναγία μου [**Panayia moo**] my God!

πούστης [**poostis**] faggot, poofter

πουτάνα [**pootana**] whore

πώ πώ! [**po po**] bloody hell!

ρε Κώστα [**reh Kosta**] Kostas, my old pal

ρε μαλάκα [**reh malaka**] you stupid wanker

σκάσε! [**skaseh**] shut up!

σκατά! [**skata**] shit!

στ'αρχίδια μου [**starkhidia moo**] I don't give a fuck

τζάμπα [**tzamba**] dirt cheap

τί γίνεται; [**ti yineteh**] how is it going?

τί νά κάνουμε; [**ti na kanoomeh**] what can you do?

τύφλα στο μεθύσι [**tifla sto meTHisi**] pissed (drunk)

A

αγάπη (η) [agapi (i)] love

αγαπημένος [agapimenos] favourite

αγαπώ [agapo] love (verb)

αγγίζω [angizo] touch (verb)

ΑΓΓΛΙΑ Αγγλία (η) [Anglia (i)] England

Αγγλίδα (η) [Anglitha (i)] Englishwoman

ΑΓΓΛΙΚΑ Αγγλικά (τα) [Anglika (ta)] English

ΑΓΓΛΙΚΟΣ Αγγλικός [Anglikos] English

άγγλος (ο) [Anglos (o)] Englishman

αγελάδα (η) [ayelatha (i)] cow

αγενής [ayenis] rude

άγκυρα (η) [angira (i)] anchor

αγκώνας (ο) [angonas (o)] elbow

ΑΓΝΟ ΠΑΡΘΕΝΟ ΜΑΛΛΙ αγνό παρθένο μαλλί pure new wool

ΑΓΟΡΑ αγορά (η) [agora (i)] market

αγοράζω [agorazo] buy (verb)

αγόρι (το) [agori (to)] boy

άγριος [agrios] wild, fierce

αγρόκτημα (το) [agroktima (to)] farm

αγρότης (ο) [agrotis (o)] farmer

αγώνας (ο) [agonas (o)] fight, struggle; game

άδεια (η) [athia (i)] licence; permission

άδεια οδηγήσεως (η) [athia othiyiseos (i)] driving licence

άδειος [athios] empty, vacant

αδελφή (η) [athelffi (i)] sister

ΑΔΕΛΦΟΙ αδελφοί brothers

αδελφός (ο) [athelfos (o)] brother

ΑΔΙΕΞΟΔΟ αδιέξοδο cul-de-sac, dead end

αδύνατος [athinatos] impossible; weak

A.E. public limited company

ΑΕΡΑΝΤΛΙΑ αεραντλία (η) air pump

αέρας (ο) [aeras (o)] air; wind; choke

ΑΕΡΟΔΡΟΜΙΟ αεροδρόμιο (το) [aerothromio (to)] airport

ΑΕΡΟΛΙΜΗΝ αερολιμήν (ο) [aerolimin (o)] airport

αεροπλάνο (το) [aeroplano (to)] plane

αεροπορική εταιρεία (η) [aeroporiki eteria (i)] airline

ΑΕΡΟΠΟΡΙΚΩΣ αεροπορικώς [aeroporikos] by air; by air mail

ΑΕΡΟΣΥΝΟΔΟΣ αεροσυνοδός (ο/η) [aerosinothos (o/i)] steward, stewardess

ΑΘΗΝΑ Αθήνα (η) [ATHina (i)] Athens

αθλητής (ο) [aTHlitis (o)] athlete

ΑΘΛΗΤΙΚΑ αθλητικά (τα) [aTHlitika (ta)] sports shop

αθλητικά παπούτσια (τα) [aTHlitika papootsia (ta)] trainers

ΑΘΛΗΤΙΚΕΣ ΕΓΚΑΤΑΣΤΑΣΕΙΣ αθλητικές εγκαταστάσεις sporting facilities αθλητική φόρμα (η) [aTHlitikí forma (i)] tracksuit

ΑΘΛΗΤΙΚΟ ΚΕΝΤΡΟ αθλητικό κέντρο (το) [aTHlitikó kendro (to)] sports centre

αθώος [aTHoos] innocent

ΑΙΓΑΙΟ Αιγαίο (το) [E-yeo (to)] Aegean

ΑΙΘΟΥΣΑ ΤΡΑΝΖΙΤ αίθουσα τράνζιτ transit lounge

αίμα (το) [ema (to)] blood

αιμορραγώ [emorago] bleed

αισθάνομαι [esTHanomeh] feel (verb)

ΑΙΤΗΣΗ αίτηση (η) [etisi (i)] application form; application

αιτία (η) [etia (i)] cause; reason

εξ αιτίας ... [exetias ...] because of ...

αιώνας (ο) [eonas (o)] century

ΑΚΑΤΑΛΛΗΛΟ ακατάλληλο adults only

Α΄ ΚΑΤΗΓΟΡΙΑΣ Α΄ κατηγορίας first class

ακολουθώ [akolooTHo] follow

ακόμα, ακόμη [akoma, akomi] still, yet; even; also

ακουστικά (τα) [akoostika (ta)] hearing aid; headphones

ΑΚΟΥΣΤΙΚΟ ακουστικό (το) [akoostiko (to)] receiver

ακούω [akoo-o] hear; listen

άκρη (η) [akri (i)] edge; end; tip

ΑΚΡΙΒΕΣ ΑΝΤΙΤΙΜΟ ΜΟΝΟ ακριβές αντίτιμο μόνο exact fare only

ακριβός [akrivos] expensive

ακροατήριο (το) [akroatirio (to)] audience

ΑΚΡΥΛΙΚΟ ακρυλικό [akriliko] acrylic

ΑΚΤΗ ακτή (η) [akti (i)] beach; coast, shore

ακυρώνω [akirono] cancel

ΑΛΒΑΝΙΑ Αλβανία (η) [Alvania (i)] Albania

αληθινός [aliTHinos] true; real

αλλά [alla] but

ΑΛΛΑΓΗ ΛΑΔΙΩΝ αλλαγή λαδιών oil change

αλλάζω [allazo] change (verb)

αλλάζω ρούχα [allazo rookha] change one's clothes

ΑΛΛΕΡΓΙΑ αλλεργία (η) [alleryia (i)] allergy

ΑΛΛΕΡΓΙΑ ΣΤΗ ΓΥΡΗ αλλεργία στη γύρη [alleryia sti yiri] hay fever

αλλεργικός σε [alleryikos seh] allergic to

άλλη [ali] other; else

άλλη μία [ali mia] another

άλλο [alo] other; else; another

όχι άλλο [okhi alo] no more

άλλο ένα [alo ena] another

άλλος [alos] other; else

άλλος ένας [alos enas] another

αλλού [aloo] elsewhere

αλμυρός [almiros] salty

άλογο (το) [alogo (to)] horse

ΑΛΟΙΦΗ αλοιφή (η) [alifi (i)] ointment

αλουμινόχαρτο (το) [aloominokharto (to)] aluminium foil

ΑΛΣΟΣ άλσος (το) [alsos (to)] wooded park, grove

αλτ! [alt!] stop!

αλυσίδα (η) [alisitha (i)] chain

ΑΜΑΞΑ άμαξα (η) [amaxa (i)] coach, car (on train)

ΑΜΑΞΙ αμάξι (το) [amaxi (to)] car (on train)

ΑΜΑΞΟΣΤΟΙΧΙΑ αμαξοστοιχία (η) [amaxostikhia (i)] train

Αμερικανίδα (η) [Amerikanitha (i)] American (woman)

Αμερικανικός [Amerikanikos] American (adj)

Αμερικανός (ο) [Amerikanos (o)] American (man)

ΑΜΕΡΙΚΗ Αμερική (η) [Ameriki (i)] America

ΑΜΕΣΟΣ ΔΡΑΣΙΣ άμεσος δράσις emergencies

αμέσως [amesos] immediately

αμμόλοφοι (οι) [amolofi (i)] sand dunes

άμμος (η) [amos (i)] sand

αμορτισέρ (το) [amortiser (to)] shock-absorber

αμπέλι (το) [ambeli (to)] vineyard

αμπέρ (το) [amper] amp

ΑΜΠΟΥΛΕΣ αμπούλες ampoules

αν [an] if

ΑΝΑΒΡΑΖΟΝΤΑ ΔΙΣΚΙΑ αναβράζοντα δισκία effervescent tablets

ανάβω [anavo] light (verb)

αναγκαίος [anangeos] necessary

ανάγκη [anangi] need

αναγνωρίζω [anagnorizo] recognize, acknowledge, admit

ανακατεύω [anakatevo] mix (verb)

ΑΝΑΚΟΙΝΩΣΗ ανακοίνωση (η) [anakinosi (i)] announcement

ΑΝΑΚΛΗΣΙΣ ανάκλησις (η) [anaklisis (i)] withdrawal

ΑΝΑΛΗΨΗ ανάληψη (η) withdrawal(s) (of money)

αναμείνατε στο ακουστικό [anaminateh sto akoostiko] hold the line please

ανάμεσα [anamesa] among; between

αναπαύομαι [anapavomeh] rest, relax

ανάπαυση (η) [anapafsi (i)] rest

αναπαυτικός [anapaftikos] comfortable

αναπηρική πολυθρόνα (η) [anapiriki politHrona (i)] wheelchair

ανάπηρος [anapiros] disabled

αναπνέω [anapneo] breathe

αναποδογυρίζω [anapothoyirizo] knock over

αναπτήρας (ο) [anaptiras (o)] lighter

αναπτύσσω [anaptiso] develop; explain

ανατολή (η) [anatoli (i)] east; dawn

ανατολή του ήλιου (η) [anatoli too ilioo (i)] sunrise

ΑΝΑΧΩΡΕΙ ΚΑΘΗΜΕΡΙΝΑ ΓΙΑ ... αναχωρεί καθημερινά γιά ... departs daily to ...

ΑΝΑΧΩΡΗΣΕΙΣ αναχωρήσεις departures

ΑΝΑΧΩΡΗΣΗ αναχώρηση (η)
[anakhorisi (i)] departure

ΑΝΑΨΥΚΤΗΡΙΟ αναψυκτήριο
refreshments

άνδρας (ο) [anthras (o)] man

ΑΝΔΡΙΚΑ ανδρικά (τα)
[anthrika (ta)] menswear

ΑΝΔΡΙΚΑ ΕΙΔΗ ΚΑΙ
ΑΞΕΣΟΥΑΡ ανδρικά είδη και
αξεσουάρ men's fashions and
accessories

ΑΝΔΡΙΚΑ ΕΝΔΥΜΑΤΑ
ανδρικά ενδύματα [anthrika
enthimata] menswear

ΑΝΔΡΙΚΑ ΕΣΩΡΟΥΧΑ
ανδρικά εσώρουχα [anthrika
esorookha] men's underwear

ΑΝΔΡΙΚΑΙ ΚΟΜΜΩΣΕΙΣ
ανδρικαί κομμώσεις [anthrikeh
komosis] men's hairdresser

ΑΝΔΡΙΚΑ ΥΠΟΔΗΜΑΤΑ
ανδρικά υποδήματα [anthrika
ipothimata] men's footwear

ΑΝΔΡΙΚΑ ΥΠΟΚΑΜΙΣΑ
ανδρικά υποκάμισα [anthrika
ipokamisa] men's shirts

ΑΝΔΡΩΝ ανδρών gents'
(toilet), men's room

ανεβαίνω [aneveno] get in (car);
get up; go up

ΑΝΕΛΚΥΣΤΗΡΑΣ
ανελκυστήρας (ο) [anelkistiras
(o)] lift, elevator

ΑΝΕΜΙΣΤΗΡΑΣ ανεμιστήρας
(ο) [anemistiras (o)] fan

άνεμος (ο) [anemos (o)] wind

ΑΝΕΞΑΡΤΗΤΟ ΔΙΑΜΕΡΙΣΜΑ
ανεξάρτητο διαμέρισμα (το)
[anexartito thiamerisma (to)] self-

catering apartment

ανεξάρτητος [anexartitos]
independent

άνεργος [anergos] unemployed

ανήκω [aniko] belong

ανησυχώ [anisikho] be anxious,
be worried

ανησυχώ για [anisikho ya]
worry about

ανηψιά (η) [anipsia (i)] niece

ανηψιός (ο) [anipsios (o)]
nephew

ΑΝΘΟΠΩΛΕΙΟ ανθοπωλείο
(το) [anтнopolio (to)] florist's

άνθρωποι (οι) [anтнropi (i)]
people

αν και [an keh] although

ΑΝΟΔΟΣ άνοδος (η) [anothos
(i)] ascent, way up

ανοίγω [anigo] open (verb);
switch on

ανοίγω τις βαλίτσες [anigo tis
valitses] unpack

ΑΝΟΙΚΤΑ ανοικτά [anikta]
open

ΑΝΟΙΚΤΟ ΑΠΟ ... ΩΣ ...
ανοικτό από ... ως ... [anikto
apo ... os ...] open from ...
to ...

ΑΝΟΙΚΤΟΝ ανοικτόν [anikton]
open (adj)

ανοικτός [aniktos] open (adj);
on (light)

άνοιξη (η) [anixi (i)] spring
(season)

ανοιχτήρι (το) [anikhtiri (to)] tin
opener; corkscrew

ΑΝΟΙΧΤΟ ανοιχτό [anikhto]
open; light (colour)

ΑΝΤΑΛΛΑΚΤΙΚΑ
ανταλλακτικά (τα) spare parts
ΑΝΤΑΛΛΑΚΤΙΚΑ
ΑΥΤΟΚΙΝΗΤΩΝ
ανταλλακτικά αυτοκινήτων (τα)
auto spares
ανταλλάσω [andalaso]
exchange (verb)
άντε! [andeh!] come on!
αντέχω [andekho] endure,
tolerate
αντί [andi] instead of
ΑΝΤΙΒΙΟΤΙΚΟ αντιβιοτικό
(το) [andiviotiko (to)] antibiotic
ΑΝΤΙ-ΙΣΤΑΜΙΝΙΚΟ
ΦΑΡΜΑΚΟ αντι-ισταμινικό
φάρμακο (το) [andi-istaminiko
farmako (to)] antihistamine
αντίκα (η) [andika (i)] antique
ΑΝΤΙΚΕΣ αντίκες [andikes]
antiques
αντίο [andio] goodbye
αντιπαθητικός [andipaτHitikos]
obnoxious
ΑΝΤΙΠΡΟΣΩΠΕΙΑ
ΑΥΤΟΚΙΝΗΤΩΝ
αντιπροσωπεία αυτοκινήτων
(η) [andiprosopia aftokiniton (i)]
car dealer
ΑΝΤΙΠΡΟΣΩΠΟΣ
αντιπρόσωπος (ο) [andiprosopos
(o)] agent
αντιπυρετικό [andipiretiko] anti-
fever
ΑΝΤΙΣΗΠΤΙΚΟ αντισηπτικό
(το) [andisiptiko (to)] antiseptic
ΑΝΤΙΣΥΛΛΗΠΤΙΚΟ
αντισυλληπτικό (το)
[andisiliptiko (to)] contraceptive

ΑΝΤΙΣΥΛΛΗΠΤΙΚΟ ΧΑΠΙ
αντισυλληπτικό χάπι (το)
[andisiliptiko khapi (to)]
contraceptive pill
ΑΝΤΙΤΙΜΟ (ΔΙΑΔΡΟΜΗΣ)
αντίτιμο (διαδρομής) (το)
[anditimo (thiathromis) (to)] fare
ΑΝΤΙΦΛΕΓΜΩΔΕΣ
αντιφλεγμώδες anti-
inflammation
αντλία (η) [andlia (i)] pump
ΑΝΤΛΙΑ ΒΕΝΖΙΝΗΣ αντλία
βενζίνης petrol/gas pump
ΑΝΤΛΙΑ ΝΤΙΖΕΛ αντλία
ντίζελ diesel pump
ΑΝΩ άνω [ano] up
ΑΞΕΣΟΥΑΡ ΑΥΤΟΚΙΝΗΤΩΝ
αξεσουάρ αυτοκινήτων (τα)
auto accessories
άξονας (ο) [axonas (o)] axle
ΑΠΑΓΟΡΕΥΕΤΑΙ
απαγορεύεται it is
prohibited
ΑΠΑΓΟΡΕΥΕΤΑΙ Η ΕΙΣΟΔΟΣ
απαγορεύεται η είσοδος no
entry, no admission
ΑΠΑΓΟΡΕΥΕΤΑΙ Η
ΚΑΤΑΠΟΣΙΣ απαγορεύεται η
κατάποσις do not swallow
ΑΠΑΓΟΡΕΥΕΤΑΙ Η
ΚΑΤΑΣΚΗΝΩΣΗ
απαγορεύεται η κατασκήνωση
no camping
ΑΠΑΓΟΡΕΥΕΤΑΙ Η
ΚΟΛΥΜΒΗΣΗ απαγορεύεται
η κολύμβηση no swimming
ΑΠΑΓΟΡΕΥΕΤΑΙ Η ΛΗΨΙΣ
ΔΙΑ ΤΟΥ ΣΤΟΜΑΤΟΣ
απαγορεύεται η λήψις διά του

στόματος not to be taken
orally
ΑΠΑΓΟΡΕΥΕΤΑΙ Η
ΣΤΑΘΜΕΥΣΗ απαγορεύεται
η στάθμευση no parking
ΑΠΑΓΟΡΕΥΕΤΑΙ Η ΣΤΑΣΗ
απαγορεύεται η στάση no
waiting, no stopping
ΑΠΑΓΟΡΕΥΕΤΑΙ Η
ΧΟΡΗΓΗΣΗ ΑΝΕΥ
ΣΥΝΤΑΓΗΣ ΙΑΤΡΟΥ
απαγορεύεται η χορήγηση
άνευ συνταγής ιατρού available
on prescription only
ΑΠΑΓΟΡΕΥΕΤΑΙ Ο
ΓΥΜΝΙΣΜΟΣ απαγορεύεται ο
γυμνισμός nudism prohibited
ΑΠΑΓΟΡΕΥΟΝΤΑΙ ΟΙ
ΚΑΤΑΔΥΣΕΙΣ απαγορεύονται
οι καταδύσεις no diving
ΑΠΑΓΟΡΕΥΕΤΑΙ ΤΟ
ΚΑΜΠΙΝΓΚ απαγορεύεται το
κάμπινγκ no camping
ΑΠΑΓΟΡΕΥΕΤΑΙ ΤΟ
ΚΑΠΝΙΖΕΙΝ απαγορεύεται το
καπνίζειν no smoking
ΑΠΑΓΟΡΕΥΕΤΑΙ ΤΟ
ΚΑΠΝΙΣΜΑ απαγορεύεται το
κάπνισμα no smoking
ΑΠΑΓΟΡΕΥΕΤΑΙ ΤΟ
ΚΥΝΗΓΙ απαγορεύεται το
κυνήγι no hunting
ΑΠΑΓΟΡΕΥΕΤΑΙ ΤΟ
ΠΡΟΣΠΕΡΑΣΜΑ
απαγορεύεται το προσπέρασμα
no overtaking, no passing
ΑΠΑΓΟΡΕΥΕΤΑΙ ΤΟ
ΨΑΡΕΜΑ απαγορεύεται το
ψάρεμα no fishing

ΑΠΑΓΟΡΕΥΜΕΝΗ ΠΕΡΙΟΧΗ
απαγορευμένη περιοχή
restricted area
απαγορευμένος [apagorevmenos]
forbidden
απαίσιος [apesios] appalling
απαιτώ [apeto] demand (verb)
απαλός [apalos] soft
απαντάω [apandao] answer
(verb)
απάντηση (η) [apandisi (i)]
answer
απένταρος [apendaros] broke
απίθανος [apiΤHanos] incredible
ΑΠΛΗ ΒΕΝΖΙΝΗ απλή
βενζίνη (η) [apli venzini (i)]
two-star petrol/gas
ΑΠΛΗ ΔΙΑΔΡΟΜΗ απλή
διαδρομή (η) [apli thiathromi (i)]
single/one-way fare
ΑΠΛΟ ΕΙΣΙΤΗΡΙΟ απλό
εισιτήριο (το) [aplo isitirio (to)]
single/one-way ticket
απλός [aplos] simple
απλώνω [aplono] stretch (verb)
από [apo] from; since; than
από το ... στο ... [apo to ... sto ...]
from ... to ...
από κάτω [apo kato] below,
under
από πάνω [apo pano] over,
above
αποβιβάζομαι [apovivazomeh]
land (verb)
απογειώνομαι [apoyionomeh]
take off (verb)
απόγευμα (το) [apoyevma (to)]
afternoon
το απόγευμα [to apoyevma] in

the afternoon
ΑΠΟΓΕΥΜΑΤΙΝΗ
ΠΑΡΑΣΤΑΣΗ απογευματινή
παράσταση (η) ⟦apoyevmatini
parastasi (i)⟧ matinee

απογοητευμένος ⟦apogo-
itevmenos⟧ disappointed

ΑΠΟΔΕΙΞΗ απόδειξη (η)
⟦apothixi (i)⟧ receipt, evidence

ΑΠΟ ΔΕΥΤΕΡΟ ΧΕΡΙ από
δεύτερο χέρι ⟦apo theftero kheri⟧
second-hand

ΑΠΟΛΥΜΑΝΤΙΚΟ
απολυμαντικό (το) ⟦apolimandiko
(to)⟧ disinfectant

ΑΠΟΣΚΕΥΕΣ αποσκευές (οι)
⟦aposkeves (i)⟧ luggage,
baggage

ΑΠΟΣΜΗΤΙΚΟ αποσμητικό
(το) ⟦aposmitiko (to)⟧ deodorant

ΑΠΟΣΤΟΛΕΑΣ αποστολέας
⟦apostoleas⟧ sender

απότομος ⟦apotomos⟧ steep

απότομος βράχος (ο) ⟦apotomos
vrakhos (o)⟧ cliff

αποφασίζω ⟦apofasizo⟧ decide

απόψε ⟦apopseh⟧ tonight

ΑΠΡΙΛΙΟΣ Απρίλιος (ο)
⟦Aprilios (o)⟧ April

Α΄ ΠΡΟΒΟΛΗΣ α΄ προβολής
major cinema/movie
theater

απρόσμενος ⟦aprosmenos⟧
surprising

ΑΠΩΛΕΣΘΕΝΤΑ
ΑΝΤΙΚΕΙΜΕΝΑ
απωλεσθέντα αντικείμενα
⟦apolesThenda adikimena⟧ lost
property

αράχνη (η) ⟦arakhni (i)⟧ spider

αργά ⟦arga⟧ late; slowly

αργίες (οι) ⟦aryies (i)⟧ public
holidays

αργός ⟦argos⟧ slow

αργότερα ⟦argotera⟧ later

αργώ ⟦argo⟧ arrive late; go
slowly

ΑΡΙΘΜΟΣ αριθμός (ο)
⟦ariTHmos (o)⟧ number

ΑΡΙΘΜΟΣ ΘΕΣΕΩΣ αριθμός
θέσεως ⟦ariTHmos THeseos⟧ seat
number

αριστερά ⟦aristera⟧ left

αριστερόχειρας ⟦aristerokhiras⟧
left-handed

αρκετά ⟦arketa⟧ enough; quite

αρκετοί ⟦arketi⟧ several

αρνητικό (το) ⟦arnitiko (to)⟧
negative

αρουραίος (ο) ⟦arooreos (o)⟧ rat

αρραβωνιασμένος
⟦aravoniasmenos⟧ engaged (to be
married)

αρραβωνιαστικιά (η)
⟦aravoniastikia (i)⟧ fiancée

αρραβωνιαστικός (ο)
⟦aravoniastikos (o)⟧ fiancé

αρρενωπός ⟦arenopos⟧ manly;
macho

αρρώστια (η) ⟦arostia (i)⟧ disease

άρρωστος ⟦arostos⟧ ill, sick

ΑΡΤΟΠΟΙΕΙΟ αρτοποιείο (το)
⟦artopi-io (to)⟧ bakery

αρχαιολογία (η) ⟦arkheoloyia (i)⟧
archaeology

αρχαίος ⟦arkheos⟧ ancient

αρχαιότητες (οι) ⟦arkheotites (i)⟧
ruins

A
B
Γ
Δ
E
Z
H
Θ
I
K
Λ
M
N
Ξ
O
Π
P
Σ
T
Y
Φ
X
Ψ
Ω

αρχάρια (η) [arkharia (i)]
beginner

αρχάριος (ο) [arkharios (o)]
beginner

αρχή (η) [arkhi (i)] beginning

αρχίζω [arkhizo] begin

αρχιτέκτων (ο/η) [arkhitekton (o/i)] architect

άρωμα (το) [aroma (to)] perfume

ΑΣΑΝΣΕΡ ασανσέρ (το) [asanser (to)] lift, elevator

ασετόν (το) [aseton (to)] nail varnish remover

ΑΣΗΜΕΝΙΟΣ ασημένιος [asimenios] silver

ΑΣΗΜΙΚΑ ασημικά (τα) [asimika (ta)] silver(ware)

ΑΣΘΕΝΟΦΟΡΟ ασθενοφόρο (το) [asTHenoforo (to)] ambulance

ΑΣΘΜΑ άσθμα (το) [asTHma (to)] asthma

ΑΣΠΙΡΙΝΗ ασπιρίνη (η) [aspirini (i)] aspirin

άσπρος [aspros] white

άστατος [astatos] changeable

αστείο (το) [astio (to)] joke

αστείος [astios] funny, amusing

αστέρι (το) [asteri (to)] star

αστράγαλος (ο) [astragalos (o)] ankle

ΑΣΤΥΝΟΜΙΑ αστυνομία (η) [astinomia (i)] police

ΑΣΤΥΝΟΜΙΚΟ ΤΜΗΜΑ αστυνομικό τμήμα (το) [astinomiko tmima (to)] police station

αστυφύλακας (ο) [astifilakas (o)] policeman

αστυνομικός (η) [astinomikos (i)] policewoman

ΑΣΦΑΛΕΙΑ ασφάλεια (η) [asfalia (i)] fuse; insurance

ΑΣΦΑΛΕΙΑΙ ασφάλειαι [asfali-eh] insurance

ασφαλής [asfalis] safe

άσχημα [askhima] badly

άσχημος [askhimos] ugly

ατζέντα (η) [atzenda (i)] address book

ατμόπλοιο (το) [atmoplio (to)] steamer

άτομο (το) [atomo (to)] person

ΑΥΓΟΥΣΤΟΣ Αύγουστος (ο) [Avgoostos (o)] August

αυθεντικός [afTHendikos] genuine

αύριο [avrio] tomorrow

Αυστραλέζα (η) [Afstraleza (i)] Australian (woman)

Αυστραλέζικος [Afstralezikos] Australian (adj)

ΑΥΣΤΡΑΛΙΑ Αυστραλία (η) [Afstralia (i)] Australia

Αυστραλός (ο) [Afstralos (o)] Australian (man)

αυτά, αυτές [afta, aftes] these; they; them

αυτή [afti] she; this (one)

αυτής [aftis] of her

αυτί (το) [afti (to)] ear

αυτό [afto] it; this

αυτό εδώ [afto etho] this one

αυτοί [afti] these; they

ΑΥΤΟΚΙΝΗΤΟ αυτοκίνητο (το) [aftokinito (to)] car

αυτόματος [aftomatos] automatic (adj)

αυτό που [afto poo] what
αυτός [aftos] he; this (one)
αυτός ο ίδιος [aftos o ithios]
  himself
αυτού [aftoo] of him, of it
αυτούς [aftoos] them
ΑΥΤ/ΤΟ αυτ/το car
αυτών [afton] of them
αφεντικό (το) [afendiko (to)] boss
ΑΦΕΤΗΡΙΑ αφετηρία (η)
  [afetiria (i)] terminus
αφήνω [afino] leave (verb)
ΑΦΙΞΕΙΣ αφίξεις arrivals
ΑΦΙΞΗ άφιξη (η) [afixi (i)]
  arrival
αφίσα (η) [afisa (i)] poster
ΑΦΟΙ. αφοί. bros.
ΑΦΟΡΟΛΟΓΗΤΑ
  αφορολόγητα (τα) [aforoloyita
  (ta)] duty-free
αφροδίσιο νόσημα (το) [afrothisio
  nosima (to)] VD
ΑΦΡΟΣ ΞΥΡΙΣΜΑΤΟΣ αφρός
  ξυρίσματος (ο) [afros xirismatos
  (o)] shaving foam
αφρός (ο) [afros (o)] surf
αχθοφόρος (ο) [akhTHoforos (o)]
  doorman
αχινός (ο) [akhinos (o)] sea
  urchin

B
∎

ΒΑΓΟΝΙ βαγόνι (το) [vagoni
  (to)] coach, car (train)
ΒΑΓΚΟΝ-ΛΙ βαγκόν-λι [vagon-
  li] sleeper, sleeping car
βάζο (το) [vazo (to)] vase

βάζω [vazo] put
ΒΑΘΙΑ ΝΕΡΑ βαθιά νερά
  deep water
βάθος: στο βάθος [sto vaTHos] in
  the background; at the
  bottom
βαθύς [vaTHis] deep
βαλβίδα (η) [valvitha (i)] valve
βαλίτσα (η) [valitsa (i)] bag,
  suitcase
ΒΑΜΒΑΚΕΡΟ βαμβακερό (το)
  [vamvakero (to)] cotton
βαρετός [varetos] boring
ΒΑΡΚΑ βάρκα (η) [varka (i)]
  small boat; dinghy
βάρκα με κουπιά [varka meh
  koopia] rowing boat
βάρκα με μηχανή [varka meh
  mikhani] motorboat
ΒΑΡΟΣ βάρος (το) [varos (to)]
  weight
βαρύς [varis] heavy; rich (food)
βασιλιάς (ο) [vasilias (o)] king
βασίλισσα (η) [vasilisa (i)]
  queen
ΒΑΦΗ βαφή (η) [vafi (i)] hair
  dye
βάφω [vafo] paint; tint (verb)
βγάζω φωτογραφία [vgazo
  fotografia] photograph (verb)
βγαίνω [vgeno] go out
ΒΓΑΛΤΕ ΤΗΝ ΚΑΡΤΑ βγάλτε
  την κάρτα remove the card
βέβαια [veveh-a] of course
βελόνα (η) [velona (i)] needle
βελτιώνω [veltiono] improve
ΒΕΝΖΙΝΑΔΙΚΟ βενζινάδικο
  (το) [venzinathiko (to)] petrol
  station, gas station

ΒΕΝΖΙΝΗ βενζίνη (η) [venzini
(i)] petrol, gas(oline)
βεντιλατέρ (το) [vendilater (to)]
fan belt
ΒΕΡΝΙΚΙ ΠΑΠΟΥΤΣΙΩΝ
βερνίκι παπουτσιών (το) [verniki
papootsion (to)] shoe polish
ΒΗΧΑΣ βήχας (ο) [vikhas (o)]
cough
βήχω [vikho] cough (verb)
βιάζομαι [viazomeh] hurry (verb)
βιάσου! [viasoo!] hurry up!
βιασμός (ο) [viasmos (o)] rape
βιβλίο (το) [vivlio (to)] book
βιβλίο διαλόγων [vivlio thialogon]
phrase book
ΒΙΒΛΙΟΘΗΚΗ βιβλιοθήκη (η)
[vivliotHiki (i)] library
ΒΙΒΛΙΟΠΩΛΕΙΟ βιβλιοπωλείο
(το) [vivliopolio (to)] bookshop,
bookstore
ΒΙΔΑ βίδα (η) [vitha (i)] screw
ΒΙΖΑ βίζα (η) [viza (i)] visa
βίλλα (η) [vila (i)] villa
βίντεο (το) [video (to)] video
ΒΙΤΑΜΙΝΕΣ βιταμίνες (οι)
[vitamines (i)] vitamins
Β΄ ΚΑΤΗΓΟΡΙΑΣ
Β΄ κατηγορίας second class
βλάβη (η) [vlavi (i)] breakdown
(car)
βλάκας (ο) [vlakas (o)] idiot;
stupid
βλέπω [vlepo] see
βοήθεια (η) [voiTHia (i)] help
βοηθώ [vo-iTHo] help (verb)
βόμβα (η) [vomva (i)] bomb
Βόρειος Ιρλανδία (η) [vorios
Irlanthia (i)] Northern Ireland

ΒΟΥΛΓΑΡΙΑ Βουλγαρία (η)
[voolgaria (i)] Bulgaria
Βουλγαρικός [voolgarikos]
Bulgarian (adj)
βουλιάζω [vooliazo] sink (verb)
ΒΟΥΛΚΑΝΙΖΑΤΕΡ
βουλκανιζατέρ [voolkanizater]
tyre repairs
βουνό (το) [voono (to)]
mountain
βούρτσα (η) [voortsa (i)] brush
βουτάω [vootao] dive (verb)
Β΄ ΠΡΟΒΟΛΗΣ β΄ προβολής
local cinema/movie theater
βράδυ (το) [vrathi (to)] evening
το βράδυ [to vrathi] in the
evening
βραδυά (η) [vrathia (i)] evening
ΒΡΑΔΥΝΗ ΠΑΡΑΣΤΑΣΗ
βραδυνή παράσταση evening
performance
βράζω [vrazo] boil (verb)
βράχια (τα) [vrakhia (ta)] rocks;
cliffs
βραχιόλι (το) [vrakhioli (to)]
bracelet
βράχος (ο) [vrakhos (o)] rock
ΒΡΕΤΑΝΝΙΑ Βρεταννία (η)
[vretania (i)] Britain
Βρεταννίδα (η) [vretanitha (i)]
Briton (woman)
Βρεταννικός [vretanikos] British
Βρεταννός (ο) [vretanos (o)]
Briton (man)
βρέχει [vrekhi] it's raining
βρίσκω [vrisko] find (verb)
βροντή (η) [vrondi (i)] thunder
βροχή (η) [vrokhi (i)] rain
βρύση (η) [vrisi (i)] tap, faucet

βρώμικος [vromikos] dirty

βυζαίνω [vizeno] breastfeed

βυθός (ο) [víthos (o)] bottom (of sea)

Γ

γάιδαρος (ο) [gaitharos (o)] donkey

ΓΑΛΑΚΤΟΠΩΛΕΙΟ γαλακτοπωλείο (το) [galaktopolio (to)] shop/take-away café selling dairy products

ΓΑΛΑΚΤΩΜΑ ΚΑΘΑΡΙΣΜΟΥ γαλάκτωμα καθαρισμού (το) [galaktoma katharismoo (to)] cleansing lotion

ΓΑΛΛΙΑ Γαλλία (η) [galia (i)] France

Γαλλικός [galikos] French (adj)

γάμος (ο) [gamos (o)] wedding

γαμπρός (ο) [gambros (o)] bridegroom; son-in-law; brother-in-law

γάντια (τα) [gandia (ta)] gloves

γάτα (η) [gata (i)] cat

γειά σου! [yia soo!] hello!; bless you!; cheers!

γείτονας (ο) [yitonas (o)] neighbour

γελοίο [yelio] ridiculous

γελώ [yelo] laugh (verb)

γεμάτος [yematos] full

γεμίζω [yemizo] fill (verb)

γενέθλια (τα) [yenethlia (ta)] birthday

γένια (τα) [yenia (ta)] beard

γενναίος [yeneos] brave

ΓΕΡΜΑΝΙΑ Γερμανία (η) [Yermania (i)] Germany

Γερμανικός [Yermanikos] German (adj)

γέρος [yeros] old (person)

ΓΕΥΜΑ γεύμα (το) [yevma (to)] meal

γεύση (η) [yefsi (i)] flavour; taste

ΓΕΦΥΡΑ γέφυρα (η) [yefira (i)] bridge

ΓΗΠΕΔΟ γήπεδο (το) [yipetho (to)] football pitch

ΓΗΠΕΔΟ ΤΕΝΝΙΣ γήπεδο τέννις [yipetho tenis] tennis court

για [ya] for

για μένα [ya mena] for me

γιαγιά (η) [yaya (i)] grandmother

ΓΙΑ ΕΞΩΤΕΡΙΚΗ ΧΡΗΣΗ ΜΟΝΟΝ για εξωτερική χρήση μόνον for external use only

ΓΙΑ ΕΣΩΤΕΡΙΚΗ ΧΡΗΣΗ ΜΟΝΟΝ για εσωτερική χρήση μόνον for internal use only

γιακάς (ο) [yakas (o)] collar

γιατί; [yati?] why?

ΓΙΑ ΤΟ ΣΠΙΤΙ για το σπίτι [ya to spiti] to take away, to go (food)

ΓΙΑΤΡΟΣ γιατρός (ο/η) [yatros (o/i)] doctor

γίνομαι [yinomeh] become; happen

τι γίνεται; [ti yineteh?] what's happening?

ΓΙΟΡΤΗ ΚΡΑΣΙΟΥ γιορτή κρασιού (η) [yorti krasioo (i)] wine festival

γιός (ο) [yos (o)] son

γιώτ (το) [yot (to)] yacht

γκάζι (το) [gazi (to)] gas; accelerator

ΓΚΑΛΕΡΙ γκαλερί (η) [galeri (i)] art gallery

ΓΚΑΡΑΖ γκαράζ (το) [garaz (to)] garage (for parking/repairs)

ΓΚΑΡΝΤΑΡΟΜΠΑ γκαρνταρόμπα (η) [gardaroba (i)] cloakroom (for coats)

Γ΄ ΚΑΤΗΓΟΡΙΑΣ Γ΄ κατηγορίας third class

γκολφ (το) [golf (to)] golf

γκρίζος [grizos] grey

γκρουπ (το) [groop (to)] group

γλάρος (ο) [glaros (o)] seagull

ΓΛΙΦΙΤΖΟΥΡΙ γλιφιτζούρι (το) [glifidzoori (to)] lollipop

ΓΛΥΚΟ γλυκό (το) [gliko (to)] sweet, candy

γλυκός [glikos] sweet (adj)

γλυστερός [glisteros] slippery

γλυστράω [glistrao] skid (verb)

γλώσσα (η) [glosa (i)] language; tongue

γνωρίζω [gnorizo] know

δεν γνωρίζω [then gnorizo] I don't know

γόνατο (το) [gonato (to)] knee

γονείς (οι) [gonis (i)] parents

γουίντσερφ (το) [gooindserf (to)] sailboard

ΓΟΥΝΑΡΙΚΑ γουναρικά (τα)

[goonarika (ta)] furrier

ΓΟΥΝΕΣ γούνες [goones] furs

γουόκμαν (το) [goo-okman (to)] personal stereo

γουρούνι (το) [goorooni (to)] pig

γοφός (ο) [gofos (o)] hip

γραβάτα (η) [gravata (i)] tie, necktie

γράμμα (το) [grama (to)] letter

γράμματα (τα) [gramata (ta)] post, mail

γραμματική (η) [gramatiki (i)] grammar

ΓΡΑΜΜΑΤΟΚΙΒΩΤΙΟ γραμματοκιβώτιο (το) [gramatokivotio (to)] letterbox, mailbox

γραμματόσημο (το) [gramatosimo (to)] stamp

ΓΡΑΜΜΕΣ ΤΡΑΙΝΟΥ γραμμές τραίνου railway crosses road

ΓΡΑΜΜΗ γραμμή (η) [grami (i)] route, line

γρασίδι (το) [grasithi (to)] lawn

γραφείο (το) [grafio (to)] office

ΓΡΑΦΕΙΟ ΤΑΞΙΔΙΩΝ γραφείο ταξιδίων [grafio taxithion] travel agency

γραφομηχανή (η) [grafomikhani (i)] typewriter

γράφω [grafo] write

γρήγορα [grigora] quick; quickly

γρήγορος [grigoros] fast

ΓΡΙΠΠΗ γρίππη (η) [gripi (i)] flu

γρύλλος (ο) [grilos (o)] jack

γυαλί (το) [yali (to)] glass

(material)
ΓΥΑΛΙΑ γυαλιά (τα) [yalia (ta)]
glasses, eyeglasses
ΓΥΑΛΙΑ ΗΛΙΟΥ γυαλιά ηλίου
[yalia ilioo] sunglasses
ΓΥΜΝΑΣΙΟ γυμνάσιο (το)
[yimnasio (to)] secondary
school
γυμνασμένος [yimnasmenos] fit
(healthy)
ΓΥΜΝΑΣΤΗΡΙΟ γυμναστήριο
(το) [yimnastirio (to)] gym
γυμνός [yimnos] naked
γυναίκα (η) [yineka (i)] woman;
wife
ΓΥΝΑΙΚΕΙΑ γυναικεία (τα)
[yinekia (ta)] ladies' wear
ΓΥΝΑΙΚΕΙΑΙ ΚΟΜΜΩΣΕΙΣ
γυναικείαι κομμώσεις (οι)
[yinekieh komosis (i)] ladies'
salon
ΓΥΝΑΙΚΕΙΑ ΦΟΡΕΜΑΤΑ
γυναικεία φορέματα [yinekia
foremata] ladies' dresses
ΓΥΝΑΙΚΕΙΕΣ ΚΑΛΤΣΕΣ -
ΚΑΛΣΟΝ γυναικείες κάλτσες
- καλσόν [yinekies kaltses -
kalson] ladies' socks –
stockings
ΓΥΝΑΙΚΩΝ γυναικών ladies'
(toilet), ladies' room
γυρνώ [yirno] turn (verb)
γυρνώ πίσω [yirno piso] arrive
back, return; take back
γυρνώ σπίτι [yirno spiti] return
home

Δ

δακτυλίδι (το) [thaktilithi (to)]
ring (on finger)
δανείζομαι [thanizomeh] borrow
δανείζω [thanizo] lend
δασκάλα (η) [thaskala (i)]
instructor; teacher
δάσκαλος (ο) [thaskalos (o)]
instructor; teacher
δάσος (το) [thasos (to)] forest
δάχτυλο (το) [thakhtilo (to)]
finger
δάχτυλο του ποδιού [thakhtilo too
pothioo] toe
δε [theh] ξου
Δ.Ε.Η. public electricity
company
δείκτης (ο) [thiktis (o)] gauge;
index finger
ΔΕΙΠΝΟ δείπνο (το) [thipno
(to)] evening meal
δείχνω [thikhno] show (verb)
δέκα [theka] ten
δεκαεννιά [theka-enia] nineteen
δεκαέξι [theka-exi] sixteen
δεκαεπτά [theka-epta]
seventeen
δεκαοχτώ [theka-okhto]
eighteen
δεκαπενθήμερο
[thekapenTHimero] fortnight
δεκαπέντε [thekapendeh] fifteen
ΔΕΚΑΡΙΚΟ δεκάρικο (το)
[thekariko (to)] 10-drachma
coin
δεκατέσσερα [thekatesera]
fourteen

A
B
Γ
Δ
E
Z
H
Θ
I
K
Λ
M
N
Ξ
O
Π
P
Σ
T
Y
Φ
X
Ψ
Ω

141

δέκατος [thekatos] tenth

δεκατρία [thekatria] thirteen

ΔΕΚΕΜΒΡΙΟΣ Δεκέμβριος (ο) [thekemvrios (o)] December

δέμα (το) [thema (to)] parcel

ΔΕΜΑΤΑ δέματα parcels, packages

δεν [then] not

δένδρο (το) [thenthro (to)] tree

ΔΕΝ ΛΕΙΤΟΥΡΓΕΙ δεν λειτουργεί [then litooryi] out of order

ΔΕΝ ΣΙΔΕΡΩΝΕΤΑΙ δεν σιδερώνεται do not iron

δεξιός, δεξιά [thexios, thexia] right (side)

δεξίωση (η) [thexiosi (i)] reception (party)

ΔΕΡΜΑ δέρμα (το) [therma (to)] skin; leather

ΔΕΡΜΑΤΑ δέρματα (τα) [thermata (ta)] leather goods

ΔΕΣΠΟΙΝΙΔΑ δεσποινίδα (η) [thespinitha (i)] young woman; Miss; Ms

ΔΕΣΠΟΙΝΙΣ δεσποινίς [thespinis] Miss; Ms

ΔΕΥΤΕΡΑ Δευτέρα (η) [theftera (i)] Monday

ΔΕΥΤΕΡΗ ΘΕΣΗ δεύτερη θέση second class

δευτερόλεπτο (το) [thefterolepto (to)] second

δεύτερος [thefteros] second (adj)

ΔΕΥΤΕΡΟ ΧΕΡΙ δεύτερο χέρι [theftero kheri] second-hand

δέχομαι [thekhomeh] accept; receive

δηλητηρίαση (η) [thilitiriasi (i)] poisoning

δηλητήριο (το) [thilitirio (to)] poison

ΔΗΜΑΡΧΕΙΟ δημαρχείο (το) [thimarkhio (to)] town hall

ΔΗΜΟΣΙΑ ΛΟΥΤΡΑ δημόσια λουτρά (τα) [thimosia lootra (ta)] public baths

δημόσιος [thimosios] public

δημοσιογράφος (ο/η) [thimosiografos (o/i)] reporter

δημοτική μουσική (η) [thimotiki moosiki (i)] folk music

διαβάζω [thiavazo] read

ΔΙΑΒΑΣΗ ΠΕΖΩΝ διάβαση πεζών (η) [thiavasi pezon (i)] pedestrian crossing

ΔΙΑΒΑΤΗΡΙΟ διαβατήριο (το) [thiavatirio (to)] passport

διαβητικός (ο) [thiavitikos (o)] diabetic

διαβητική (η) [thiaviti ki (i)] diabetic

ΔΙΑΔΡΟΜΗ ΜΕΤ' ΕΠΙΣΤΡΟΦΗΣ διαδρομή μετ' επιστροφής (η) [thiathromi met' epistrofis (i)] return/round trip fare

διάδρομος (ο) [thiathromos (o)] corridor

διάθεση (η) [thiaτнesi (i)] mood

δίαιτα (η) [thieta (i)] diet

διακοπές (οι) [thiakopes (i)] holiday, vacation

διακοπή (η) [thiakopi (i)] interruption; power cut

διακόπτης (ο) [thiakoptis (o)] switch

διακόπτω [thiakopto] interrupt

διακόσια [thiakosia] two hundred

διαλέγω [thialego] choose

ΔΙΑΛΕΙΜΜΑ διάλειμμα (το) [thialima (to)] interval, intermission

διάλεκτος (η) [thialektos (i)] dialect

ΔΙΑΛΥΜΑ διάλυμα (το) [thialima (to)] solution

διαμάντι (το) [thiamandi (to)] diamond

Διαμαρτυρόμενος (ο) [thiamartiromenos (o)] Protestant

ΔΙΑΜΕΡΙΣΜΑ διαμέρισμα (το) [thiamerisma (to)] apartment, flat

διά μέσου [thia mesoo] through

διαμονή (η) [thiamoni (i)] accommodation; stay

ΔΙΑΝΥΚΤΕΡΕΥΟΝ διανυκτερεύον open all night

διάρκεια (η) [thiarkia (i)] duration

ΔΙΑΡΚΕΙΑ ΠΤΗΣΕΩΣ διάρκεια πτήσεως [thiarkia ptiseos] flight time

διαρροή (η) [thiaroi (i)] leak

ΔΙΑΡΡΟΙΑ διάρροια (η) [thiaria (i)] diarrhoea

διάσημος [thiasimos] famous

ΔΙΑΣΤΑΥΡΩΣΗ διασταύρωση (η) [thiastavrosi (i)] junction, crossroads, intersection

διασχίζω [thiaskhizo] go through

ΔΙΑΤΗΡΕΙΤΑΙ ΣΕ ΨΥΓΕΙΟ διατηρείται σε ψυγείο keep refrigerated

διαφημιστικό (το) [thiafimistiko (to)] leaflet; advertisements (on TV); trailer (cinema)

διαφορετικά [thiaforetika] otherwise

διαφορετικός [thiaforetikos] different

διάφραγμα (το) [thiafragma (to)] shutter (in camera)

διαχειριστής (ο) [thiakhiristis (o)] manager

διαχειρίστρια (η) [thiakhiristria (i)] manageress

διδάσκω [thithasko] teach

δίδυμοι (οι) [thithimi (i)] twins

ΔΙΕΥΘΥΝΣΗ διεύθυνση (η) [thiefthinsi (i)] address

δίκαιος [thikeos] fair, just

δικά μας [thika mas] ours

δικά μου [thika moo] mine

δικά σας, δικά σου [thika sas, thika soo] yours

ΔΙΚΑΣΤΗΡΙΟ δικαστήριο (το) [thikastirio (to)] law court

δικά της [thika tis] hers

δικά του [thika too] his, its

δικά τους [thika toos] theirs

δικηγόρος (ο/η) [thikigoros (o/i)] lawyer

δική μας [thiki mas] ours

δική μου [thiki moo] mine

δική σας, δική σου [thiki sas, thiki soo] yours

δική του [thiki too] his

δική τους [thiki toos] theirs

ΔΙΚΛΙΝΟ ΔΩΜΑΤΙΟ δίκλινο δωμάτιο (το) [thiklino thomatio (to)] double room

δικό μας [thiko mas] ours

A
B
Γ
Δ
E
Z
H
Θ
I
K
Λ
M
N
Ξ
O
Π
P
Σ
T
Y
Φ
X
Ψ
Ω

δικό μου [thiko moo] mine

δικό σας, δικό σου [thiko sas, thiko soo] yours

δικό τους [thiko toos] theirs

δικό της [thiko tis] hers

δικό του [thiko too] his; its

δικός μας [thikos mas] ours

δικός μου [thikos moo] mine

δικός σας, δικός σου [thikos sas, thikos soo] yours

δικός του [thikos too] his

δικός τους [thikos toos] theirs

δίνω [thino] give

ΔΙΟΔΙΑ διόδια (τα) [thiothia (ta)] toll

διορθώνω [thiorThono] mend, correct

ΔΙΠΛΗ ΤΑΡΙΦΑ διπλή ταρίφα (η) double tariff

διπλό [thiplo] double

ΔΙΠΛΟ ΔΩΜΑΤΙΟ διπλό δωμάτιο (το) [thiplo thomatio (to)] double room

διπλό κρεβάτι (το) [thiplo krevati (to)] double bed

ΔΙΣ. δις. Miss

ΔΙΣΚΑΔΙΚΟ δισκάδικο (το) [thiskathiko (to)] record shop

ΔΙΣΚΟΙ - ΚΑΣΕΤΕΣ δίσκοι - κασέτες [thiski - kasetes] records – cassettes

δίσκος (ο) [thiskos (o)] record; tray

Δ΄ ΚΑΤΗΓΟΡΙΑΣ Δ΄ κατηγορίας fourth class

δοκιμάζω [thokimazo] taste (verb); try (on)

ΔΟΛΛΑΡΙΟ δολλάριο (το) [tholario (to)] dollar

δόντι (το) [thondi (to)] tooth

ΔΟΣΟΛΟΓΙΑ ΕΝΗΛΙΚΩΝ δοσολογία ενηλίκων adult dosage

ΔΟΣΟΛΟΓΙΑ ΠΑΙΔΩΝ δοσολογία παίδων children's dosage

δουλειά (η) [thoolia (i)] job; work

δουλειές (οι) [thoolies (i)] business

δουλεύω [thoolevo] work (verb)

δεν δουλεύει [then thoolevi] it's not working

ΔΡΑΧΜΗ δραχμή (η) [thrakhmi (i)] drachma

ΔΡΟΜΟΛΟΓΙΑ δρομολόγια (τα) [thromoloyia (ta)] timetable, (US) schedule

δρόμος (ο) [thromos (o)] road; street

δροσερός [throseros] cool

ΔΡΧ. δρχ. drachma

δυνατός [thinatos] loud; possible; strong

δύο [thio] two

ΔΥΟ ΠΑΡΑΣΤΑΣΕΙΣ δύο παραστάσεις two shows

δυσάρεστος [thisarestos] unpleasant

δύση του ήλιου (η) [thisi too ilioo (i)] sunset

ΔΥΣΚΟΙΛΙΑ δυσκοίλια (η) [thiskilia (i)] constipation

δύσκολος [thiskolos] difficult

ΔΥΣΠΕΨΙΑ δυσπεψία (η) [thispepsia (i)] indigestion

δυστύχημα (το) [thistikhima (to)] accident

δυστυχώς [thistikhos]
  unfortunately
δώδεκα [thotheka] twelve
ΔΩΔΕΚΑΔΑ δωδεκάδα (η)
  [thothekatha (i)] dozen
ΔΩΜΑΤΙΟ δωμάτιο (το)
  [thomatio (to)] room
ΔΩΡΑ δώρα gifts
ΔΩΡΕΑΝ δωρεάν [thorean] free
  (of charge)
δώρο (το) [thoro (to)] gift
ΔΩΡΟ ΠΑΣΧΑ Δώρο Πάσχα
  [thoro Paskha] Easter
  supplement paid to taxi
  drivers
ΔΩΡΟ ΧΡΙΣΤΟΥΓΕΝΝΩΝ
  Δώρο Χριστουγέννων [thoro
  khristooyenon] Christmas
  supplement paid to taxi
  drivers

Ε

Ε.Α.Σ. Athens Public
  Transport Corporation
εβδομάδα (η) [evthomatha (i)]
  week
εβδομήντα [evthominda] seventy
έβδομος [evthomos] seventh
Εβραίος [Evreos] Jewish
έγγραφο (το) [engrafo (to)]
  document
εγγύηση (η) [egi-isi (i)]
  guarantee
έγινε! [eyineh!] OK, coming
  up!
εγκαίρως [engeros] on time
έγκαυμα από τον ήλιο (το)

[engavma apo ton ilio (to)]
  sunburn
έγκυος [engios] pregnant
έγκυρος [engiros] valid
έγχρωμο φιλμ (το) [enkhromo film
  (to)] colour film
εγώ [ego] I
εγώ ο ίδιος [ego o ithios] myself
εδώ [etho] here
έθιμο (το) [ethimo (to)] custom
ΕΘΝΙΚΗ ΟΔΟΣ εθνική οδός
  (η) [ethniki othos (i)] motorway,
  highway, freeway
ΕΘΝΙΚΗ ΠΙΝΑΚΟΘΗΚΗ
  Εθνική Πινακοθήκη [Ethniki
  Pinakothiki] National Art
  Gallery
ΕΘΝΙΚΟΤΗΤΑ εθνικότητα (η)
  [ethnikotita (i)] nationality
ΕΙΔΗ είδη (τα) [ithi (ta)] goods
ΕΙΔΗ ΑΥΤΟΚΙΝΗΤΟΥ είδη
  αυτοκινήτου auto accessories
ΕΙΔΗ ΔΩΡΩΝ είδη δώρων gifts
ΕΙΔΗ ΜΠΕΜΠΕ είδη μπεμπέ
  [ithi bebeh] babywear
ΕΙΔΗ ΡΟΥΧΙΣΜΟΥ είδη
  ρουχισμού [ithi roukhismoo]
  clothes
ΕΙΔΗ ΣΠΟΡ είδη σπορ [ithi
  spor] sports equipment,
  sportswear
ΕΙΔΗ ΧΑΡΤΟΠΩΛΕΙΟΥ είδη
  χαρτοπωλείου [ithi khartopolioo]
  stationery
ΕΙΔΙΚΗ ΠΡΟΣΦΟΡΑ ειδική
  προσφορά special price,
  special offer
ειδικώς [ithikos] especially
είχες [ikhes] you had

ΕΙΚΟΣΑΡΙΚΟ εικοσάρικο [ikosariko] 20-drachma coin

είκοσι [ikosi] twenty

ειλικρινής [ilikrinis] sincere

είμαι [imeh] I am

είμαστε [imasteh] we are

είναι [ineh] he/she/it is; they are

είστε [isteh] you are

ΕΙΣΑΓΩΓΗΣ εισαγωγής imported

είσαι [iseh] you are

ΕΙΣΙΤΗΡΙΟ εισιτήριο (το) [isitirio (to)] ticket

ΕΙΣΙΤΗΡΙΟ ΜΕ ΕΠΙΣΤΡΟΦΗ εισιτήριο με επιστροφή [isitirio meh epistrofi] return/round trip ticket

ΕΙΣΟΔΟΣ είσοδος (η) [isothos (i)] entrance, way in

ΕΙΣΟΔΟΣ ΕΛΕΥΘΕΡΑ είσοδος ελευθέρα admission free

ΕΙΣΟΔΟΣ ΠΡΑΤΗΡΙΟΥ είσοδος πρατηρίου entrance to petrol/gas station

ΕΙΣΠΡΑΚΤΩΡ εισπράκτωρ (ο) ticket collector

είχα [ikha] I had

είχαμε [ikhameh] we had

είχαν [ikhan] they had

είχατε [ikhateh] you had

είχε [ikheh] he/she/it had

είχες [ikhes] you had

Ε´ ΚΑΤΗΓΟΡΙΑΣ Ε´ κατηγορίας fifth class

εκατό [ekato] hundred

εκατομμύριο: ένα εκατομμύριο [ena ekatomirio] one million

ΕΚΔΟΣΗ ΕΙΣΙΤΗΡΙΩΝ έκδοση εισιτηρίων [ekthosi isitirion] ticket office

εκεί [eki] there, over there

εκεί κάτω [eki kato] down there

εκείνα, εκείνες [ekina, ekines] those

εκείνη, εκείνο [ekini, ekino] that

εκείνοι [ekini] those

εκείνος [ekinos] that

ΕΚΘΕΣΗ έκθεση (η) [ekthesi (i)] exhibition, showroom

ΕΚΚΛΗΣΙΑ εκκλησία (η) [eklisia (i)] church

Ε.Κ.Ο. Greek state petrol company

εκπληκτικός [ekpliktikos] surprising

έκπληξη (η) [ekplixi (i)] surprise

ΕΚΠΤΩΣΕΙΣ εκπτώσεις (οι) sales

ΕΚΤΑΚΤΗ ΑΝΑΓΚΗ έκτακτη ανάγκη (η) [ektakti anangi (i)] emergency

εκτός [ektos] except

έκτος [ektos] sixth

έλα! [ela!] you don't say!; come on!, hurry up!

ΕΛ.ΑΣ. Greek police

ΕΛΑΣΤΙΚΑ ελαστικά tyres

ελαστικός [elastikos] elastic

ελατήριο (το) [elatirio (to)] spring (in seat etc)

ελαττωματικός [elatomatikos] faulty

ΕΛΑΤΤΩΣΑΤΕ ΤΑΧΥΤΗΤΑ ελαττώσατε ταχύτητα reduce speed

ελαφρός [elafros] light (not

heavy)

ελάχιστος [elakhistos] smallest; few

ελεγκτής (ο) [elenktis (o)] inspector (bus)

ΕΛΕΓΧΟΣ έλεγχος (ο) [elenkhos (o)] check, inspection

ΕΛΕΓΧΟΣ ΑΠΟΣΚΕΥΩΝ έλεγχος αποσκευών baggage control

ΕΛΕΓΧΟΣ ΔΙΑΒΑΤΗΡΙΩΝ έλεγχος διαβατηρίων passport control

ΕΛΕΓΧΟΣ ΕΙΣΙΤΗΡΙΩΝ έλεγχος εισιτηρίων ticket inspection

ΕΛΕΓΧΟΣ ΕΠΙΒΑΤΩΝ έλεγχος επιβατών passenger control

ΕΛΕΥΘΕΡΑ ΕΙΣΟΔΟΣ ελευθέρα είσοδος [eleftHera isothos] admission free

ΕΛΕΥΘΕΡΟΝ ελεύθερον [elefтHeron] free; for hire (taxi)

ελεύθερος [elefтHeros] free; single (unmarried)

ελιά (η) [elia (i)] olive; spot (blemish)

ελικόπτερο (το) [elikoptero (to)] helicopter

ελκυστικός [elkistikos] attractive

ΕΛΛΑΔΑ Ελλάδα (η) [Elatha (i)] Greece

Έλληνας (ο) [Elinas (o)] Greek (man)

Ελληνίδα (η) [Elinitha (i)] Greek (woman)

ΕΛΛΗΝΙΚΑ Ελληνικά (τα) [Elinika (ta)] Greek (language)

ΕΛΛΗΝΙΚΗ ΑΣΤΥΝΟΜΙΑ Ελληνική Αστυνομία (η) Greek police

ΕΛΛΗΝΙΚΗ ΡΑΔΙΟΦΩΝΙΑ Ελληνική Ραδιοφωνία Greek radio

ΕΛΛΗΝΙΚΗ ΤΗΛΕΟΡΑΣΗ Ελληνική Τηλεόραση Greek television

ΕΛΛΗΝΙΚΗΣ ΚΑΤΑΣΚΕΥΗΣ Ελληνικής κατασκευής made in Greece

ΕΛΛΗΝΙΚΟ ΠΡΟΙΟΝ Ελληνικό προϊόν produce of Greece

ΕΛΛΗΝΙΚΟΣ Ελληνικός [Elinikos] Greek (adj)

Ε.Λ.Π.Α. [E.L.P.A.] Greek motoring organization

ελπίζω [elpizo] hope (verb)

ΕΛ.ΤΑ. Greek Post Office

εμάς [emas] us

εμβολιασμός (ο) [emvoliasmos (o)] vaccination

εμβόλιο (το) [emvolio (to)] vaccine

εμείς [emis] we

εμένα [emena] me

ΕΜΠΟΡΙΚΟ ΚΕΝΤΡΟ εμπορικό κέντρο (το) [emboriko kendro (to)] shopping centre

εμπρός [ebros] come in; hello (response on phone)

ένα(ν) [ena(n)] a; one

εναντίον [enandion] against

ένας [enas] a; one

ένατος [enatos] ninth

ενδιαφέρον [enthiaferon] interesting

ενενήντα [eneninda] ninety

ένεση (η) [enesi (i)] injection

ενήλικη (η) [eniliki (i)] adult

ΕΝΗΛΙΚΟΣ ενήλικος (ο) [enilikos (o)] adult

ΕΝΘΥΜΙΟ ενθύμιο (το) [enThimio (to)] souvenir

εννιά [enia] nine

εννοώ [enoo] mean (verb)

ΕΝΟΙΚΙΑΖΟΝΤΑΙ ενοικιάζονται [enikiazondeh] for hire, to rent

ΕΝΟΙΚΙΑΖΟΝΤΑΙ ΑΥΤΟΚΙΝΗΤΑ ενοικιάζονται αυτοκίνητα car rental

ΕΝΟΙΚΙΑΖΟΝΤΑΙ ΒΑΡΚΕΣ ενοικιάζονται βάρκες boats for hire

ΕΝΟΙΚΙΑΖΟΝΤΑΙ ΔΩΜΑΤΙΑ ενοικιάζονται δωμάτια rooms to let

ΕΝΟΙΚΙΑΣΗ ΑΥΤΟΚΙΝΗΤΩΝ ενοικίαση αυτοκινήτων car rental

ενοίκιο (το) [enikio (to)] rent

ενός [enos] of a

ενοχλητικός [enokhlitikos] annoying

ενοχλώ [enokhlo] disturb

εντάξει [endaxi] that's all right; OK

έντεκα [endeka] eleven

έντομο (το) [endomo (to)] insect

ΕΝΤΥΠΑ έντυπα printed matter

ενώ [eno] while

εξαιρετικός [exeretikos] terrific

εξ αιτίας [ex etias] because of

εξαρτάται [exartateh] it depends

ΕΞΑΤΜΙΣΗ εξάτμιση (η) [examtisi (i)] exhaust

εξαφανίζομαι [exafanizomeh] disappear

ΕΞΕΤΑΣΕΙΣ εξετάσεις (οι) [exetasis (i)] check-up; exams

εξηγώ [exigo] explain

εξήντα [exinda] sixty

έξι [exi] six

ΕΞΟΔΟΣ έξοδος (η) [exothos (i)] exit; gate (at airport); door

ΕΞΟΔΟΣ ΑΥΤ/ΤΩΝ έξοδος αυτ/των vehicle exit

ΕΞΟΔΟΣ ΚΙΝΔΥΝΟΥ έξοδος κινδύνου emergency exit

εξοχή (η) [exokhi (i)] countryside

έξοχος [exokhos] excellent

ΕΞΠΡΕΣ εξπρές [expres] special delivery; express

εξυπηρετώ [exipireto] serve (verb), assist

έξυπνος [exipnos] clever, intelligent

έξω! [exo!] get out!

ΕΞΩΣΤΗΣ εξώστης [exostis] circle (in cinema etc)

εξωτερικός [exoterikos] external στο εξωτερικό [sto exoteriko] abroad

ΕΞΩΤΕΡΙΚΟΥ εξωτερικού postage abroad

εξωφρενικός [exofrenikos] shocking

E.O.K. [E.O.K.] EEC, EU

E.O.T. [E.O.T.] National Tourist Agency

επαληθεύω [epaliTHevo] check (verb), verify

επαναλαμβάνω [epanalamvano] repeat

επαφή: έρχομαι σε επαφή [erkhomeh seh epafi] contact (verb)

Ε.Π.Ε. Ltd

επείγον [epigon] urgent

επειδή [epithi] because

επέκταση (η) [epektasi (i)] extension lead

επέτειος (η) [epetios (i)] anniversary

ΕΠΙΒΑΤΗΣ επιβάτης (ο/η) [epivatis (o/i)] passenger

επιβεβαιώνω [epiveveono] confirm

επίδεσμος (ο) [epithesmos (o)] bandage

επίθεση (η) [epiTHesi (i)] attack (noun)

επιθετικός [epiTHetikos] aggressive

ΕΠΙΘΕΤΟ επίθετο (το) [epiTHeto (to)] surname

επικίνδυνος [epikinthinos] dangerous

ΕΠΙΛΕΞΑΤΕ ΤΟΝ ΑΡΙΘΜΟ επιλέξατε τον αριθμό dial the number

επίπεδος [epipethos] flat (even)

έπιπλα (τα) [epipla (ta)] furniture

ΕΠΙΠΛΩΜΕΝΑ ΔΩΜΑΤΙΑ επιπλωμένα δωμάτια furnished rooms

επίσης [episis] too, also

επισκέπτομαι [episkeptomeh] visit (verb)

ΕΠΙΣΚΕΥΑΖΟΝΤΑΙ ΥΠΟΔΗΜΑΤΑ επισκευάζονται υποδήματα shoe repairs

επισκευή (η) [episkevi (i)] repair

επίσκεψη (η) [episkepsi (i)] visit

επιστήμη (η) [epistimi (i)] science

ΕΠΙΣΤΟΛΕΣ επιστολές letters

επιστρέφω [epistrefo] give back; arrive back

ΕΠΙΣΤΡΕΦΩ ΣΕ 5′ επιστρέφω σε 5′ back in 5 minutes

ΕΠΙΤΑΓΗ επιταγή (η) [epitayi (i)] cheque, (US) check

επιτέλους [epiteloos] at last

επίτηδες [epitithes] deliberately

επιτρέπω [epitrepo] let (allow)

επιτρέπεται [epitrepeteh] it is permitted

επιτυχία (η) [epitikhia (i)] success

επόμενος (ο) [epomenos (o)] next

εποχή (η) [epokhi (i)] season

επτά [epta] seven

E.P.A. Greek radio

ΕΡΓΑ έργα roadworks

ΕΡΓΑ ΕΠΙ ΤΗΣ ΟΔΟΥ ΣΕ ΜΗΚΟΣ ... ΧΙΛ. έργα επί της οδού σε μήκος ... χιλ. roadworks for ... kms

εργάζομαι [ergazomeh] work (verb)

ΕΡΓΑΛΕΙΑ ΠΥΡΑΣΦΑΛΕΙΑΣ εργαλεία πυρασφάλειας fire-fighting equipment εργαλείο (το) [ergalio (to)] tool

ΕΡΓΑΣΤΗΡΙΟ ΗΛΕΚΤΡΟΝΙΚΩΝ εργαστήριο ηλεκτρονικών electronics

εργένης (ο) [eryenis (o)] bachelor

εργοστάσιο (το) [ergostasio (to)] factory

ερυθρά (η) [eriTHra (i)] German measles

έρχομαι [erkhomeh] come

έρωτας (ο) [erotas (o)] love

κάνω έρωτα [kano erota] make love

ερώτηση (η) [erotisi (i)] question

εσάς, εσείς, εσένα [esas, esis, esena] you

ΕΣΤΙΑΤΟΡΙΟ εστιατόριο (το) [estiatorio (to)] restaurant

εσύ [esi] you

Ε.Σ.Υ. National Health Service

εσώρουχα (τα) [esorookha (ta)] underwear

ΕΣΩΡΟΥΧΑ ΓΥΝΑΙΚΕΙΑ εσώρουχα γυναικεία [esorookha yinekia] ladies' underwear

ΕΣΩΤΕΡΙΚΟΥ εσωτερικού inland postage

Ε.Τ. Greek television

εταιρεία (η) [eteria (i)] company

ετικέτα (η) [etiketa (i)] label

ΕΤΟΙΜΑ ΓΥΝΑΙΚΕΙΑ έτοιμα γυναικεία ladies' clothing

ετοιμάζω [etimazo] prepare

ΕΤΟΙΜΑ ΠΑΙΔΙΚΑ έτοιμα παιδικά children's clothing

έτοιμος [etimos] ready

έτσι [etsi] so; like this

έτσι κι έτσι [etsi ki etsi] so-so

ευαίσθητος [evesTHitos] sensitive

ευγενικός [evyenikos] kind; polite

ευγνώμων [evgnomon] grateful

ΕΥΚΑΙΡΙΑ ευκαιρία (η) [efkeria (i)] bargain

ΕΥΚΑΙΡΙΕΣ ευκαιρίες bargains

εύκολος [efkolos] easy

ΕΥΡΩΠΑΪΚΟΣ Ευρωπαϊκός [Evropa-ikos] European

ΕΥΡΩΠΗ Ευρώπη (η) [Evropi (i)] Europe

ευτυχισμένος [eftikhismenos] happy

ευτυχώς [eftikhos] fortunately

ευχαριστημένος [efkharistimenos] glad; pleased

ευχάριστος [efkharistos] pleasant

ευχαριστώ [efkharisto] thank you

ΕΦΗΜΕΡΙΔΑ εφημερίδα (η) [efimeritha (i)] newspaper

εφημεριδοπώλης (ο) [efimerithopolis (o)] newsagent

ΕΦΟΡΙΑ εφορία (η) tax office

έχει [ekhi] he/she/it has

έχεις [ekhis] you have

έχεις ...; [ekhis ...?] do you have ...?

έχετε [ekheteh] you have

έχετε ...; [ekheteh ...?] do you have ...?

έχουμε **[ekhoomeh]** we have
έχουν **[ekhoon]** they have
έχω **[ekho]** I have

Z
▬

ζακέτα (η) **[zaketa (i)]** cardigan
ΖΑΧΑΡΟΠΛΑΣΤΕΙΟ
ζαχαροπλαστείο (το)
[zakharoplastio (to)] cake shop
  or café selling cakes and soft
  drinks
ζέστη (η) **[zesti (i)]** heat
κάνει ζέστη **[kani zesti]** it's
  warm
ΖΕΣΤΟ ζεστό **[zesto]** hot
ΖΕΣΤΟ ΝΕΡΟ ζεστό νερό
[zesto nero] hot water
ζεστός **[zestos]** hot; warm
ζευγάρι (το) **[zevgari (to)]** pair
ζηλιάρης **[ziliaris]** jealous
ζημιά (η) **[zimia (i)]** damage
ζημιές: κάνω ζημιές **[kano
  zimies]** break (verb)
ζητάω συγγνώμη **[zitao signomi]**
  apologize
ζω **[zo]** live (verb)
ζωγραφίζω **[zografizo]** paint
  (verb: pictures)
ζωγραφική (η) **[zografiki (i)]**
  painting
ζωή (η) **[zoi (i)]** life
ζώνη (η) **[zoni (i)]** belt
ζώνη ασφαλείας (η) **[zoni asfalias
  (i)]** seat belt
ζωντανός **[zondanos]** alive
ζώο (το) **[zo-o (to)]** animal
ΖΩΟΛΟΓΙΚΟΣ ΚΗΠΟΣ

ζωολογικός κήπος (ο)
[zo-oloyikos kipos (o)] zoo

Η
▬

η **[i]** the
ή **[i]** or
ή ... ή ... **[i ... i ...]** either ...
  or ...
ήδη **[ithi]** already
ήθελα: θα ήθελα **[tha itHela]** I
  would like
ηθοποιός (ο/η) **[itHopios (o/i)]**
  actor, actress
ΗΛ/ΓΕΙΟ ηλ/γειο electrical
  goods
ΗΛΕΚΤΡΙΚΑ ΕΙΔΗ ηλεκτρικά
  είδη **[ilektrika ithi]** electrical
  goods
ηλεκτρική σκούπα (η) **[ilektriki
  skoopa (i)]** vacuum cleaner
ηλεκτρικό ρεύμα (το) **[ilektriko
  revma (to)]** electricity
ΗΛΕΚΤΡΙΚΟΣ ηλεκτρικός (ο)
[ilektrikos (o)] underground,
  (US) subway
ηλεκτρικό σίδερο (το) **[ilektriko
  sithero (to)]** iron (for ironing)
ηλεκτρικός **[ilektrikos]** electric
ΗΛΕΚΤΡΟΛΟΓΟΣ
ηλεκτρολόγος (ο) **[ilektrologos
  (o)]** electrician
ηλίαση (η) **[iliasi (i)]** sunstroke
ηλικία (η) **[ilikia (i)]** age
ηλιοθεραπεία: κάνω
  ηλιοθεραπεία **[kano ilioTHerapia]**
  sunbathe
ηλιόλουστος **[ilioloostos]** sunny

ήλιος (o) [**ilios** (o)] sun
ήμαστε [**imasteh**] we were
ημέρα (η) [**imera** (i)] day
ημερολόγιο (το) [**imeroloyio** (to)]
calendar, diary
ημερομηνία (η) [**imerominia** (i)]
date (time)
ΗΜΕΡΟΜΗΝΙΑ ΛΗΞΗΣ
ημερομηνία λήξης best before
ΗΜΕΡΟΜΗΝΙΑ
ΠΑΡΑΣΚΕΥΗΣ ημερομηνία
παρασκευής date of
manufacture
ΗΜΙΔΙΑΤΡΟΦΗ ημιδιατροφή
(η) [**imithiatrofi** (i)] half board
ΗΜΙΣΚΛΗΡΟΙ ΦΑΚΟΙ
ΕΠΑΦΗΣ ημίσκληροι φακοί
επαφής (οι) [**imiskliri faki epafis**
(i)] gas permeable lenses
ήμουν [**imoon**] I was
ΗΝΩΜΕΝΕΣ ΠΟΛΙΤΕΙΕΣ
ΑΜΕΡΙΚΗΣ Ηνωμένες
Πολιτείες Αμερικής (οι)
[**Inomenes Polities Amerikis** (i)]
United States of America
Η.Π.Α. (οι) [**I.P.A.** (i)] USA
ηρεμώ [**iremo**] calm down
ΗΡΩΩΝ ηρώων (το) [**iro-on** (to)]
war memorial
ήσουν, ήστε [**isoon, isteh**] you
were
ΗΣΥΧΙΑ ησυχία [**isikhia**]
quiet
ήσυχος [**isikhos**] quiet
ήταν [**itan**] he/she/it was; they
were

Θ

θάλασσα (η) [**THalasa** (i)] sea
ΘΑΛΑΣΣΙΑ ΣΠΟΡ θαλάσσια
σπορ water sports
ΘΑΛΑΣΣΙΟ ΣΚΙ θαλάσσιο σκι
(το) [**THalasio ski** (to)]
waterskiing
θάνατος (o) [**THanatos** (o)] death
θα σε δω! [**THa seh tho!**] see you!
θαυμάσιος [**THavmasios**]
wonderful
θεά (η) [**THea** (i)] goddess
θέα (η) [**THea** (i)] view
ΘΕΑΤΡΙΚΟ ΕΡΓΟ θεατρικό
έργο (το) [**THeh-atriko ergo** (to)]
play (theatre)
ΘΕΑΤΡΟ θέατρο (το) [**THeatro**
(to)] theatre
θεία (η) [**THia** (i)] aunt
θείος (o) [**THios** (o)] uncle
θέλετε ...; [**THeleteh ...?**] do you
want ...?
θέλω [**THelo**] want (verb)
θεός (o) [**THeos** (o)] God
ΘΕΡΙΝΟΣ θερινός (o) open-
air cinema/movie theater
θέρμανση (η) [**THermansi** (i)]
heating
θερμοκρασία (η) [**THermokrasia**
(i)] temperature
θερμόμετρο (το) [**THermometro**
(to)] thermometer
θερμός (το) [**THermos** (to)]
Thermos® flask
ΘΕΣΕΙΣ θέσεις seats
ΘΕΣΕΙΣ ΚΑΘΗΜΕΝΩΝ
θέσεις καθημένων seats

ΘΕΣΕΙΣ ΟΡΘΙΩΝ θέσεις
ορθίων standing room
θέση (η) [THesi (i)] seat
κλείνω θέση [klino THesi] book
a seat
ΘΕΩΡΕΙΑ θεωρεία [THeoria]
boxes (in theatre)
θλιμμένος [THlimenos]
depressed; sad
θορυβώδης [THorivothis] noisy
θρησκεία (η) [THriskia (i)]
religion
θύελλα (η) [THiela (i)] storm;
thunderstorm
θυμάμαι [THimameh] remember
θυμωμένος [THimomenos] angry
θυρωρός (ο) [THiroros (o)]
doorman; caretaker

I
■

ΙΑΜΑΤΙΚΕΣ ΠΗΓΕΣ
ιαματικές πηγές [iamatikes
piyes] spa
ΙΑΝΟΥΑΡΙΟΣ Ιανουάριος (ο)
[Ianooarios (o)] January
ιδέα (η) [ithea (i)] idea
ιδιοκτήτης (ο) [ithioktitis (o)]
owner
ιδιοκτήτρια (η) [ithioktitria (i)]
owner
ΙΔΙΟΚΤΗΤΟ ΠΑΡΚΙΝΓΚ
ιδιόκτητο πάρκινγκ private
parking
ίδιος [ithios] same
ΙΔΙΩΤΙΚΗ/ΚΡΑΤΙΚΗ
ΙΔΙΟΚΤΗΣΙΑ
ιδιωτική/κρατική ιδιοκτησία

private/state property
ΙΔΙΩΤΙΚΗ ΠΙΝΑΚΟΘΗΚΗ
ιδιωτική πινακοθήκη private
art gallery
ΙΔΙΩΤΙΚΟΣ ιδιωτικός
[ithiotikos] private
ΙΔΙΩΤΙΚΟΣ ΔΡΟΜΟΣ
ιδιωτικός δρόμος private road
ιδρώνω [ithrono] sweat (verb)
ιλαρά (η) [ilara (i)] measles
ΙΝΣΤΙΤΟΥΤΟ ΑΙΣΘΗΤΙΚΗΣ
ινστιτούτο αισθητικής (το)
[institooto esTHitikis (to)] beauty
salon
ΙΟΥΛΙΟΣ Ιούλιος (ο) [Ioolios
(o)] July
ΙΟΥΝΙΟΣ Ιούνιος (ο) [Ioonios
(o)] June
ιππασία (η) [ipasia (i)] horse-
riding
ΙΠΠΟΔΡΟΜΟΣ ιππόδρομος (ο)
[ipothromos (o)] race course (for
horses)
Ιρλανδέζα (η) [Irlantheza (i)]
Irishwoman
ΙΡΛΑΝΔΙΑ Ιρλανδία (η)
[Irlanthia (i)] Ireland
Ιρλανδικός [Irlanthikos] Irish
Ιρλανδός (ο) [Irlanthos (o)]
Irishman
ίσια [isia] straight
ΙΣΟΓΕΙΟ ισόγειο (το) [isoyio
(to)] ground floor, (US) first
floor
ΙΣΟΠΕΔΟΣ ΔΙΑΒΑΣΙΣ
ισόπεδος διάβασις level
crossing
ΙΣΠΑΝΙΑ Ισπανία (η) [ispania
(i)] Spain

Ισπανικός [Ispanikos] Spanish (adj)

ιστιοπλοΐα (η) [istioploia (i)] sailing

ιστιοπλοϊκό σκάφος (το) [istioplo-iko skafos (to)] sailing boat

ΙΣΤΙΟΦΟΡΟ ιστιοφόρο (το) [istioforo (to)] sailing boat

ιστορία (η) [istoria (i)] story; history

ίσως [isos] maybe, perhaps

ΙΤΑΛΙΑ Ιταλία (η) [Italia (i)] Italy

Ιταλικός [Italikos] Italian (adj)

ΙΧΘΥΟΠΩΛΕΙΟ ιχθυοπωλείο (το) [ikhTHiopolio (to)] fishmonger's

K

K. κ. Mr

ΚΑ. κα. Mrs

ΚΑΖΙΝΟ καζίνο (το) [kazino (to)] casino

καθαρίζω [kaTHarizo] clean

ΚΑΘΑΡΙΣΤΗΡΙΟ καθαριστήριο (το) [kaTHaristirio (to)] laundry and dry cleaner's

ΚΑΘΑΡΙΣΤΙΚΟ ΔΕΡΜΑΤΟΣ καθαριστικό δέρματος (το) [kaTHaristiko thermatos (to)] skin cleanser

ΚΑΘΑΡΟ ΒΑΡΟΣ καθαρό βάρος net weight

καθαρός [kaTHaros] clean (adj)

ΚΑΘΑΡΤΙΚΟ καθαρτικό (το) [kaTHartiko (to)] laxative

κάθε [kaTHeh] every

καθεμία, καθένα, καθένας [kaTHemia, kaTHena, kaTHenas] each

κάθε τι [kaTHeh ti] everything

καθηγητής (ο) [kaTHiyitis (o)] teacher, professor

καθηγήτρια (η) [kaTHiyitria (i)] teacher, professor

ΚΑΘΗΜΕΡΙΝΑ καθημερινά [kaTHimerina] daily

καθήστε [kaTHisteh] please sit down

ΚΑΘΟΔΟΣ κάθοδος [kaTHothos] way down, descent

καθολικός [kaTHolikos] Catholic (adj)

καθόλου [kaTHoloo] not at all; none; any

κάθομαι [kaTHomeh] sit down

καθρέφτης (ο) [kaTHreftis (o)] mirror

καθρέφτης αυτοκινήτου (ο) [kaTHreftis aftokinitoo (o)] rearview mirror

ΚΑΘΥΣΤΕΡΗΣΗ καθυστέρηση (η) [kaTHisterisi (i)] delay

καθυστερώ [kaTHistero] delay (verb); be late

και [keh] and

και εγώ επίσης [k ego episis] me too

και οι δύο [k i thio] both of them

ΚΑΙ ΛΟΙΠΑ και λοιπά etc

καινούργιο [kenooryio] brand-new

ευτυχισμένος ο καινούργιος χρόνος! ⟦eftikhismenos o kenooryios khronos!⟧ happy New Year!

καιρός (ο) ⟦keros (o)⟧ weather

καίω ⟦keo⟧ burn (verb)

κακός ⟦kakos⟧ bad

καλά ⟦kala⟧ well

καλά! ⟦kala!⟧ good!

καλάθι (το) ⟦kalaтНi (to)⟧ basket

καλεί ⟦kali⟧ it's ringing

ΚΑΛΕΣΑΤΕ καλέσατε dial

ΚΑΛΕΣΤΕ ΤΟΝ ΑΡΙΘΜΟ καλέστε τον αριθμό dial number

καλή διασκέδαση ⟦kali thiaskethasi⟧ have fun

καλημέρα ⟦kalimera⟧ good morning

καληνύχτα ⟦kalinikhta⟧ good night

καλησπέρα ⟦kalispera⟧ good afternoon; good evening

καλλιτέχνηδα (η) ⟦kalitekhnitha (i)⟧ artist

καλλιτέχνης (ο) ⟦kalitekhnis (o)⟧ artist

ΚΑΛΛΥΝΤΙΚΑ καλλυντικά (τα) ⟦kalindika (ta)⟧ perfume and cosmetics

ΚΑΛΟΚΑΙΡΙ καλοκαίρι (το) ⟦kalokeri (to)⟧ summer

καλοκαιρινές διακοπές (οι) ⟦kalokerines thiakopes (i)⟧ summer holidays/vacation

καλοριφέρ (το) ⟦kalorifer (to)⟧ radiator (heater)

καλός ⟦kalos⟧ good; kind

καλοψημένος ⟦kalopsimenos⟧ well-done (meat)

κάλσον (το) ⟦kalson (to)⟧ tights, pantyhose

κάλτσες (οι) ⟦kaltses (i)⟧ socks

καλύτερος (ο) ⟦kaliteros (o)⟧ the best

καλύτερος ⟦kaliteros⟧ better

καλύτερος από ⟦kaliteros apo⟧ better than

καλώς ήλθατε! ⟦kalos ilтнateh!⟧ welcome!

ΚΑΛΩΣ ΩΡΙΣΑΤΕ ΣΤΗΝ ... καλώς ωρίσατε στην ... welcome to ...

καμαριέρα (η) ⟦kamariera (i)⟧ chambermaid

καμμία ⟦kamia⟧ no-one

καμμιά φορά ⟦kamia fora⟧ sometimes

καμπάνα (η) ⟦kabana (i)⟧ bell

ΚΑΜΠΙΝΑ καμπίνα (η) ⟦kabina (i)⟧ cabin (on ship)

ΚΑΜΠΙΝΓΚ κάμπινγκ (το) ⟦camping (to)⟧ campsite, caravan site, trailer park

ΚΑΜΠΙΝΕΣ καμπίνες ⟦kabines⟧ changing rooms

ΚΑΝΑΔΑΣ Καναδάς (ο) ⟦Kanathas (o)⟧ Canada

Καναδή (η) ⟦Kanathi (i)⟧ Canadian (woman)

Καναδικός ⟦Kanathikos⟧ Canadian (adj)

Καναδός (ο) ⟦Kanathos (o)⟧ Canadian (man)

κανάτα (η) ⟦kanata (i)⟧ jug

κάνει ... ⟦kani ...⟧ it is ..., it costs ...

κάνεις ⟦kanis⟧ you do

τι κάνεις; [ti kanis?] how are you?, how do you do?

κανένα [kanena] nothing

κανένας [kanenas] no-one, nobody

κάνετε [kaneteh] you do

τι κάνετε; [ti kaneteh?] how are you?, how do you do?

κανό (το) [kano (to)] canoe

κάνω [kano] do; make

καπάκι (το) [kapaki (to)] lid, cap (of bottle)

καπαρντίνα (η) [kapardina (i)] raincoat

καπέλο (το) [kapelo (to)] hat, cap

ΚΑΠΕΤΑΝΙΟΣ καπετάνιος (ο) [kapetanios (o)] captain (of ship)

ΚΑΠΝΙΖΟΝΤΕΣ καπνίζοντες [kapnizondes] smoking

καπνίζω [kapnizo] smoke (verb)

ΚΑΠΝΙΣΤΕΣ καπνιστές [kapnistes] smokers

ΚΑΠΝΙΣΤΗΡΙΟ καπνιστήριο (το) [kapnistirio (to)] smoking room

ΚΑΠΝΟΠΩΛΕΙΟ καπνοπωλείο (το) [kapnopolio (to)] tobacconist's

ΚΑΠΝΟΣ καπνός (ο) [kapnos (o)] smoke; tobacco

καπό (το) [kapo (to)] bonnet (car), (US) hood

κάποιος [kapios] somebody

κάπου [kapoo] somewhere

ΚΑΡΑΜΕΛΑ καραμέλα (η) [karamela (i)] caramel

καρδιά (η) [karthia (i)] heart

καρδιακή προσβολή (η) [karthiaki prosvoli (i)] heart attack

καρέκλα (η) [karekla (i)] chair

καρμπιρατέρ (το) [karbirater (to)] carburettor

καρνέ επιταγών (το) [karneh epitagon (to)] cheque book, (US) check book

καροτσάκι (το) [karotsaki (to)] pram; pushchair, buggy

καρπός (ο) [karpos (o)] wrist

ΚΑΡΤΑ κάρτα (η) [karta (i)] postcard; business card

κάρτα επιβιβάσεως (η) [karta epivivaseos (i)] boarding pass

κάρτα επιταγών (η) [karta epitagon (i)] cheque card, (US) check card

ΚΑΡΤΠΟΣΤΑΛ καρτποστάλ (η) [kartpostal (i)] postcard

καρφί (το) [karfi (to)] nail (in wall)

καρφίτσα (η) [karfitsa (i)] pin; brooch

κασκόλ (το) [kaskol (to)] scarf (for neck)

ΚΑΣΣΕΤΑ κασσέτα (η) [kaseta (i)] cassette, tape

κασσεττόφωνο (το) [kasetofono (to)] cassette player

καστόρι (το) [kastori (to)] suede

κάστρο (το) [kastro (to)] castle

κατά [kata] against; about

κάταγμα (το) [katagma (to)] fracture

καταδύσεις (οι) [katathisis (i)] skin-diving

ΚΑΤΑΘΕΣΗ κατάθεση (η) [kataτHesi (i)] deposit

καταλαβαίνω [katalaveno]

understand

δεν καταλαβαίνω [then katalaveno] I don't understand

ΚΑΤΑΛΛΗΛΟ κατάλληλο suitable for all ages

κατάλογος (ο) [katalogos (o)] list; menu

ΚΑΤΑΝΑΛΩΣΗ ΠΡΙΝ ... κατανάλωση πριν ... consume before ...

καταπίνω [katapino] swallow (verb)

καταρράκτης (ο) [kataraktis (o)] waterfall

ΚΑΤΑΣΚΕΥΑΖΟΝΤΑΙ ΚΛΕΙΔΙΑ κατασκευάζονται κλειδιά keys cut here

κατασκήνωση (η) [kataskinosi (i)] camping

ΚΑΤΑΣΤΗΜΑ ΑΦΟΡΟΛΟΓΗΤΩΝ κατάστημα αφορολογήτων (το) [katastima aforoloyiton (to)] duty-free shop

καταστροφή (η) [katastrofi (i)] disaster

ΚΑΤΑΣΤΡΩΜΑ κατάστρωμα (το) [katastroma (to)] deck

κατά τη διάρκεια [kata ti thiarkia] while, during

καταψύκτης (ο) [katapsiktis (o)] freezer

κατάψυξη (η) [katapsixi (i)] freezer compartment

κατεβαίνω [kateveno] get off; go down

ΚΑΤΕΙΛΗΜΜΕΝΟΣ κατειλημμένος [katilimenos] engaged, occupied

ΚΑΤΕΠΕΙΓΟΝ κατεπείγον [katepigon] express

κατευθείαν [katefтнian] direct

ΚΑΤΕΨΥΓΜΕΝΑ κατεψυγμένα (τα) [katepsigmena (ta)] frozen food

ΚΑΤΕΨΥΓΜΕΝΟ κατεψυγμένο [katepsigmeno] frozen (food)

κάτι [kati] something

κάτι άλλο [kati alo] something else

ΚΑΤΟΛΙΣΘΗΣΕΙΣ κατολισθήσεις falling rocks

ΚΑΤΟΣΤΑΡΙΚΟ κατοστάρικο (το) [katostariko (to)] 100-drachma note/bill

κατσαβίδι (το) [katsavithi (to)] screwdriver

κατσαρόλα (η) [katsarola (i)] saucepan

κατσίκα (η) [katsika (i)] goat

ΚΑΤΩ κάτω [kato] down; downstairs

κάτω από [kato apo] under

καυτερός [kafteros] spicy, hot

καυτός [kaftos] hot (to taste)

καφέ [kafe] brown

ΚΑΦΕΚΟΠΤΕΙΟ καφεκοπτείο (το) [kafekoptio (to)] coffee shop

ΚΑΦΕΝΕΙΟ καφενείο (το) [kafenio (to)] coffee house, where Greek coffee is served with traditional sweets

ΚΑΦΕΤΕΡΙΑ καφετέρια (η) [kafeteria (i)] café, coffee shop

κάψιμο (το) [kapsimo (to)] burn

ΚΕΛΣΙΟΥ Κελσίου [Kelsioo]
centigrade

κέλυφος (το) [kelifos (to)] shell

ΚΕΝΤΗΜΑΤΑ κεντήματα (τα)
[kendimata (ta)] embroidery

κεντρική θέρμανση (η) [kendriki
THermansi (i)] central heating

ΚΕΝΤΡΟ κέντρο (το) [kendro
(to)] centre

κέντρο της πόλης [kendro tis
polis] city centre

ΚΕΡΑΜΙΚΑ κεραμικά (τα)
[keramika (ta)] ceramics

κερδίζω [kerthizo] earn; win
(verb)

κερί (το) [keri (to)] candle

ΚΕΡΚΥΡΑ Κέρκυρα (η)
[Kerkira (i)] Corfu

ΚΕΡΜΑ κέρμα (το) [kerma (to)]
coin

ΚΕΡΜΑΤΑ κέρματα [kermata]
coins

ΚΕΣ. κες. Mrs

κεφάλι (το) [kefali (to)] head

κηδεία (η) [kithia (i)] funeral

ΚΗΠΟΘΕΑΤΡΟ κηποθέατρο
(το) open-air theatre

ΚΗΠΟΣ κήπος (ο) [kipos (o)]
garden, park

κιβώτιο ταχυτήτων (το) [kivotio
takhititon (to)] gearbox

κιθάρα (η) [kiThara (i)] guitar

ΚΙΛΟ κιλό (το) [kilo (to)] kilo

ΚΙΝΔΥΝΟΣ κίνδυνος (ο)
[kinthinos (o)] danger; caution

ΚΙΝΔΥΝΟΣ ΠΥΡΚΑΓΙΑΣ
κίνδυνος πυρκαγιάς fire risk

κινηματογραφική μηχανή (η)
[kinimatografiki mikhani (i)]
camcorder

ΚΙΝΗΜΑΤΟΓΡΑΦΟΣ
κινηματογράφος (ο)
[kinimatografos (o)] cinema,
movie theater

κίτρινος [kitrinos] yellow

ΚΚ. κκ. Messrs

κλαίω [kleo] cry (verb)

κλάξον (το) [klaxon (to)] horn (in
car)

κλέβω [klevo] steal

κλειδαριά (η) [klitharia (i)] lock

κλειδί (το) [klithi (to)] key;
spanner, wrench

ΚΛΕΙΔΙΑ κλειδιά keys cut
here

κλειδώνω [klithono] lock (verb)

ΚΛΕΙΝΕΤΕ ΤΗΝ ΠΟΡΤΑ
κλείνετε την πόρτα close the
door

κλείνω [klino] close (verb);
switch off

ΚΛΕΙΣΤΑ κλειστά [klista]
closed

ΚΛΕΙΣΤΟ ΑΠΟ ... ΩΣ ...
κλειστό από ... ως ... [klisto apo
... os ...] closed from ...
to ...

ΚΛΕΙΣΤΟΝ κλειστόν [kliston]
closed

κλειστός [klistos] closed; off
(lights)

κλέφτης (ο) [kleftis (o)] thief

κλέφτρα (η) [kleftra (i)] thief

κλίμα (το) [klima (to)] climate

ΚΛΙΜΑΤΙΖΟΜΕΝΟΣ
κλιματιζόμενος [klimatizomenos]
air-conditioned

ΚΛΙΜΑΤΙΣΜΟΣ κλιματισμός

(ο) [klimatismos (o)] air-
conditioning

κλοπή (η) [klopi (i)] theft

Κ.Λ.Π. κλπ etc

ΚΛΩΣΤΗ κλωστή (η) [klosti (i)]
thread

κόβω [kovo] cut (verb)

κοιλάδα (η) [kilatha (i)] valley

κοιμάμαι [kimameh] sleep
(verb); be asleep

ΚΟΙΜΗΤΗΡΙΟ κοιμητήριο
(το) [kimitirio (to)] cemetery

ΚΟΙΝΟΤΙΚΟ ΓΡΑΦΕΙΟ
κοινοτικό γραφείο (το) local
government office

κοκκαλιάρης [kokaliaris] skinny

κόκκαλο (το) [kokalo (to)] bone

κόκκινος [kokinos] red

κόλλα (η) [kola (i)] glue

κολλιέ (το) [kolie (to)] necklace

κόλπος (ο) [kolpos (o)] vagina;
gulf

ΚΟΛΥΜΒΗΤΗΡΙΟ
κολυμβητήριο (το) [kolimvitirio
(to)] swimming pool

κολυμπάω [kolibao] swim (verb)

κολύμπι (το) [kolibi (to)]
swimming

κολυμπώ [kolibo] swim (verb)

κολώνια (η) [kolonia (i)] eau de
toilette

κολώνια μετά το ξύρισμα
[kolonia meta to xirisma]
aftershave

κομμάτι (το) [komati (to)] piece

ΚΟΜΜΩΣΕΙΣ κομμώσεις (οι)
[komosis (i)] hairdresser's

ΚΟΜΜΩΤΗΡΙΟ κομμωτήριο
(το) [komotirio (to)] hairdresser's

κομμώτρια (η) [komotria (i)]
hairdresser

κομπιουτεράκι (το) [kombi-
ooteraki (to)] calculator

κομπολόι (το) [komboloi (to)]
worry beads

κοντά [konda] near, close by

κοντέρ (το) [konder (to)]
speedometer

ΚΟΝΤΙΣΙΟΝΕΡ κοντίσιονερ
(το) [kondisioner (to)]
conditioner

κοντός [kondos] short (person)

ΚΟΡΔΟΝΙΑ ΠΑΠΟΥΤΣΙΩΝ
κορδόνια παπουτσιών (τα)
[korthonia papootsion (ta)]
shoelaces

κόρη (η) [kori (i)] daughter

κορίτσι (το) [koritsi (to)] girl

κόρνα (η) [korna (i)] horn (in
car)

κορυφή (η) [korifi (i)] top

ΚΟΣΜΗΜΑΤΑ κοσμήματα
(τα) [kosmimata (ta)] jewellery

ΚΟΣΜΗΜΑΤΟΠΩΛΕΙΟ
κοσμηματοπωλείο (το)
[kosmimatopolio (to)] jeweller's

κόσμος (ο) [kosmos (o)] world;
people, crowd

κοστίζει [kostizi] it costs

κόστος (το) [kostos (to)] cost

κουβάς (ο) [koovas (o)] bucket

κουβέρτα (η) [kooverta (i)]
blanket

κουδούνι (το) [koothooni (to)] bell
(for door)

ΚΟΥΖΙΝΑ κουζίνα (η) [koozina
(i)] cooker; kitchen

ΚΟΥΚΕΤΑ κουκέτα (η)

[kooketa (i)] couchette
κουκέτες (οι) [kooketes (i)] bunk beds
κούκλα (η) [kookla (i)] doll
κουμπί (το) [koobi (to)] button
κουνέλι (το) [kooneli (to)] rabbit
κούνια (η) [koonia (i)] cot
κουνούπι (το) [koonoopi (to)] mosquito
κουπέ (το) [koopeh (to)] compartment
κουρασμένος [koorasmenos] tired
ΚΟΥΡΕΑΣ κουρέας (ο) [kooreas (o)] barber
ΚΟΥΡΕΙΟ κουρείο (το) [koorio (to)] barber's shop
κούρεμα (το) [koorema (to)] haircut
κουρτίνα (η) [koortina (i)] curtain
κουστούμι (το) [koostoomi (to)] suit
κουτάλι (το) [kootali (to)] spoon
ΚΟΥΤΑΛΙΕΣ ΓΛΥΚΟΥ κουταλιές γλυκού teaspoonfuls
ΚΟΥΤΑΛΙΕΣ ΣΟΥΠΑΣ κουταλιές σούπας tablespoonfuls
κουτί (το) [kooti (to)] box; can
κουφός [koofos] deaf
ΚΡΑΓΙΟΝ κραγιόν (το) [krayon (to)] lipstick
κράμπα (η) [kramba (i)] cramp
κρανίο (το) [kranio (to)] skull
κρατάω [kratao] hold; keep
ΚΡΑΤΗΣΕΙΣ ΘΕΣΕΩΝ κρατήσεις θέσεων

reservations; seat reservations
κράτηση θέσης (η) [kratisi THesis (i)] reservation
κρεβάτι (το) [krevati (to)] bed
ΚΡΕΜΑ ΠΡΟΣΩΠΟΥ κρέμα προσώπου (η) [krema prosopoo (i)] moisturizer
κρεμάστρα (η) [kremastra (i)] coathanger; peg
ΚΡΕΟΠΩΛΕΙΟ κρεοπωλείο (το) [kreopolio (to)] butcher's
κρίμα: είναι κρίμα [ineh krima] it's a pity
κρουαζιέρα (η) [kroo-aziera (i)] cruise
κρύβομαι [krivomeh] hide (oneself)
κρύβω [krivo] hide (something)
κρύο (το) [krio (to)] cold
κάνει κρύο [kani krio] it's cold
ΚΡΥΟ ΝΕΡΟ κρύο νερό [krio nero] cold water
κρύος [krios] cold (adj)
κρύωμα (το) [krioma (to)] cold (illness)
Κ.Τ.Ε.Λ. long-distance bus station
κτηνίατρος (ο/η) [ktiniatros (o/i)] vet
κτίριο (το) [ktirio (to)] building
κυβέρνηση (η) [kivernisi (i)] government
κυκλοφορία (η) [kikloforia (i)] traffic
κυκλοφοριακή συμφόρηση (η) [kikloforiaki simforisi (i)] traffic jam
ΚΥΛΙΚΕΙΟ κυλικείο (το) [kilikio (to)] snackbar

ΚΥΛΟΤΕΣ κυλότες (οι) [kilotes
(i)] panties; underpants
κύμα (το) [kima (to)] wave
κυνηγώ [kinigo] hunt (verb),
chase
ΚΥΠΡΟΣ Κύπρος (η) [Kipros (i)]
Cyprus
Κυρία (η) [Kiria (i)] Mrs; Ms
κυρία (η) [kiria (i)] lady; madam
ΚΥΡΙΑΚΕΣ ΚΑΙ ΕΟΡΤΕΣ
Κυριακές και Εορτές Sundays
and holidays
ΚΥΡΙΑΚΗ Κυριακή (η) [Kiriaki
(i)] Sunday
ΚΥΡΙΑΚΗ ΤΟΥ ΠΑΣΧΑ
Κυριακή του Πάσχα (η) [Kiriaki
too Paskha (i)] Easter Sunday
κύριε [kiri-eh] sir
ΚΥΡΙΕΣ κυρίες [kiries] Mrs
ΚΥΡΙΟΙ κύριοι Messrs
ΚΥΡΙΟΣ Κύριος [Kirios] Mr
κύριος (ο) [kirios (o)] gentleman
κύριος [kirios] main
κύστη (η) [kisti (i)] bladder
κυττάζω [kitazo] look (verb)
ΚΩΔΙΚΟΣ κωδικός (ο) [kothikos
(o)] code
ΚΩΔΙΚΟΣ ΑΡΙΘΜΟΣ κωδικός
αριθμός [kothikos ariTHmos]
dialling code

Λ

ΛΑΔΙ λάδι (το) [lathi (to)] oil
ΛΑΔΙΑ λάδια (τα) [lathia (ta)]
engine oil
ΛΑΔΙ ΜΑΥΡΙΣΜΑΤΟΣ λάδι
μαυρίσματος [lathi mavrismatos]
suntan oil
λάθος (το) [laTHos (to)] mistake
λάθος [laTHos] wrong
λάθος νούμερο [laTHos noomero]
wrong number
λαιμός (ο) [lemos (o)] neck;
throat
λακ (η) [lak (i)] hairspray
λάμπα (η) [lamba (i)] light bulb;
lamp
λαστιχάκι (το) [lastikhaki (to)]
rubber band
λάστιχο (το) [lastikho (to)]
rubber (material); tyre
λεβιές ταχυτήτων (ο) [levies
takhititon (o)] gear lever
λείπω [lipo] be missing; be
out; be away
λειτουργία (η) [litooryia (i)] mass
(chuch)
λεκές (ο) [lekes (o)] stain
ΛΕΜΒΟΣ λέμβος (η) [lemvos
(i)] lifeboat
λένε: λένε ότι [leneh oti] they
say that
με λένε ... [meh leneh ...] my
name is ...
πως σε λένε; [pos seh leneh?]
what's your name?
λέξη (η) [lexi (i)] word
λεξικό (το) [lexiko (to)]
dictionary
λεπτό (το) [lepto (to)] minute
λεπτός [leptos] slim
λέσχη (η) [leskhi (i)] club
λευκοπλάστ (το) [lefkoplast (to)]
(sticking) plaster, Bandaid®
ΛΕΦΤΑ λεφτά (τα) [lefta (ta)]
money

λέω [leo] say

ΛΕΩΦΟΡΕΙΟ λεωφορείο (το) [leoforio (to)] bus

ΛΕΩΦΟΡΕΙΟ ΥΠ' ΑΡΙΘΜ ... λεωφορείο υπ' αριθμ ... bus number ...

ΛΕΩΦΟΡΟΣ λεωφόρος (η) [leoforos (i)] avenue

ΛΗΓΕΙ ΤΗΝ ... λήγει την ... expires on ...

λιακάδα (η) [liakatha (i)] sunshine

λίγα [liga] a few

λίγο [ligo] a little bit

ΣΕ ΛΙΓΟ σε λίγο [seh ligo] in a little while

λίγος [ligos] little, short

λιγότερος [ligoteros] fewer

λιγότερο [ligotero] less

ΛΙΜΑΝΙ λιμάνι (το) [limani (to)] harbour

λίμα νυχιών (η) [lima nikhion (i)] nailfile

ΛΙΜΕΝΑΡΧΕΙΟ λιμεναρχείο (το) port authorities

ΛΙΜΕΝΑΡΧΗΣ λιμενάρχης (ο) harbour master

ΛΙΜΕΝΙΚΗ ΑΣΤΥΝΟΜΙΑ Λιμενική Αστυνομία (η) [limeniki Astinomia (i)] harbour police

ΛΙΜΗΝ λιμήν (ο) [limin (o)] port

λίμνη (η) [limni (i)] lake

λιμνούλα (η) [limnoola (i)] pond

λίμπρα (η) [libra (i)] pound (weight)

λιπαρός [liparos] greasy

λιποθυμώ [lipoTHimo] faint (verb)

ΛΙΡΑ ΑΓΓΛΙΑΣ λίρα Αγγλίας (η) [lira Anglias (i)] pound sterling

ΛΙΤΑΝΕΙΑ λιτανεία (η) litany

ΛΙΤΡΟ λίτρο (το) [litro (to)] litre

ΛΟΓΑΡΙΑΣΜΟΣ λογαριασμός (ο) [logariasmos (o)] bill, (US) check

λογικός [loyikos] sensible

ΛΟΓΙΣΤΗΡΙΟ λογιστήριο (το) [loyistirio (to)] purser's office

ΛΟΝΔΙΝΟ Λονδίνο (το) [Lonthino (to)] London

λόξυγγας (ο) [loxingas (o)] hiccups

λουλούδι (το) [looloothi (to)] flower

λούσιμο (το) [loosimo (to)] wash

ΛΟΥΤΡΟ λουτρό (το) [lootro (to)] bathroom

λόφος (ο) [lofos (o)] hill

λυπάμαι [lipameh] I'm sorry

λυπημένος [lipimenos] sad

ΛΥΡΙΚΗ ΣΚΗΝΗ λυρική σκηνή (η) [liriki skini (i)] opera house

M

μαγαζί (το) [magazi (to)] shop

μαγειρεύω [mayirevo] cook (verb)

μαγειρικά σκεύη (τα) [mayirika skevi (ta)] cooking utensils

μαγείρισσα (η) [mayirisa (i)] cook

μάγειρος (ο) [mayiros (o)] cook

μάγκας (ο) [mangas (o)]

streetwise/smart person

μαγιό (το) [mayo (to)] swimming trunks

μάγουλο (το) [magoolo (to)] chin

μαζί [mazi] together

μαζί με [mazi meh] with, together with

μαθαίνω [maтHeno] learn

μάθημα (το) [maтHima (to)] lesson

κάνω μάθημα [kano maтHima] teach; take a lesson

ΜΑΘΗΜΑΤΑ ΣΚΙ μαθήματα σκι [maтHimata ski] skiing lessons

ΜΑΙΟΣ Μάιος (ο) [Maios (o)] May

μακριά [makria] far, at a distance

μαλάκας (ο) [malakas (o)] arsehole, wanker

μακρύς [makris] long

ΜΑΛΑΚΟΙ ΦΑΚΟΙ μαλακοί φακοί (οι) [malaki faki (i)] soft lenses

μάλιστα [malista] yes, certainly

μάλιστα! [malista!] well!

ΜΑΛΛΙ μαλλί (το) [mali (to)] wool

μαλλιά (τα) [malia (ta)] hair

ΜΑΛΛΙΝΟ μάλλινο [malino] wool

μάλλον [malon] rather; probably

μαλώνω [malono] fight (verb)

μαμά (η) [mama (i)] mum

ΜΑΝΑΒΗΣ μανάβης (ο) [manavis (o)] greengrocer's

ΜΑΝΟ μανό (το) [mano (to)] nail polish

μανταλάκι (το) [mandalaki (to)] clothes peg

μαντήλι (το) [mandili (to)] handkerchief; headscarf

μαξιλάρι (το) [maxilari (to)] pillow

μαραγκός (ο) [marangos (o)] carpenter

ΜΑΡΙΝΑ μαρίνα (η) [marina (i)] marina

μαρκαδόρος (ο) [markathoros (o)] felt-tip pen

ΜΑΡΤΙΟΣ Μάρτιος (ο) [Martios (o)] March

μάρτυρας (ο) [martiras (o)] witness

μασέλα (η) [masela (i)] dentures

μας [mas] us; our

μάτι (το) [mati (to)] eye; ring (on cooker)

ματς (το) [mats (to)] match (sport)

μαυρίζω [mavrizo] tan (verb)

μαύρισμα (το) [mavrisma (to)] tan (colour)

μαύρισμα από τον ήλιο [mavrisma apo ton ilio] suntan

μαύρος [mavros] black

μαχαίρι (το) [makheri (to)] knife

μαχαιροπήρουνα (τα) [makheropiroona (ta)] cutlery

με [meh] with; by; me

με αυτοκίνητο [meh aftokinito] by car

ΜΕΓΑΛΗ ΒΡΕΤΑΝΝΙΑ Μεγάλη Βρεταννία (η) [Megali Vretania (i)] Great Britain

Μεγάλη Παρασκευή (η) [Megali

Paraskevi (i)] Good Friday

μεγάλος [megalos] big

μεγαλύτερος [megaliteros] bigger

ΜΕΓΕΘΟΣ μέγεθος (το) [meyeTHos (to)] size

μεγέθυνση (η) [meyeTHinsi (i)] enlargement

ΜΕΓΙΣΤΟ ΒΑΡΟΣ μέγιστο βάρος maximum permitted weight

μέγιστος (ο) [meyistos (o)] biggest

μεζ (η) [mez (i)] highlights (in hair)

μεθαύριο [meTHavrio] the day after tomorrow

μεθυσμένος [meTHismenos] drunk

μέικ απ (το) [meik ap (to)] make-up

μελανιά (η) [melania (i)] bruise

μέλλον (το) [melon (to)] future

ΜΕ ΜΠΑΝΙΟ με μπάνιο [meh banio] with bathroom

ΜΕ ΝΤΟΥΣ με ντους [meh doos] with shower

μένω [meno] live (in town etc); stay (in hotel etc)

μέρα (η) [mera (i)] day

μερίδα (η) [meritha (i)] portion

μερικά, μερικές, μερικοί [merika, merikes, meriki] some

μέρος (το) [meros (to)] part, place; WC

μέσα [mesa] in; inside

μεσάνυχτα (τα) [mesanikhta (ta)] midnight

μέση (η) [mesi (i)] middle; waist

μεσημέρι (το) [mesimeri (to)] midday

Μεσόγειος (η) [Mesoyios (i)] Mediterranean

μετά [meta] after; afterwards

μετά από σας [meta apo sas] after you

μετά μεσημβρίας [meta mesimvrias] pm

μετακινούμαι [metakinoomeh] move (verb)

μέταλλο (το) [metalo (to)] metal

ΜΕΤΑΞΙ μετάξι (το) [metaxi (to)] silk

μεταξύ [metaxi] between

μεταφέρω [metafero] carry

μεταφράζω [metafrazo] translate

μετεωρολογικό δελτίο (το) [meteoroloyiko theltio (to)] weather forecast

ΜΕΤΡΗΤΑ μετρητά [metrita] cash

ΤΟΙΣ ΜΕΤΡΗΤΟΙΣ τοις μετρητοίς [tis metritis] in cash

μετρητής βενζίνης (ο) [metritis venzinis (o)] fuel gauge

μέτριο μέγεθος [metrio meyeTHos] medium-sized

ΜΕΤΡΙΟΣ μέτριος [metrios] medium; average

ΜΕΤΡΟ μέτρο (το) [metro (to)] metre

μέτωπο (το) [metopo (to)] forehead

μέχρι [mekhri] until

ΜΗ μη do not

ΜΗ ΒΓΑΖΕΤΕ ΤΗΝ ΚΑΡΤΑ μη βγάζετε την κάρτα do not remove the card yet μηδέν [mithen] zero

ΜΗΝ ΚΑΠΝΙΖΕΤΕ μην καπνίζετε no smoking

ΜΗ ΚΑΠΝΙΖΟΝΤΕΣ μη καπνίζοντες [mi kapnizondes] non-smoking

ΜΗ ΚΑΠΝΙΣΤΕΣ μη καπνιστές [mi kapnistes] non-smokers

μήκος (το) [mikos (to)] length

μήνας (ο) [minas (o)] month

μήνας του μέλιτος [minas too melitos] honeymoon

ΜΗΝ ΕΝΟΧΛΕΙΤΕ μην ενοχλείτε do not disturb

ΜΗΝ ΟΜΙΛΕΙΤΕ ΣΤΟΝ ΟΔΗΓΟ μην ομιλείτε στον οδηγό do not speak to the driver

ΜΗΝ ΠΑΤΑΤΕ ΤΟ ΧΟΡΤΟ μην πατάτε το χόρτο keep off the grass

ΜΗ ΠΟΣΙΜΟ (ΝΕΡΟ) μη πόσιμο (νερό) not for drinking (water)

μητέρα (η) [mitera (i)] mother

ΜΗ ΤΟΞΙΚΟ μη τοξικό non-toxic

μητρόπολη (η) [mitropoli (i)] cathedral

μηχανάκι (το) [mikhanaki (to)] moped

μηχανή (η) [mikhani (i)] engine

μηχανικός (ο) [mikhanikos (o)] mechanic; engineer

μία [mia] a; one

μία φορά [mia fora] once

μιάς [mias] of a

μίζα (η) [miza (i)] ignition

ΜΙΚΡΟ ΟΝΟΜΑ μικρό όνομα (το) [mikro onoma (to)] Christian name

ΜΙΚΡΟΣ μικρός [mikros] little, small

ΜΙΚΤΟ ΒΑΡΟΣ μικτό βάρος gross weight

μικρότερος [mikroteros] smaller

ΜΙΛΑΕΙ μιλάει [milai] engaged, occupied

μιλάω [milao] speak

μιλάτε ...; [milateh ...?] do you speak ...?

μισός [misos] half

ΜΙΣΟΤΙΜΗΣ μισοτιμής half-price

μισώ [miso] hate (verb)

μ.μ. [m.m.] pm

μνημείο (το) [mnimio (to)] monument

μόδα (η) [motha (i)] fashion

της μόδας [tis mothas] fashionable

ΜΟΔΕΣ μόδες fashions

μοιάζει [miazi] it looks/seems

μοιράζομαι [mirazomeh] share (verb)

μοκέτα (η) [moketa (i)] carpet

μολύβι (το) [molivi (to)] pencil

μόλυνση (η) [molinsi (i)] infection

ΜΟΛΥΣΜΕΝΑ ΥΔΑΤΑ μολυσμένα ύδατα polluted water

μολυσμένος [molismenos] polluted

ΜΟΝΑΔΕΣ μονάδες units

ΜΟΝΑΔΙΚΗ ΕΥΚΑΙΡΙΑ

μοναδική ευκαιρία (η) special
offer
μονή [moni] monastery
μόνο [mono] only
ΜΟΝΟΔΡΟΜΟΣ μονόδρομος
one-way street
ΜΟΝΟ ΔΩΜΑΤΙΟ μονό
δωμάτιο (το) [mono thomatio (to)]
single room
ΜΟΝΟΚΛΙΝΟ ΔΩΜΑΤΙΟ
μονόκλινο δωμάτιο (το)
[monoklino thomatio (to)] single
room
μονό κρεβάτι [mono krevati]
single bed
μονοπάτι (το) [monopati (to)]
path
μόνος [monos] alone
μοντέρνος [mondernos] modern
μοτοσυκλέτα (η) [motosikleta (i)]
motorbike
μου [moo] my
ΜΟΥΣΕΙΟ μουσείο (το)
[moosio (to)] museum
ΜΟΥΣΙΚΑ ΟΡΓΑΝΑ μουσικά
όργανα [moosika organa]
musical instruments
μουσική (η) [moosiki (i)] music
μουσική ποπ (η) [moosiki pop (i)]
pop music
μουστάκι (το) [moostaki (to)]
moustache
μπαίνω [beno] go in, enter
ΜΠΑΚΑΛΙΚΟ μπακάλικο (το)
[bakaliko (to)] grocer's
μπαλκόνι (το) [balkoni (to)]
balcony
μπάλλα (η) [bala (i)] ball (large)
μπαλλάκι (το) [balaki (to)] ball

(small)
μπαμπάς (ο) [babas (o)] dad
μπανιέρα (η) [baniera (i)]
bathtub
ΜΠΑΝΙΟ μπάνιο (το) [banio
(to)] bath
κάνω μπάνιο [kano banio] swim
(verb); have a bath
πάω για μπάνιο [pao ya banio]
go swimming
ΜΠΑΡ μπαρ (το) [bar (to)] bar
μπάρμαν (ο) [barman (o)]
barman
μπάρ γούμαν (η) [bar woman (i)]
barmaid
μπαταρία (η) [bataria (i)] battery
μπεζ [bez] beige
μπέιμπι-σίττερ (η) [baby-sitter (i)]
babysitter
μπερδεμένος [berthemenos]
complicated
μπικίνι (το) [bikini (to)] bikini
μπλε [bleh] blue
μπλούζα (η) [blooza (i)] blouse
μπλουζάκι (το) [bloozaki (to)] T-
shirt
μπόρα (η) [bora (i)] shower (rain)
μπορείς [boris] you can
μπορείς να ...; [boris na ...?] can
you ...?
μπορείτε [boriteh] you can
μπορείτε να ...; [boriteh na ...?]
can you ...?
μπρος [bros] forwards; in front
of
βάζω μπρος [vazo bros] switch
on (engine)
μπορώ [boro] I can
μπότα (η) [bota (i)] boot (shoe)

μπουγάδα (η) [boogatha (i)] washing

βάζω μπουγάδα [vazo boogatha] do the washing

μπουζί (το) [boozi (to)] spark plug

ΜΠΟΥΖΟΥΚΙΑ μπουζούκια (τα) [boozookia (ta)] club with bouzouki music

μπουκάλι (το) [bookali (to)] bottle

μπουκιά (η) [bookia (i)] bite

μπούτι (το) [booti (to)] thigh

ΜΠΟΥΤΙΚ μπουτίκ (η) [bootik (i)] boutique

μπροστινό μέρος (το) [brostino meros (to)] front (part)

ΜΠΥΡΑ μπύρα [bira] beer, lager

μπωλ (το) [bol (to)] bowl

μύγα (η) [miga (i)] fly

μυθιστόρημα (το) [miτHistorima (to)] novel

μυρίζω [mirizo] smell (verb)

μυρμήγκι (το) [mirmingi (to)] ant

μυρωδιά (η) [mirothia (i)] smell

μυστικός [mistikos] secret

μυς (ο) [mis (o)] muscle

μύτη (η) [miti (i)] nose

μύωπας [miopas] shortsighted

μωβ [mov] purple

μωρό (το) [moro (to)] baby

Ν

να [na] here is/are

ναι [neh] yes

ναι, ναι! [neh neh!] oh yes I do!

νάιτκλαμπ (το) [nightclub (to)] nightclub

ΝΑ ΛΑΜΒΑΝΕΤΑΙ ΜΟΝΟΝ ΑΠΟ ΤΟ ΣΤΟΜΑ να λαμβάνεται μόνον από το στόμα to be taken orally only

ΝΑ ΛΑΜΒΑΝΕΤΑΙ ... ΦΟΡΕΣ ΗΜΕΡΗΣΙΩΣ να λαμβάνεται ... φορές ημερησίως to be taken ... times daily

ναρκωτικά (τα) [narkotika (ta)] drugs (narcotics)

ΝΑ ΦΥΛΑΣΣΕΤΑΙ ΜΑΚΡΙΑ ΑΠΟ ΠΑΙΔΙΑ να φυλάσσεται μακριά από παιδιά keep out of reach of children

νέα (η) [nea (i)] teenager

νέα (τα) [nea (ta)] news

ΝΕΑ ΖΗΛΑΝΔΙΑ Νέα Ζηλανδία (η) [Nea Zilanthia (i)] New Zealand

ΝΕΚΡΟΤΑΦΕΙΟ νεκροταφείο (το) [nekrotafio (to)] cemetery

Νέο Έτος (το) [Neo Etos (to)] New Year

ΝΕΟΖΗΛΑΝΔΕΖΑ Νεοζηλανδέζα (η) [Neozilantheza (i)] New Zealander

ΝΕΟΖΗΛΑΝΔΟΣ Νεοζηλανδός (ο) [Neozilanthos (o)] New Zealander

νέοι (οι) [nei (i)] young people

νέος (ο) [neos (o)] teenager

νέος [neos] new; young

ΝΕΡΟ νερό (το) [nero (to)] water

νεροχύτης (ο) [nerokhitis (o)] sink

νευρικός [nevrikos] nervous

νεφρά (τα) [nefra (ta)] kidneys

νησί (το) [nisi (to)] island

νιπτήρας (ο) [niptiras (o)] washbasin

νιώθω [nioTHo] feel

ΝΟΕΜΒΡΙΟΣ Νοέμβριος (ο) [Noemvrios (o)] November

νοικιάζω [nikiazo] rent (verb)

ΝΟΜΑΡΧΙΑ νομαρχία (η) local government office

νομίζω [nomizo] think

ΝΟΜΟΣ νομός (ο) county

νόμος (ο) [nomos (o)] law

ΝΟΣΟΚΟΜΕΙΟ νοσοκομείο (το) [nosokomio (to)] hospital

νόστιμο [nostimo] tasty

νοστιμώτατο [nostimotato] delicious

ΝΟΥΜΕΡΟ νούμερο (το) [noomero (to)] number

ΝΤΕΜΙ ΠΑΝΣΙΟΝ ντεμί πανσιόν (η) [demi pansion (i)] half board

ντεπόζιτο (το) [ndepozito (to)] tank

ΝΤΗΖΕΛ ντήζελ (το) [dizel (to)] diesel

ντισκοτέκ (η) [ndiskotek (i)] disco

ντιστριμπυτέρ (το) [ndistribiter (to)] distributor

ντουλάπι (το) [ndoolapi (to)] cupboard

ΝΤΟΥΣ ντους (το) [doos (to)] shower (in bathroom)

ΝΤΡΑΙΒ - ΙΝ ντραιβ - ιν

drive-in

ντροπαλός [ndropalos] shy

ντύνομαι [ndinomeh] dress (oneself)

ντύνω [ndino] dress (verb: someone)

νύφη (η) [nifi (i)] daughter-in-law; sister-in-law; bride

νύχι (το) [nikhi (to)] fingernail

νυχοκόπτης (ο) [nikhokoptis (o)] nail clippers

νύχτα (η) [nikhta (i)] night

ΝΥΧΤΕΡΙΝΟ ΚΕΝΤΡΟ νυχτερινό κέντρο [nikhterino kendro] nightclub

νυχτικό (το) [nikhtiko (to)] nightdress

νωρίς [noris] early

Ξ

ξαδέλφη (η) [xathelfi (i)] cousin

ξάδελφος (ο) [xathelfos (o)] cousin

ξανά [xana] again

ξανθός [xanTHos] blond

ξαπλώνω [xaplono] lie down

ξαφνικά [xafnika] suddenly

ξεκουράζομαι [xekoorazomeh] relax

ξεναγός (ο/η) [xenagos (o/i)] guide

ΞΕΝΟΔΟΧΕΙΟ ξενοδοχείο (το) [xenothokhio (to)] hotel

ξένος [xenos] foreign

ΞΕΝΩΝΑΣ ξενώνας (ο) [xenonas (o)] guesthouse

ΞΕΝΩΝΑΣ ΝΕΟΤΗΤΑΣ

ξενώνας νεότητας [xenonas neotitas] youth hostel
ΞΕΝΩΝΑΣ ΝΕΩΝ ξενώνας νέων [xenonas neon] youth hostel
ΞΕΠΟΥΛΗΜΑ ξεπούλημα closing-down sale
ξέρω [xero] know
δεν ξέρω [then xero] I don't know
ξεφωνίζω [xefonizo] scream (verb)
ξεχνώ [xekhno] leave (verb); forget
ξεχωριστά [xekhorista] separately
ξηρός [xiros] dry
ξοδεύω [xothevo] spend
ξύλο (το) [xilo (to)] wood
ξινός [xinos] sour
ξυπνάω [xipnao] wake up
ξυπνητήρι (το) [xipnitiri (to)] alarm clock
ξύπνιος [xipnios] awake
ξυραφάκι (το) [xirafaki (to)] razor
ξυρίζομαι [xirizomeh] shave (verb)
ξύρισμα (το) [xirisma (to)] shave
ξυριστική μηχανή (η) [xiristiki mikhani (i)] electric shaver

Ο

ο [o] the
Ο.Α. Olympic Airways
Ο/Γ ferry
ογδόντα [ogthonda] eighty

όγδοος [ogthoos] eighth
οδηγάω [othigao] drive
οδηγός (ο/η) [othigos (o/i)] driver
ΟΔΙΚΑ ΕΡΓΑ οδικά έργα roadworks
ΟΔΟΝΤΙΑΤΡΟΣ οδοντίατρος (ο/η) [othondiatros (o/i)] dentist
οδοντόβουρτσα (η) [othondovoortsa (i)] toothbrush
ΟΔΟΝΤΟΓΙΑΤΡΟΣ οδοντογιατρός (ο/η) [othondoyatros (o/i)] dentist
ΟΔΟΝΤΙΑΤΡΕΙΟ οδοντιατρείο (το) [othondiatrio (to)] dentist's
ΟΔΟΝΤΟΚΡΕΜΑ οδοντόκρεμα (η) [othondokrema (i)] toothpaste
ΟΔΟΣ οδός (η) [othos (i)] road, street
ΟΔΟΣ ΑΝΕΥ ΣΗΜΑΝΣΕΩΣ ΣΕ ΜΗΚΟΣ ... ΧΙΛ. οδός άνευ σημάνσεως σε μήκος ... χιλ no road markings for ... kms
οδυνηρός [othiniros] painful
όζα (η) [oza (i)] nail polish
Ο.Η.Ε. UN
ΟΧΙ ΕΠΙΤΑΓΕΣ όχι επιταγές no cheques/checks
οι [i] the
οικογένεια (η) [ikoyenia (i)] family
ΟΚΤΩΒΡΙΟΣ Οκτώβριος (ο) [Oktovrios (o)] October
όλα [ola] all
όλα καλά [ola kala] that'll do nicely, everything's fine
όλα πληρωμένα [ola pliromena] all inclusive

όλες, όλη [oles, oli] all
ΟΛΙΣΘΗΡΟ ΟΔΟΣΤΡΩΜΑ
ολισθηρό οδόστρωμα slippery
road surface
όλο [olo] amμ
όλοι [oli] everyone; all
ολόκληρος [olokliros] whole
όλος [olos] all
Ο.Λ.Π. Piraeus Port
Authorities
ΟΛΥΜΠΙΑΚΗ ΑΕΡΟΠΟΡΙΑ
Ολυμπιακή Αεροπορία
Olympic Airways
ομάδα (η) [omatha (i)] group;
team
ομάδα αίματος (η) [omatha
ematos (i)] blood group
ομίχλη (η) [omikhli (i)] fog
όμοιος [omios] similar
όμορφος [omorfos] fine,
beautiful
ομοφυλόφιλος (ο) [omofilofilos
(o)] gay
ομπρέλλα (η) [ombrella (i)]
umbrella
όνειρο (το) [oniro (to)] dream
ΟΝΟΜΑ όνομα (το) [onoma
(to)] name; first name
οπά! [opa!] watch it!
ΟΠΕΡΑ όπερα (η) [opera (i)]
opera
όπισθεν (η) [opisTHen (i)] reverse
(gear)
όπλο (το) [oplo (to)] gun; rifle
ΟΠΤΙΚΑ οπτικά (τα) [optika
(ta)] optician's
ΟΠΤΙΚΟΣ οπτικός (ο) [optikos
(o)] optician
ΟΠΩΡΟΠΩΛΕΙΟ

οπωροπωλείο (το) [oporopolio
(to)] grocer's
όπως [opos] like; as
όπως και νάναι [opos keh naneh]
anyway
ΟΡΓΑΝΙΣΜΟΣ ΗΝΩΜΕΝΩΝ
ΕΘΝΩΝ Οργανισμός
Ηνωμένων Εθνών United
Nations Organization
οργανωμένη εκδρομή (η)
[organomeni ekthromi (i)]
package tour
οργανώνω [organono] organize
όρεξη (η) [orexi (i)] appetite
καλή όρεξη! [kali orexi!] enjoy
your meal!, bon appetit!
ΟΡΘΙΩΝ ορθίων standing
ΟΡΙΟ ΤΑΧΥΤΗΤΑΣ όριο
ταχύτητας (το) speed limit
ορίστε; [oristeh?] can I help
you?
όροφος (ο) [orofos (o)] floor,
storey
ΟΡΥΚΤΕΛΑΙΟ ορυκτέλαιο
(το) [orikteleo (to)] engine oil
ορχήστρα (η) [orkhistra (i)]
orchestra
Ο.Σ.Ε. Greek Railways
όταν [otan] when
Ο.Τ.Ε. Greek
Telecommunications
Company
ότι [oti] that
οτιδήποτε [otithipoteh] anything
Ο.Υ. water authorities
Ουαλλή (η) [Ooali (i)]
Welshwoman
ΟΥΑΛΛΙΑ Ουαλλία (η) [Ooalia
(i)] Wales

Ουαλλικός [Ooalikos] Welsh (adj)

Ουαλλός (ο) [Ooalos (o)] Welshman

ΟΥΖΕΡΙ ουζερί [oozeri] bar serving ouzo and beer with snacks or full meals

ούλο (το) [oolo (to)] gum (in mouth)

ΟΥΡΑ ουρά (η) [oora (i)] queue; tail; queue here

κάνω ουρά [kano oora] queue (verb)

ουρανός (ο) [ooranos (o)] sky

ούτε ... ούτε ... [oote ... oote ...] neither ... nor ...

ΟΦΘΑΛΜΙΑΤΡΟΣ οφθαλμίατρος (ο/η) eye specialist

όχημα (το) [okhima (to)] vehicle

ΟΧΙ όχι [okhi] no; not

όχι άλλο [okhi allo] no more

ΟΧΙ ΥΠΕΡΑΣΤΙΚΑ όχι υπεραστικά no long-distance calls

οχτώ [okhto] eight

Π

ΠΑΓΟΣ πάγος (ο) [pagos (o)] ice

ΠΑΓΩΤΟ παγωτό (το) [pagoto (to)] ice cream

ΠΑΓΩΤΟ ΞΥΛΑΚΙ παγωτό ξυλάκι (το) [pagoto xilaki (to)] ice lolly

πάει: πώς πάει; [pos pai?] how are things?

ΠΑΖΑΡΙ παζάρι (το) [pazari (to)] bazaar

ΠΑΘΟΛΟΓΟΣ παθολόγος (ο/η) [paTHologos (o/i)] doctor, general practitioner

ΠΑΙΔΙ παιδί (το) [pethi (to)] child

ΠΑΙΔΙΑΤΡΟΣ παιδίατρος (ο/η) paediatrician

ΠΑΙΔΙΚΑ παιδικά (τα) [pethika (ta)] children's wear

ΠΑΙΔΙΚΑ ΕΙΔΗ παιδικά είδη (τα) [pethika ithi (ta)] children's department

ΠΑΙΔΙΚΑ ΕΣΩΡΟΥΧΑ παιδικά εσώρουχα [pethika esorookha] children's underwear

ΠΑΙΔΙΚΑ ΦΟΡΜΑΚΙΑ παιδικά φορμάκια [pethika formakia] babywear, toddlers' clothes

ΠΑΙΔΙΚΟ παιδικό [pethiko] children's (adj)

παίζω [pezo] play (verb)

παίρνω [perno] get; take

παίρνω τηλέφωνο [perno tilefono] phone (verb)

ΠΑΙΧΝΙΔΙ παιχνίδι (το) [pekhnithi (to)] game; toy

ΠΑΚΕΤΟ πακέτο (το) [paketo (to)] package; packet

ΠΑΛΑΙΟΠΩΛΕΙΟ παλαιοπωλείο (το) [paleopolio (to)] antique shop

παλαιός [paleos] old, ancient, antique

παλάτι (το) [palati (to)] palace

παλίρροια (η) [paliria (i)] tide

παλτό (το) [palto (to)] coat
πάνα (η) [pana (i)] nappy, diaper
ΠΑΝΕΠΙΣΤΗΜΙΟ
πανεπιστήμιο (το) [panepistimio
(to)] university
ΠΑΝΗΓΥΡΙ πανηγύρι (το)
[paniyiri (to)] fair, funfair
πανί (το) [pani (to)] sail
ΠΑΝ/ΜΙΟ παν/μιο university
ΠΑΝΣΙΟΝ πανσιόν (η) [pansion
(i)] guesthouse
πάντα [panda] always; still
πανταλόνι (το) [pandaloni (to)]
trousers, (US) pants
παντζούρια (τα) [pandzooria (ta)]
shutters
ΠΑΝΤΟΠΩΛΕΙΟ παντοπωλείο
(το) [pandopolio (to)] grocery
store
πάντοτε [pandoteh] always
παντού [pandoo] everywhere
παντόφλες (οι) [pandofles (i)]
slippers
παντρεμένος [pandremenos]
married
παντρεμένη [pandremeni]
married
πάνω [pano] on; up; upstairs
πάνω από [pano apo] above
παξιμάδι (το) [paximathi (to)] nut
(for bolt)
παπάς (ο) [papas (o)] priest
πάπια (η) [papia (i)] duck
πάπλωμα (το) [paploma (to)] quilt
παπούτσι (το) [papootsi (to)]
shoe
παππούς (ο) [pappoos (o)]
grandfather
παραγγελία (η) [parangelia (i)]

message
παραγγέλνω [paragelno] order
(verb: in restaurant)
παράδειγμα (το) [parathigma (to)]
example
παραδείγματος χάρι
[parathigmatos khari] for
example
παράδοση (η) [parathosi (i)]
tradition
παραδοσιακός [parathosiakos]
traditional
παράθυρο (το) [paraThiro (to)]
window
παρακαλώ [parakalo] please;
excuse me; don't mention it
παρακαλώ; [parakalo?] can I
help you?
ΠΑΡΑΚΑΜΠΤΗΡΙΟΣ
παρακαμπτήριος (η) diversion
ΠΑΡΑΛΑΒΗ ΑΠΟΣΚΕΥΩΝ
παραλαβή αποσκευών (η)
[paralavi aposkevon (i)] baggage
claim
ΠΑΡΑΛΙΑ παραλία (η) [paralia
(i)] beach
κοντά στην παραλία [konda stin
paralia] at the seaside
παραμάνα (η) [paramana (i)]
safety pin
παραμένω [parameno] stay
(verb), remain
παράξενος [paraxenos] strange
παραπονούμαι [paraponoomeh]
complain
ΠΑΡΑΣΚΕΥΗ Παρασκευή (η)
[Paraskevi (i)] Friday
παρατηρώ [paratiro] watch
(verb)

παρατσούκλι (το) [paratsookli (to)] nickname

παρεξήγηση (η) [parexiyisi (i)] misunderstanding

παρκάρω [parkaro] park (verb)

ΠΑΡΚΙΝΓΚ πάρκινγκ (το) [parking (to)] car park, parking lot

πάρκο (το) [parko (to)] park

ΠΑΡΟΔΟΣ πάροδος (η) [parothos (i)] side street

παρπρίζ (το) [parpriz (to)] windscreen

πάρτυ (το) [parti (to)] party, celebration

παστίλιες λαιμού (οι) [pastili-es lemoo (i)] throat pastilles

Πάσχα (το) [Paskha (to)] Easter

πατέρας (ο) [pateras (o)] father

πατερίτσες (οι) [pateritses (i)] crutches

πάτωμα (το) [patoma (to)] floor (of room)

ΠΑΥΣΙΠΟΝΟ παυσίπονο (το) [pafsipono (to)] painkiller

πάχος (το) [pakhos (to)] fat (on meat)

παχύς [pakhis] fat; thick

πάω [pao] go (verb)

πεζοδρόμιο (το) [pezothromio (to)] pavement, sidewalk

ΠΕΖΟΔΡΟΜΟΣ πεζόδρομος (ο) pedestrian precinct

ΠΕΖΟΙ πεζοί pedestrians

πεθαίνω [petHeno] die

πεθαμένος [petHamenos] dead

πεθερά (η) [petHera (i)] mother-in-law

πεθερός (ο) [petHeros (o)] father-in-law

πειράζει [pirazi] it matters

θα σε πείραζε αν ...; [tHa seh pirazeh an ...?] do you mind if I ...?

δεν πειράζει [then pirazi] it doesn't matter

ΠΕΙΡΑΙΑΣ Πειραιάς [Pireas] Piraeus

ΠΕΜΠΤΗ Πέμπτη (η) [Pempti (i)] Thursday

πέμπτος [pemptos] fifth

πενήντα [peninda] fifty

ΠΕΝΗΝΤΑΡΙΚΟ πενηντάρικο (το) [penindariko (to)] 50-drachma coin or note/bill

πενικιλλίνη (η) [penikilini (i)] penicillin

πέννα (η) [pena (i)] pen

πένσα (η) [pensa (i)] pliers

ΠΕΝΤΑΚΟΣΑΡΙΚΟ πεντακοσάρικο (το) [pendakosariko (to)] 500-drachma note/bill

πέντε [pendeh] five

πέος (το) [peos (to)] penis

περάστε [perasteh] come in; come back

ΠΕΡΙΕΧΟΜΕΝΟ περιεχόμενο contains

περίμενε [perimeneh] wait

περιμένω [perimeno] wait (for); expect

ΠΕΡΙΟΔΙΚΟ περιοδικό (το) [periothiko (to)] magazine

περίοδος (η) [periothos (i)] period

περιοχή (η) [periokhi (i)] area

περίπατος (ο) [peripatos (o)] walk

πάω περίπατο [pao peripato] go for a walk

περίπου [peripoo] about, approximately

ΠΕΡΙΠΤΕΡΟ περίπτερο [periptero] newspaper kiosk

ΣΕ ΠΕΡΙΠΤΩΣΗ ΑΝΑΓΚΗΣ ΣΠΑΣΤΕ ΤΟ ΤΖΑΜΙ σε περίπτωση ανάγκης σπάστε το τζάμι [seh periptosi anangis spasteh to tzami] in emergency break glass

περισσότερο [perisotero] more, most (of)

περισσότερος [perisoteros] more, most (of)

ΠΕΡΜΑΝΑΝΤ περμανάντ (η) [permanand (i)] perm

περνάω [pernao] cross, go through

περπατάω [perpatao] walk (verb)

πέρσυ [persi] last year

πετάλι (το) [petali (to)] pedal

πετάω [petao] throw away (verb)

πέτρα (η) [petra (i)] stone

πετσέτα (η) [petseta (i)] napkin; towel

πετσέτα κουζίνας [petseta koozinas] tea towel

πετώ [peto] fly (verb)

πέφτω [pefto] fall (verb)

πηγή (η) [piyi (i)] fountain

πηγούνι (το) [pigooni (to)] chin

πηδάω [pithao] jump (verb)

πηρούνι (το) [pirooni (to)] fork

πιάνω [piano] catch (verb)

πιατάκι (το) [piataki (to)] saucer

πιατικά (τα) [piatika (ta)] crockery

πιάτο (το) [piato (to)] dish; plate

ΠΙΕΣΗ ΑΙΜΑΤΟΣ πίεση αίματος (η) blood pressure

πιθανώς [pithanos] probably

πικάντικος [pikandikos] spicy

πικάπ (το) [pikap (to)] record player

πικνίκ (το) [piknik (to)] picnic

πικρός [pikros] bitter

πιλότος (ο) [pilotos (o)] pilot

πινακίδες (οι) [pinakithes (i)] number plates

ΠΙΝΑΚΟΘΗΚΗ πινακοθήκη (η) [pinakoTHiki (i)] art gallery

πινγκ-πονγκ (το) [ping-pong (to)] table tennis

πινέλο (το) [pinelo (to)] paintbrush

πινέλο γιά ξύρισμα [pinelo ya xirisma] shaving brush

πίνω [pino] drink (verb)

πίπα (η) [pipa (i)] pipe (for smoking)

ΠΙΣΙΝΑ πισίνα (η) [pisina (i)] swimming pool

πιστεύω [pistevo] believe

πιστολάκι (το) [pistolaki (to)] hairdryer

πιστόλι (το) [pistoli (to)] gun, pistol

πιστοποιητικό (το) [pistopi-itiko (to)] certificate

ΠΙΣΤΩΤΙΚΗ ΚΑΡΤΑ πιστωτική κάρτα (η) [pistotiki karta (i)] credit card

πίσω [piso] back; behind

πίσω φώτα (τα) 【piso fota (ta)】 rear lights

ΠΙΤΣΑΡΙΑ πιτσαρία (η) 【pitsaria (i)】 pizzeria

πλαστική σακούλα (η) 【plastiki sakoola (i)】 plastic bag

πλαστικός 【plastikos】 plastic

ΠΛΑΤΕΙΑ πλατεία (η) 【platia (i)】 square (in town); stalls (in theatre)

πλάτη (η) 【plati (i)】 back (of person)

πλατύς 【platis】 wide

ΠΛΑΤΦΟΡΜΑ πλατφόρμα (η) 【platforma (i)】 platform, (US) track

πλέκω 【pleko】 knit

πλένομαι 【plenomeh】 wash (oneself)

πλένω 【pleno】 wash (verb: something)

πλευρά (η) 【plevra (i)】 side

πλευρό (το) 【plevro (to)】 rib

πληγή (η) 【pliyi (i)】 wound

πλήθος (το) 【pliThos (to)】 crowd

ΠΛΗΡΕΣ πλήρες no vacancies, full

ΠΛΗΡΟΦΟΡΙΕΣ πληροφορίες (οι) 【plirofories (i)】 information; directory enquiries

ΠΛΗΡΩΜΑ πλήρωμα (το) 【pliroma (to)】 crew

πληρώνω 【plirono】 pay (verb)

πλοίο (το) 【plio (to)】 boat, ship

πλούσιος 【ploosios】 rich

πλυντήριο (το) 【plindirio (to)】 washing machine

ΠΛΥΝΤΗΡΙΟ ΑΥΤΟΚΙΝΗΤΩΝ πλυντήριο αυτοκινήτων car wash

ΠΛΥΝΤΗΡΙΟ ΡΟΥΧΩΝ πλυντήριο ρούχων 【plindirio rookhon】 launderette, laundromat

ΠΛΥΣΙΜΟ ΜΕ ΤΟ ΧΕΡΙ πλύσιμο με το χέρι handwash only

πλύσιμο των πιάτων (το) 【plisimo ton piaton (to)】 washing up

πνεύμονες (οι) 【pnevmones (i)】 lungs

ποδηλασία (η) 【pothilasia (i)】 cycling

ποδηλάτης (ο/η) 【pothilatis (o/i)】 cyclist

ΠΟΔΗΛΑΤΟ ποδήλατο (το) 【pothilato (to)】 bicycle

πόδι (το) 【pothi (to)】 foot; leg

με τα πόδια 【meh ta pothia】 on foot

ποδόσφαιρο (το) 【pothosfero (to)】 football

ποιά; 【pia?】 who?

ποιανού; 【pianoo?】 whose?

ποιό; 【pio?】 which?

ποιός; 【pios?】 who?

ποιός είναι; 【pios ineh?】 who is it?

πόλεμος (ο) 【polemos (o)】 war

πόλη (η) 【poli (i)】 city, town

πολιτεία (η) 【politia (i)】 state

πολιτικά (τα) 【politika (ta)】 politics

πολιτικός 【politikos】 political; politician

πολλά, πολλές, πολλή, πολλοί 【pola, poles, poli, poli】 many, a lot (of) πολύ [poli] a lot of; very; too much

πάρα πολύ [para poli] too much; very much

πολυσύχναστος [polisikhnastos] busy (place)

πολύς [polis] a lot (of)

ΠΟΛΥΤΕΛΕΙΑΣ πολυτελείας luxury class, four-star (hotel)

πονάει [ponai] hurt

πονόδοντος (ο) [ponothondos (o)] toothache

πονοκέφαλος (ο) [ponokefalos (o)] headache

πόνος (ο) [ponos (o)] ache, pain

ποντίκι (το) [pondiki (to)] mouse

πόνυ (το) [poni (to)] pony

πορεία (η) [poria (i)] route

πόρτα (η) [porta (i)] door

πορτ-μπαγκάζ (το) [port-bangaz (to)] boot (car), (US) trunk

πορτ-μπε-μπέ (το) [port-be-be (to)] carrycot

πορτοκαλί [portokali] orange (colour)

πορτοφολάς (ο) [portofolas (o)] pickpocket

πορτοφόλι (το) [portofoli (to)] wallet

πόσα;, πόσες;, [posa?, poses?] how many?

ΠΟΣΙΜΟ ΝΕΡΟ πόσιμο νερό (το) [posimo nero (to)] drinking water

πόσο; [poso?] how much?

πόσοι; [posi?] how many?

πόστερ (το) [poster (to)] poster

ΠΟΣΤ ΡΕΣΤΑΝΤ ποστ ρεστάντ [post restant] poste restante

ποτάμι (το) [potami (to)] river

ποτέ [poteh] never

πότε; [poteh?] when?

έχετε ποτέ ...; [ekheteh poteh ...?] have you ever ...?

ποτήρι (το) [potiri (to)] glass

ΠΟΤΟΠΩΛΕΙΟ ποτοπωλείο (το) [potopolio (to)] off-licence, liquor store

που [poo] who, which, that

πού; [poo?] where?

πούδρα ταλκ (η) [poothra talk (i)] talcum powder

πουθενά [pooTHena] nowhere

πουκάμισο (το) [pookamiso (to)] shirt

πουλί (το) [pooli (to)] bird

ΠΟΥΛΜΑΝ πούλμαν (το) [poolman (to)] bus, coach

πουλόβερ (το) [poolover (to)] jumper

πουλώ [poolo] sell

πούρο (το) [pooro (to)] cigar

πράγμα (το) [pragma (to)] thing

πραγματικά [pragmatika] really

πρακτικός [praktikos] practical

πρακτορείο (το) [praktorio (to)] agency

ΠΡΑΚΤΟΡΕΙΟ ΕΦΗΜΕΡΙΔΩΝ πρακτορείο εφημερίδων newsagent, news vendor

ΠΡΑΚΤΟΡΕΙΟ ΛΕΩΦΟΡΕΙΩΝ πρακτορείο λεωφορείων [praktorio leoforion] bus station

πράσινος [prasinos] green

ΠΡΑΤΗΡΙΟ ΒΕΝΖΙΝΗΣ πρατήριο βενζίνης (το) [pratirio venzinis (to)] petrol station, gas station

πρέπει να ... [**pre**pi na ...] I
must ...

ΠΡΕΣΒΕΙΑ πρεσβεία (η)
[presv**i**a (i)] embassy

πρησμένος [prism**e**nos] swollen

πρίγκηπας (ο) [pr**i**ngipas (o)]
prince

πριγκίπισσα (η) [pring**i**pisa (i)]
princess

πρίζα (η) [pr**i**za (i)] socket; plug

πρίζα ταυ (η) [pr**i**za taf (i)]
adaptor

πριν [prin] before; ago

πριν τρεις μέρες [prin tris m**e**res]
three days ago

προάστια (τα) [pro**a**stia (ta)]
suburbs

πρόβατο (το) [pr**o**vato (to)] sheep

πρόβλημα (το) [pr**o**vlima (to)]
problem

ΠΡΟΒΛΗΤΑ προβλήτα (η)
[provl**i**ta (i)] quay

προβολείς (οι) [provol**i**s (i)]
headlights

ΠΡΟΓΕΥΜΑ πρόγευμα (το)
[pr**o**yevma (to)] breakfast

πρόγονος (ο/η) [pr**o**gonos (o/i)]
ancestor

ΠΡΟΓΡΑΜΜΑ πρόγραμμα (το)
[pr**o**grama (to)] timetable, (US)
schedule; programme

προκαταβάλλω [prokatav**a**lo]
advance (verb)

προκαταβολικά [prokatavolik**a**] in
advance

ΠΡΟΞΕΝΕΙΟ προξενείο (το)
[prox**e**nio (to)] consulate

ΠΡΟΟΡΙΣΜΟΣ προορισμός
[pro-orism**o**s] destination

προσβάλλω [prosv**a**lo] offend

ΠΡΟΣ ΓΚΑΡΑΖ προς γκαράζ
to car deck

ΠΡΟΣΔΕΘΗΤΕ προσδεθήτε
fasten your seat belt

προσεκτικός [prosektik**o**s]
careful

πρόσεξε! [pr**o**sexeh!] look out!

ΠΡΟΣΕΧΕ! πρόσεχε!
[pr**o**sekheh!] look out!

προσέχω [pros**e**kho] take care
of

ΠΡΟΣΕΧΩΣ προσεχώς
coming soon

πρόσθετο (το) [pr**o**sτΗeto (to)]
supplementary

προσκαλώ [proskal**o**] invite

πρόσκληση (η) [pr**o**sklisi (i)]
invitation

ΠΡΟΣ ΟΡΟΦΟΥΣ προς
ορόφους to all floors

ΠΡΟΣΟΧΗ! προσοχή!
caution!

ΠΡΟΣΟΧΗ ΑΡΓΑ προσοχή
αργά caution: slow

ΠΡΟΣΟΧΗ ΕΞΟΔΟΣ
ΟΧΗΜΑΤΩΝ προσοχή
έξοδος οχημάτων caution:
vehicle exit

ΠΡΟΣΟΧΗ ΕΥΦΛΕΚΤΟΝ
προσοχή εύφλεκτον caution:
highly inflammable

ΠΡΟΣΟΧΗ ΚΙΝΔΥΝΟΣ
προσοχή κίνδυνος caution:
danger

προσοχή παρακαλώ [pros**o**khi
parakal**o**] attention please

ΠΡΟΣΟΧΗ ΣΚΥΛΟΣ προσοχή
σκύλος beware of the dog

ΠΡΟΣ ΠΑΡΑΣΚΗΝΙΑ προς
παρασκήνια to dressing
rooms

προσπέκτους (το) [prospektoos
(to)] brochure

προσπερνώ [prosperno]
overtake

προστατεύω [prostatevo] protect

ΠΡΟΣΤΙΜΟ πρόστιμο (το)
[prostimo (to)] fine

προσφέρω [prosfero] offer
(verb); give

ΠΡΟΣΦΟΡΑ προσφορά special
bargain

πρόσωπο (το) [prosopo (to)] face

προς [pros] towards

προτείνω [protino] recommend

ΠΡΟΤΕΡΑΙΟΤΗΤΑ
προτεραιότητα (η) right of
way

προτιμώ [protimo] prefer

προφανής [profanis] obvious

προφέρω [profero] pronounce

προφορά (η) [profora (i)] accent

προφυλακτήρας (ο) [profilaktiras
(o)] bumper, fender

ΠΡΟΦΥΛΑΚΤΙΚΑ
προφυλακτικά contraceptives

ΠΡΟΦΥΛΑΚΤΙΚΟ
προφυλακτικό (το) [profilaktiko
(to)] condom

προχτές [prokhtes] the day
before yesterday

πρωί (το) [proi (to)] morning
το πρωί [to proi] in the
morning

ΠΡΩΙΝΟ πρωινό (το) [pro-ino
(to)] breakfast

πρώτα [prota] first, firstly

ΠΡΩΤΕΣ ΒΟΗΘΕΙΕΣ πρώτες
βοήθειες (οι) [protes voiTHi-es (i)]
first aid

ΠΡΩΤΗ ΘΕΣΗ πρώτη θέση
first class

πρώτο! [proto!] great!

ΠΡΩΤΟ ΠΑΤΩΜΑ πρώτο
πάτωμα (το) [proto patoma (to)]
first floor, (US) second floor

πρώτος [protos] first

ΠΡΩΤΟΣ ΟΡΟΦΟΣ πρώτος
όροφος [protos orofos] first
floor, (US) second floor

Πρωτοχρονιά (η) [Protokhronia
(i)] New Year's Day

ΠΤΗΣΕΙΣ ΕΞΩΤΕΡΙΚΟΥ
πτήσεις εξωτερικού
international flights

ΠΤΗΣΕΙΣ ΕΣΩΤΕΡΙΚΟΥ
πτήσεις εσωτερικού domestic
flights

ΠΤΗΣΗ πτήση (η) [ptisi (i)]
flight

ΠΤΗΣΗ ΤΣΑΡΤΕΡ πτήση
τσάρτερ charter flight

πυζάμες (οι) [pizames (i)]
pyjamas

πυξίδα (η) [pixitha (i)] compass

πύργος (ο) [pirgos (o)] tower

πυρετός (ο) [piretos (o)] fever

πυρκαγιά (η) [pirkaya (i)] fire

ΠΥΡΟΣΒΕΣΤΗΡ πυροσβεστήρ
(ο) fire extinguisher

ΠΥΡΟΣΒΕΣΤΗΡΑΣ
πυροσβεστήρας (ο) fire
extinguisher

ΠΥΡΟΣΒΕΣΤΙΚΗ ΣΩΛΗΝΑ
πυροσβεστική σωλήνα (η) fire
hose

ΠΥΡΟΣΒΕΣΤΙΚΗ
(ΥΠΗΡΕΣΙΑ) πυροσβεστική
(υπηρεσία) (η) [pirosvestiki
ipiresia (i)] fire brigade
πυροτεχνήματα (τα)
[pirotekhnimata (ta)] fireworks
πυτζάμες (οι) [pitzames (i)]
pyjamas
ΠΩΛΕΙΤΑΙ πωλείται for sale
ΠΩΛΗΣΗ πώληση (η) sale
πώς; [pos?] how?; what?

Ρ

ράβω [ravo] sew
ραδιόφωνο (το) [rathiofono (to)]
radio
ραντεβού (το) [randevoo (to)]
appointment
ράντζο (το) [randzo (to)]
campbed
ΡΑΦΕΙΟ ραφείο (το) [rafio (to)]
tailor's
ρεζέρβα (η) [rezerva (i)] spare
tyre
ΡΕΣΕΨΙΟΝ ρεσεψιόν (η)
[resepsion (i)] reception
ρεσεψιονίστ (ο/η) [resepsionist
(o/i)] receptionist
ρε συ! [reh si!] you there!, oy
you!
ρεύμα (το) [revma (to)] current;
draught
ρευματισμοί (οι) [revmatismi (i)]
rheumatism
ρίχνω [rikhno] throw (verb)
ρόδα (η) [rotha (i)] wheel
ροζ [roz] pink

ρόκ (η) [rok (i)] rock music
ρολόι (το) [roloi (to)] clock;
watch
ρόμπα (η) [roba (i)] dressing
gown
ΡΟΥΦ - ΓΚΑΡΝΤΕΝ Ρουφ -
Γκάρντεν [Roof - garden] roof
garden
ρούχα (τα) [rookha (ta)] clothes
ροχαλίζω [rokhalizo] snore
ρυμούλκα (η) [rimoolka (i)]
trailer (for car)
ρυμουλκό [rimoolko] trailer (for
car etc)
ρωτώ [roto] ask

Σ

ΣΑΒΒΑΤΟ Σάββατο (το)
[Savato (to)] Saturday
σαββατοκύριακο (το)
[savatokiriako (to)] weekend
ΣΑΓΙΟΝΑΡΕΣ σαγιονάρες
[sayonares] beach sandals,
flip-flops
σαγόνι (το) [sagoni (to)] jaw
σακάκι (το) [sakaki (to)] jacket
σακβουαγιάζ (το) [sakvooayaz
(to)] hand luggage, hand
baggage
σακίδιο (το) [sakithio (to)]
rucksack
σάκος (ο) [sakos (o)] backpack,
rucksack
ΣΑΛΟΝΙ σαλόνι (το) [saloni
(to)] lounge
ΣΑΜΠΟΥΑΝ σαμπουάν (το)
[sampooan (to)] shampoo

σαμπρέλα (η) [sabrela (i)] inner tube

σαν [san] like, as

σανδάλια (τα) [santhalia (ta)] sandals

σάουνα (η) [saoona (i)] sauna

σάπιος [sapios] rotten

ΣΑΠΟΥΝΙ ΠΙΑΤΩΝ σαπούνι πιάτων (το) [sapooni piaton (to)] washing-up liquid

ΣΑΠΟΥΝΙ σαπούνι (το) [sapooni (to)] soap

σαράντα [saranda] forty

σας [sas] you; your

σβήνω [svino] switch off (engine); put out (fire)

ΣΒΗΣΤΕ ΤΗΝ ΜΗΧΑΝΗ σβήστε την μηχανή switch off engine

σβήστρα (η) [svistra (i)] rubber, eraser

σγουρά [sgoora] curly

σε [seh] you; to; at; in

σεζ λόνγκ (η) [sez long (i)] deckchair

ΣΕΙΡΑ σειρά (η) [sira (i)] row (of seats)

σελίδα (η) [selitha (i)] page

ΣΕΛΛΟΤΕΗΠ σέλλοτεηπ (το) [selloteip (to)] Sellotape®, Scotch tape®

ΣΕΛΦ ΣΕΡΒΙΣ σελφ σέρβις [self servis] self-service

σεντόνι (το) [sendoni (to)] sheet

σέξυ [sexi] sexy

ΣΕ ΠΕΡΙΠΤΩΣΗ ΑΝΑΓΚΗΣ ΣΠΑΣΤΕ ΤΟ ΤΖΑΜΙ σε περίπτωση ανάγκης σπάστε το τζάμι in emergency break glass

ΣΕΠΤΕΜΒΡΙΟΣ Σεπτέμβριος (ο) [Septemvrios (o)] September

ΣΕΡΒΙΕΤΕΣ σερβιέτες (οι) [servietes (i)] sanitary towels/napkins

σερβιτόρα (η) [servitora (i)] barmaid; waitress

σερβιτόρος (ο) [servitoros (o)] waiter

ΣΗΚΩΣΤΕ ΤΟ ΑΚΟΥΣΤΙΚΟ σηκώστε το ακουστικό lift receiver

σημαδούρα (η) [simathoora (i)] buoy

σημαία (η) [simea (i)] flag

σημειωματάριο (το) [simiomatario (to)] notebook

ΣΗΜΕΡΑ σήμερα [simera] today

ΣΗΜΕΡΟΝ σήμερον showing today

σήραγγα (η) [siranga (i)] tunnel

σιγά-σιγά [siga-siga] slowly; slow down

σίγουρος [sigooros] sure

σίδερο (το) [sithero (to)] iron

σιδερώνω [sitherono] iron (verb)

ΣΙΔΗΡΟΔΡΟΜΙΚΟΣ ΣΤΑΘΜΟΣ σιδηροδρομικός σταθμός (ο) [sithirothromikos staTHmos (o)] railway station

σιδηρόδρομος (ο) [sithirothromos (o)] railway

ΣΙΔΗΡΟΥΡΓΕΙΟ σιδηρουργείο (το) [sithirooryio (to)] hardware store

ΣΙΝΕΜΑ σινεμά (το) [sinema (to)] cinema, movie theater

σιωπή (η) [siopi (i)] silence

σκάλα (η) [skala (i)] ladder

ΣΚΑΛΕΣ σκάλες (οι) [skales (i)] stairs

σκέπτομαι [skeptomeh] think

ΣΚΗΝΗ σκηνή (η) [skini (i)] tent

σκιά (η) [skia (i)] shade, shadow

στη σκιά [sti skia] in the shade

ΣΚΙΑ ΜΑΤΙΩΝ σκιά ματιών (η) [skia mation (i)] eye shadow

ΣΚΛΗΡΟΙ ΦΑΚΟΙ σκληροί φακοί (οι) [skliri faki (i)] hard lenses

σκληρός [skliros] hard

ΣΚΟΝΗ ΠΛΥΝΤΗΡΙΟΥ σκόνη πλυντηρίου (η) [skoni plindirioo (i)] washing powder

σκοτεινός [skotinos] dark

σκοτώνω [skotonu] kill (verb)

σκουλαρίκια (τα) [skoolarikia (ta)] earrings

σκούπα [skoopa] broom

σκουπίδια (τα) [skoopithia (ta)] rubbish, garbage

σκουπιδοντενεκές (ο) [skoopithondenekes (o)] dustbin, trashcan

σκύλος (ο) [skilos (o)] dog

σκωληκοειδίτις (η) [skoliko-ithitis (i)] appendicitis

ΣΚΩΤΙΑ Σκωτία (η) [Skotia (i)] Scotland

Σκωτσέζικος [Skotsezikos] Scottish

σλάιντ (το) [slaid (to)] slide

σλίπ (το) [slip (to)] underpants; panties

ΣΛΙΠΙΝΓΚ ΜΠΑΓΚ σλίπινγκ

μπαγκ (το) [sliping bag (to)] sleeping bag

σοβαρός [sovaros] serious

σοκ (το) [sok (to)] shock

ΣΟΚΟΛΑΤΑ σοκολάτα (η) [sokolata (i)] chocolate

ΣΟΚΟΛΑΤΑ ΓΑΛΑΚΤΟΣ σοκολάτα γάλακτος (η) [sokolata galaktos (i)] milk chocolate

ΣΟΚΟΛΑΤΑΚΙΑ σοκολατάκια (τα) [sokolatakia (ta)] chocolates

σόλα (η) [sola (i)] sole (of shoe)

σόμπα (η) [soba (i)] oil heater

σορτς (το) [sorts (to)] shorts

σου [soo] you; your

σουγιάς (ο) [sooyas (o)] penknife

ΣΟΥΠΕΡ ΒΕΝΖΙΝΗ σούπερ βενζίνη (η) [sooper venzini (i)] four-star petrol, premium

ΣΟΥΠΕΡΜΑΡΚΕΤ σούπερμάρκετ (το) [soopermarket (to)] supermarket

σουτιέν (το) [sootien (to)] bra

ΣΠΑΓΓΟΣ σπάγγος (ο) [spangos (o)] string

σπασμένος [spasmenos] broken

σπάω [spao] break (verb)

σπηλιά (το) [spilia (to)] cave

σπιράλ (το) [spiral (to)] spiral; IUD; incense coil (mosquito repellent)

σπίρτα (τα) [spirta (ta)] matches

σπίτι (το) [spiti (to)] house

στο σπίτι [sto spiti] at home

σπορ (το) [spor (to)] sport

σπουδαίος [spootheos] important

σπρώχνω [**sprokhno**] push (verb)
σταγόνα (η) [**stagona** (i)] drop
ΣΤΑΓΟΝΕΣ σταγόνες drops
ΣΤΑΔΙΟ στάδιο (το) [**stathio** (to)] stadium
ΣΤΑΘΜΟΣ σταθμός (ο) [**staтHmos** (o)] station
ΣΤΑΘΜΟΣ ΑΝΕΦΟΔΙΑΣΜΟΥ ΘΑΛΑΜΗΓΩΝ σταθμός ανεφοδιασμού θαλαμηγών yacht refuelling station
ΣΤΑΘΜΟΣ ΛΕΩΦΟΡΕΙΩΝ σταθμός λεωφορείων [**staтHmos leoforion**] bus station
ΣΤΑΘΜΟΣ ΠΡΩΤΩΝ ΒΟΗΘΕΙΩΝ σταθμός πρώτων βοηθειών [**staтHmos proton vo-iтHion**] first aid post
ΣΤΑΘΜΟΣ ΤΑΞΙ σταθμός ταξί [**staтHmos taxi**] taxi stand
ΣΤΑΘΜΟΣ ΥΠΕΡΑΣΤΙΚΩΝ ΛΕΩΦΟΡΕΙΩΝ σταθμός υπεραστικών λεωφορείων [**staтHmos iperastikon leoforion**] bus station (long distance)
ΣΤΑΘΜΟΣ ΧΩΡΟΦΥΛΑΚΗΣ σταθμός χωροφυλακής [**staтHmos khorofilakis**] police station
σταματάω [**stamatao**] stop (verb)
ΣΤΑΣΗ στάση (η) [**stasi** (i)] stop (for bus, train)
ΣΤΑΣΗ ΑΣΤΙΚΩΝ ΣΥΓΚΟΙΝΩΝΙΩΝ στάση αστικών συγκοινωνιών city bus stop
ΣΤΑΣΗ ΛΕΩΦΟΡΕΙΟΥ στάση λεωφορείου bus stop
ΣΤΑΣΗ ΤΑΞΙ στάση ταξί [**stasi taxi**] taxi stand
ΣΤΑΣΙΣ στάσις (η) [**stasis** (i)] bus stop
στέγη (η) [**steyi** (i)] roof
ΣΤΕΓΝΟ ΚΑΘΑΡΙΣΜΑ ΜΟΝΟΝ στεγνό καθάρισμα μόνον dryclean only
ΣΤΕΓΝΟΚΑΘΑΡΙΣΤΗΡΙΟ στεγνοκαθαριστήριο (το) [**stegnokaтHaristirio** (to)] dry cleaner's
στεγνός [**stegnos**] dry
στεγνώνω [**stegnono**] dry (verb)
στέλνω [**stelno**] send
στενός [**stenos**] narrow; tight
στενοχώρια (η) [**stenokhoria** (i)] worry (verb)
στήθος (το) [**stiтHos** (to)] breast; chest
στην [**stin**] at; in; to; on
ΣΤΙΒΟΣ στίβος (ο) athletics stadium
στο [**sto**] at; in; to
στόμα (το) [**stoma** (to)] mouth
στομάχι (το) [**stomakhi** (to)] stomach
στον [**ston**] at; in; to;
ΣΤΟΠ! στοπ! stop!
στριφτό (το) [**strifto** (to)] hand-rolled cigarette
στρογγυλός [**strongilos**] round
στρόφαλος (ο) [**strofalos** (o)] crankshaft
στροφή (η) [**strofi** (i)] bend
στρώμα (το) [**stroma** (to)] mattress
στυλό (το) [**stilo** (to)] biro®
συγγενείς (οι) [**singenis** (i)] relatives

συγγνώμη [signomi] sorry;
excuse me
συγγνώμη; [signomi?] pardon
(me)?, sorry?
σύγκρουση (η) [singroosi (i)]
crash
συγχαρητήρια! [sinkharitiria!]
congratulations!
συγχωρείτε: με συγχωρείτε
[meh sinkhoriteh] excuse me
σύζυγος (o) [sizigos (o)] husband
συκότι (το) [sikoti (to)] liver
συλλαμβάνω [silamvano] arrest
συλλογή (η) [siloyi (i)]
collection
συμβαίνω [simveno] happen
συμβουλεύω [simvoolevo] advise
ΣΥΜΠΕΡΙΛΑΜΒΑΝΕΤΑΙ
συμπεριλαμβάνεται included
συμπλέκτης (o) [siblektis (o)]
clutch
συμφωνώ [simfono] agree
ΣΥΝΑΓΕΡΜΟΣ συναγερμός
(o) [sinayermos (o)] alarm
συναίσθημα (το) [sinesTHima (to)]
feeling
ΣΥΝΑΛΛΑΓΜΑ συνάλλαγμα
(το) [sinalagma (to)] foreign
exchange
ΣΥΝΑΛΛΑΓΜΑΤΙΚΗ
ΙΣΟΤΙΜΙΑ συναλλαγματική
ισοτιμία (η) [sinalagmatiki
isotimia (i)] exchange rate
συνάντηση (η) [sinandisi (i)]
meeting
συναντώ [sinando] meet
συναρπαστικός [sinarpastikos]
exciting
συναυλία (η) [sinavlia (i)]

concert
ΣΥΝ/ΓΕΙΟ συν/γειο auto
repairs
σύνδεση (η) [sinthesi (i)]
connection (electrical)
ΣΥΝΕΡΓΕΙΟ
(ΑΥΤΟΚΙΝΗΤΩΝ) συνεργείο
(αυτοκινήτων) (το) auto
repairs
συνήθεια (η) [siniTHia (i)] habit
συνηθισμένος [siniTHismenos]
usual
συνήθως [siniTHos] usually
ΣΥΝΘΕΤΙΚΟ συνθετικό
synthetic
συννεφιασμένος [sinefiasmenos]
cloudy
σύννεφο (το) [sinefo (to)] cloud
συνοδεύω [sinothevo]
accompany
ΣΥΝΟΙΚΙΑ συνοικία (η)
[sinikia (i)] district
συνολικά [sinolika] altogether
σύνορα (τα) [sinora (ta)] border
συνταγή (η) [sindayi (i)]
prescription; recipe
συνταξιούχος (o/η)
[sindaxiookhos (o/i)] old-age
pensioner
ΣΥΝΤΗΡΗΤΙΚΟ ΔΙΑΛΥΜΑ
συντηρητικό διάλυμα (το)
[sindiritiko thialima (to)] soaking
solution
σύντομα [sindoma] soon
ΣΥΡΑΤΕ σύρατε pull
σύρμα (το) [sirma (to)] wire
ΣΥΣΤΑΤΙΚΑ συστατικά
ingredients
ΣΥΣΤΗΜΕΝΑ συστημένα

[sistimena] registered mail

συστήνω [sistino] introduce; recommend

συχνά [sikhna] often

σφήγγα (η) [sfinga (i)] wasp

σφράγισμα (το) [sfrayisma (to)] filling (in tooth)

σφυρί (το) [sfiri (to)] hammer

σχάρα αυτοκινήτου (η) [skhara aftokinitoo (i)] roof rack

σχέδιο (το) [skhethio (to)] plan

σχεδόν [skhethon] almost

σχοινί (το) [skhini (to)] rope

ΣΧΟΛΕΙΟ σχολείο (το) [skholio (to)] school

σωλήνας (ο) [solinas (o)] pipe (water)

σώμα (το) [soma (to)] body

ΣΩΣΙΒΙΑ σωσίβια lifejackets

σωστός [sostos] correct

T

τα [ta] the; them

ταβάνι (το) [tavani (to)] ceiling

ΤΑΒΕΡΝΑ ταβέρνα (η) [taverna (i)] restaurant

τακούνι (το) [takooni (to)] heel (of shoe)

ΤΑΛΗΡΟ τάληρο (το) [taliro (to)] 5-drachma coin

ΤΑΜΕΙΟ ταμείο (το) [tamio (to)] box office; cash desk, till, cashier

ΤΑΜΙΕΥΤΗΡΙΟ ταμιευτήριο (το) [tami-eftirio (to)] savings bank

ΤΑΜΠΛΕΤΑ ταμπλέτα (η)

[tableta (i)] tablet

ΤΑΜΠΟΝ ταμπόν (τα) [tampon (ta)] tampons

τάξη (η) [taxi (i)] class

ΤΑΞΙ ταξί (το) [taxi (to)] taxi

ταξιδεύω [taxithevo] travel (verb)

ταξίδι (το) [taxithi (to)] journey, trip

καλό ταξίδι! [kalo taxithi!] have a good journey!, bon voyage!

ταξίδι για δουλειές [taxithi ya thoolies] business trip

ΤΑΞΙΔΙΩΤΙΚΗ ΕΠΙΤΑΓΗ ταξιδιωτική επιταγή (η) [taxithiotiki epitayi (i)] traveller's cheque/traveler's check

ΤΑΞΙΔΙΩΤΙΚΟ ΓΡΑΦΕΙΟ ταξιδιωτικό γραφείο (το) [taxithiotiko grafio (to)] travel agent's

τάπα (η) [tapa (i)] plug (in sink)

ΤΑ ΡΕΣΤΑ ΣΑΣ τα ρέστα σας your change

ΤΑΡΙΦΑ ταρίφα [tarifa] taxi tariff

τασάκι (το) [tasaki (to)] ashtray

ταύρος (ο) [tavros (o)] bull

ΤΑΥΤΟΤΗΤΑ ταυτότητα (η) [taftotita (i)] pass, identity card

ΤΑΧΥΔΡΟΜΕΙΟ ταχυδρομείο (το) [takhithromio (to)] post office

ΤΑΧΥΔΡΟΜΙΚΟΣ ΤΟΜΕΥΣ ταχυδρομικός τομεύς (ο) [takhithromikos tomefs (o)] postcode, zipcode

ταχυδρόμος (ο) [takhithromos (o)] postman

ταχυδρομώ [takhithromo] post,
mail (verb)

ταχύτητα (η) [takhitita (i)] gear
(in car)

ταχύτητα (η) [takhitita (i)] speed

τέλειος [telios] perfect

τελειώνω [teliono] finish (verb)

ΤΕΛΕΥΤΑΙΑ ΠΑΡΑΣΤΑΣΗ
τελευταία παράσταση last
performance

τελευταίος [telefteos] last

τελεφερίκ (το) [teleferik (to)]
cable car

ΤΕΛΟΣ τέλος (το) [telos (to)]
end

ΤΕΛΩΝΕΙΟ Τελωνείο (το)
[Telonio (to)] Customs

τεμπέλης [tebelis] lazy

τέννις (το) [tenis (to)] tennis

τέντα (η) [tenda (i)] tent,
marquee

τέσσερα [tesera] four

ΤΕΤΑΡΤΗ Τετάρτη (η) [Tetarti
(i)] Wednesday

τέταρτο (το) [tetarto (to)]
quarter

τέταρτος [tetartos] fourth

τέχνη (η) [tekhni (i)] art

τεχνητός [tekhnitos] artificial

ΤΕΧΝΗΤΟ ΧΡΩΜΑ τεχνητό
χρώμα artificial colouring

τζαζ (η) [tzaz (i)] jazz

τζηνς (τα) [tzins (ta)] jeans

τζόγγιγκ (το) [tzoging (to)]
jogging

τη [ti] the

τηγάνι (το) [tigani (to)] frying
pan

τηγανίζω [tiganizo] fry

ΤΗΛΕΓΡΑΦΗΜΑ
τηλεγράφημα (το) [tilegrafima
(to)] telegram

ΤΗΛΕΓΡΑΦΗΜΑΤΑ
τηλεγραφήματα telegrams

ΤΗΛΕΓΡΑΦΙΚΗ ΕΝΤΟΛΗ
τηλεγραφική εντολή [tilegrafiki
endoli] telegram

ΤΗΛΕΚΑΡΤΑ τηλεκάρτα (η)
[tilekarta (i)] phonecard

ΤΗΛΕΟΡΑΣΗ τηλεόραση (η)
[tileorasi (i)] television

ΤΗΛΕΦΩΝΗΜΑ τηλεφώνημα
[tilefonima] call

ΤΗΛΕΦΩΝΗΜΑ ΚΟΛΛΕΚΤ
τηλεφώνημα κολλέκτ (το)
[tilefonima kollekt (to)] reverse
charge call

ΤΗΛΕΦΩΝΙΚΗ ΕΝΤΟΛΗ
τηλεφωνική εντολή operator-
controlled phone call

ΤΗΛΕΦΩΝΙΚΟΣ ΘΑΛΑΜΟΣ
τηλεφωνικός θάλαμος (ο)
[tilefonikos THalamos (o)] phone
box

ΤΗΛΕΦΩΝΙΚΟΣ
ΚΑΤΑΛΟΓΟΣ τηλεφωνικός
κατάλογος (ο) [tilefonikos
katalogos (o)] phone book

ΤΗΛΕΦΩΝΟ τηλέφωνο (το)
[tilefono (to)] phone

ΤΗΛΕΦΩΝΩ τηλεφωνώ
[tilefono] ring, phone (verb)

την [tin] her; on; per; the

την εβδομάδα [tin evthomatha]
per week

της [tis] her; to her; of her

τι; [ti?] what?

ΤΙΜΗ τιμή (η) [timi (i)] price

ΤΙΜΗ ΑΓΟΡΑΣ τιμή αγοράς buying rate

ΤΙΜΗ ΑΝΕΥ ΠΟΣΟΣΤΩΝ τιμή άνευ ποσοστών price exclusive of extras

ΤΙΜΗ ΔΩΜΑΤΙΟΥ τιμή δωματίου room price

ΤΙΜΗ ΚΑΤ' ΑΤΟΜΟ τιμή κατ' άτομο price per person

ΤΙΜΗ ΚΛΙΝΗΣ τιμή κλίνης price per bed

ΤΙΜΗ ΜΕΤΑ ΠΟΣΟΣΤΩΝ τιμή μετά ποσοστών price inclusive of extras

ΤΙΜΗ ΠΩΛΗΣΗΣ τιμή πώλησης selling rate

τίμιος [timios] honest

τιμόνι (το) [timoni (to)] steering wheel

τίνος; [tinos?] whose

τίποτε [tipoteh] nothing

ΤΙΠΟΤΕ ΠΡΟΣ ΔΗΛΩΣΗ τίποτε προς δήλωση nothing to declare

τις [tis] them

ΤΜΗΜΑ τμήμα (το) [tmima (to)] department

το [to] in; it; the; per

τοις εκατό [tis ekato] per cent

ΤΟΙΣ ΜΕΤΡΗΤΟΙΣ τοις μετρητοίς cash only, no credit cards

τοίχος (ο) [tikhos (o)] wall

ΤΟ ΚΑΤΑΣΤΗΜΑ ΜΕΤΑΦΕΡΘΗΚΕ ΕΙΣ ... το κατάστημα μεταφέρθηκε εις ... we have moved to ...

ΤΟ ΚΟΜΜΑΤΙ το κομμάτι per item

ΤΟΚΟΣ τόκος (ο) [tokos (o)] interest

τολμάω [tolmao] dare (verb)

τον [ton] him; the

ΤΟΞΙΚΟ τοξικό toxic

ΤΟΠΙΚΗ ΩΡΑ τοπική ώρα local time

ΤΟΠΙΚΟ (ΤΗΛΕΦΩΝΗΜΑ) τοπικό (τηλεφώνημα) (το) [topiko tilefonima (to)] local call

τοπίο (το) [topio (to)] landscape

τόσο [toso] so (much); that much

τότε [toteh] then

του [too] his; its; to him

ΤΟΥΑΛΕΤΑ τουαλέτα (η) [tooaleta (i)] toilet, rest room

ΤΟΥΑΛΕΤΑ ΤΩΝ ΓΥΝΑΙΚΩΝ τουαλέτα των γυναικών (η) [tooaleta ton yinekon (i)] ladies' toilet, ladies' room

ΤΟΥΑΛΕΤΕΣ τουαλέτες [tooaletes] toilets, rest room

τουλάχιστον [toolakhiston] at least

του οποίου [too opioo] whose

τουρίστας (ο) [tooristas (o)] tourist

ΤΟΥΡΙΣΤΙΚΗ ΑΣΤΥΝΟΜΙΑ Τουριστική Αστυνομία (η) [Tooristiki Astinomia (i)] Tourist Police

τουριστικός οδηγός (ο) [tooristikos othigos (o)] guidebook

τουρίστρια (η) [tooristria (i)] tourist

ΤΟΥΡΚΑΛΑ τουρκάλα (η)

[toorkala (i)] Turk

ΤΟΥΡΚΙΑ Τουρκία (η) [Toorkia (i)] Turkey

Τούρκος (ο) [Toorkos (o)] Turk

ΤΟΥΡΚΙΚΟΣ Τουρκικός [Toorkikos] Turkish (adj)

τους [toos] them; to them

τραβάω [travao] pull (verb)

τραγούδι (το) [tragoothi (to)] song

τραγουδώ [tragootho] sing

ΤΡΑΠΕΖΑΡΙΑ τραπεζαρία (η) [trapezaria (i)] dining room

ΤΡΑΠΕΖΑ τράπεζα (η) [trapeza (i)] bank

τραπέζι (το) [trapezi (to)] table

τραπεζομάντηλο (το) [trapezomandilo (to)] tablecloth

τραυματίζομαι [travmatizomeh] hurt, injure

τραυματισμένος [travmatismenos] injured

τρελλός [trelos] mad

ΤΡΕΝΟ τρένο (το) [treno (to)] train

τρέχω [trekho] run (verb)

τρία [tria] three

τριακόσια [triakosia] three hundred

τριάντα [trianda] thirty

τριαντάφυλλο (το) [triandafilo (to)] rose

ΤΡΙΚΛΙΝΟ ΔΩΜΑΤΙΟ τρίκλινο δωμάτιο (το) [triklino thomatio (to)] triple room

ΤΡΙΤΗ Τρίτη (η) [Triti (i)] Tuesday

ΤΡΙΤΗ ΘΕΣΗ τρίτη θέση third class

τρίτος [tritos] third

τρόλλεϋ (το) [troleh-i (to)] trolley, trolleybus

τρομερός [tromeros] tremendous

ΤΡΟΦΗ ΓΙΑ ΔΙΑΒΗΤΙΚΟΥΣ τροφή γιά διαβητικούς [trofi ya thiavitikoos] diabetic foods

τροφική δηλητηρίαση (η) [trofiki thilitiriasi (i)] food poisoning

ΤΡΟΧΑΙΑ τροχαία (η) traffic police

τροχονόμος (ο) [trokhonomos (o)] traffic warden

τροχόσπιτο (το) [trokhospito (to)] caravan, (US) trailer

ΤΡΟΧΟΣΠΙΤΑ τροχόσπιτα (το) [trokhospita (to)] caravans, (US) trailers

τρύπα (η) [tripa (i)] hole

τρώω [troo] eat; have dinner

τσαγιέρα (η) [tsayera (i)] teapot

ΤΣΑΓΚΑΡΗΣ τσαγκάρης (ο) [tsangaris (o)] shoe repairer's

τσάντα (η) [tsanda (i)] bag; handbag, (US) purse

ΤΣΑΝΤΕΣ ΜΠΑΝΙΟΥ τσάντες μπάνιου beach bags

τσέπη (η) [tsepi (i)] pocket

ΤΣΙΓΑΡΟ τσιγάρο (το) [tsigaro (to)] cigarette

τσίμπημα (το) [tsibima (to)] bite (insect)

τσιμπιδάκι (το) [tsibithaki (to)] tweezers

τσιμπώ [tsibo] sting (verb)

ΤΣΙΠΣ τσιπς (τα) [tsips (ta)] crisps, (US) potato chips

ΤΣΙΧΛΑ τσίχλα (η) [tsikhla (i)] chewing gum

A
B
Γ
Δ
E
Z
H
Θ
I
K
Λ
M
N
Ξ
O
Π
P
Σ
T
Y
Φ
X
Ψ
Ω

τσόκ (το) [tsok (to)] choke (on car)

τσούχτρα (η) [tsookhtra (i)] jellyfish

τυλίγω [tiligo] wrap (verb)

τυφλός [tiflos] blind

τύχη (η) [tikhi (i)] luck
καλή τύχη! [kali tikhi!] good luck!

των [ton] of them

τώρα [tora] now

Υ

υαλοκαθαριστήρας (ο) [ialokaTHaristiras (o)] windscreen wiper

υγεία: στην υγειά σας/σου! [stin iya sas/soo!] your health!, cheers!

υγιής [iyi-is] healthy

ΥΓΡΑΕΡΙΟ υγραέριο (το) [igraerio (to)] camping gas

υγρός [igros] damp, wet

ΥΔΡΑΥΛΙΚΑ υδραυλικά (τα) [ithravlika (ta)] plumber

ΥΔΡΑΥΛΙΚΟΣ υδραυλικός (ο) [ithravlikos (o)] plumber

υπάρχει [iparkhi] there is

υπάρχουν [iparkhoon] there are

ΥΠΕΡΑΣΤΙΚΟ (ΤΗΛΕΦΩΝΗΜΑ) υπεραστικό (τηλεφώνημα) (το) [iperastiko tilefonima (to)] long-distance call, international call

υπερβάλλω [ipervallo] exaggerate

υπέρβαρο (το) [ipervaro (to)] excess baggage

υπερβολικά [ipervolika] too

υπερήφανος [iperifanos] proud

ΥΠΕΡΠΟΛΥΤΕΛΕΙΑΣ υπερπολυτελειας five-star (hotel)

υπεύθυνος [ipefTHinos] responsible

ΥΠΗΡΕΣΙΑ υπηρεσία (η) [ipiresia (i)] service

ύπνυ: πάω για ύπνο [pao ya ipno] go to bed

υπνοδωμάτιο (το) [ipnothomatio (to)] bedroom

ύπνος (ο) [ipnos (o)] sleep

ΥΠΝΩΤΙΚΟ ΧΑΠΙ υπνωτικό χάπι (το) [ipnotiko khapi (to)] sleeping pill

ΥΠΟΓΕΙΑ ΔΙΑΒΑΣΗ ΠΕΖΩΝ υπόγεια διάβαση πεζών (η) pedestrian subway

ΥΠΟΓΕΙΟ υπόγειο (το) [ipoyio (to)] basement

ΥΠΟΓΕΙΟΣ υπόγειος (ο) [ipoyios (o)] underground, (US) subway

υπογράφω [ipografo] sign (verb)

ΥΠΟΔΗΜΑΤΑ υποδήματα (τα) [ipothimata (ta)] shoes

ΥΠΟΔΗΜΑΤΑ ΓΥΝΑΙΚΕΙΑ υποδήματα γυναικεία [ipothimata yinekia] ladies' shoes

ΥΠΟΔΗΜΑΤΟΠΟΙΕΙΟ υποδηματοποιείο (το) [ipothimatopi-io (to)] shoe shop

υπολογιστής (ο) [ipoloyistis (o)] computer

υπόλοιπο (το) [ipolipo (to)] rest,

remainder

υπόσχομαι [iposkhomeh] promise (verb)

ΥΠΟΥΡΓΕΙΟ υπουργείο (το) ministry

ύφασμα (το) [ifasma (to)] material

ΥΦΑΣΜΑΤΑ υφάσματα [ifasmata] clothing; cloth, material

Φ

ΦΑΓΗΤΟ φαγητό (το) [fayito (to)] food; meal; lunch

φαγούρα (η) [fagoora (i)] itch

φάκελος (ο) [fakelos (o)] envelope

ΦΑΚΟΙ ΕΠΑΦΗΣ φακοί επαφής (οι) [faki epafis (i)] contact lenses

φακός (ο) [fakos (o)] lens; torch

φαλακρός [falakros] bald

φαλλοκράτης (ο) [falokratis (o)] male chauvinist

φανάρια τροχαίας (τα) [fanaria trokheas (ta)] traffic lights

φανταστικός [fandastikos] fantastic

ΦΑΡΜΑΚΕΙΟ φαρμακείο (το) [farmakio (to)] chemist's, pharmacy

φάρμακο (το) [farmako (to)] medicine

φαρμακοποιός (ο) [farmakopios (o)] chemist, pharmacist

φασαρία (η) [fasaria (i)] noise

ΦΕΒΡΟΥΑΡΙΟΣ Φεβρουάριος (ο) [Fevrooarios (o)] February

φεγγάρι (το) [fengari (to)] moon

φεμινίστρια (η) [feministria (i)] feminist

φερμουάρ (το) [fermooar (to)] zip

φέρνω [ferno] bring

ΦΕΡΡΥ ΜΠΩΤ φέρρυ μπωτ (το) [feri bot (to)] ferry

φέτα (η) [feta (i)] slice

φεύγω [fevgo] go away

φθινόπωρο (το) [fTHinoporo (to)] autumn, (US) fall

φίδι (το) [fithi (to)] snake

φιλενάδα (η) [filenatha (i)] girlfriend; friend

φιλί (το) [fili (to)] kiss

ΦΙΛΜ φιλμ (το) [film (to)] film, movie

ΦΙΛΟΔΩΡΗΜΑ φιλοδώρημα (το) [filothorima (to)] service charge; tip

φιλοξενία (η) [filoxenia (i)] hospitality

φιλοξενούμενη (η) [filoxenoomeni (i)] guest

φιλοξενούμενος (ο) [filoxenoomenos (o)] guest

φίλος (ο) [filos (o)] boyfriend; friend

φιλοφρόνηση (η) [filofronisi (i)] compliment

φίλτρο (το) [filtro (to)] filter

φιλώ [filo] kiss (verb)

φλας (το) [flas (to)] flash; indicator

φλέβα (η) [fleva (i)] vein

φλυτζάνι (το) [flitzani (to)] cup

φοβάμαι [fovameh] be afraid

φοβερός [foveros] terrible

φόβος (o) [fovos (o)] fear

φοιτητής (o) [fititis (o)] student

ΦΟΙΤΗΤΙΚΑ ΕΙΣΙΤΗΡΙΑ
φοιτητικά εισιτήρια [fititika
isitiria] student tickets

φοιτήτρια (η) [fititria (i)] student

φορά (η) [fora (i)] time,
occasion

φόρεμα (το) [forema (to)] dress

φορτηγό (το) [fortigo (to)] lorry

ΦΟΥΑΓΙΕ φουαγιέ (το) [fooaye
(to)] foyer

ΦΟΥΛ ΠΑΝΣΙΟΝ φουλ
πανσιόν (η) [fool pansion (i)] full
board

ΦΟΥΛ-ΣΑΙΖΟΝ φουλ-σαιζόν
high season

ΦΟΥΡΝΟΣ φούρνος (o)
[foornos (o)] baker's; oven

φουσκάλα (η) [fooskala (i)]
blister

φούστα (η) [foosta (i)] skirt

φρακαρισμένος [frakarismenos]
blocked; stuck

φράκτης (o) [fraktis (o)] fence

φρενάρω [frenaro] brake (verb)

φρένο (το) [freno (to)] brake

ΦΡΕΣΚΟΣ φρέσκος [freskos]
fresh

φρικτός [friktos] horrible

φρύδι (το) [frithi (to)] eyebrow

φτάνει [ftani] that's enough

φτάνω [ftano] arrive

φτέρνα (η) [fterna (i)] heel (of
foot)

φτερνίζομαι [fternizomeh]
sneeze (verb)

φτερό (το) [ftero (to)] wing

ΦΤΗΝΟΣ φτηνός [ftinos]

cheap, inexpensive

φτιάχνω τις βαλίτσες [ftiakhno tis
valitses] pack (verb)

φτυάρι (το) [ftiari (to)] spade

φτωχός [ftokhos] poor

φύγε! [fiyeh!] go away!

φύκια (τα) [fikia (ta)] seaweed

ΦΥΛΑΚΗ φυλακή (η) [filaki (i)]
prison

ΦΥΛΑΞΗ ΑΠΟΣΚΕΥΩΝ
φύλαξη αποσκευών [filaxi
aposkevon] left luggage,
baggage check

φύλλο (το) [filo (to)] leaf

φύλο (το) [filo (to)] gender

φύση (η) [fisi (i)] nature

ΦΥΣΙΚΟ ΠΡΟΪΟΝ φυσικό
προϊόν natural product

ΦΥΣΙΚΟΣ φυσικός [fisikos]
natural

ΦΥΣΙΚΟ ΧΡΩΜΑ φυσικό
χρώμα natural colouring

φυσιολογικός [fisioloyikos]
normal

ΦΥΤΟ φυτό (το) [fito (to)] plant

φωνάζω [fonazo] call; shout
(verb)

φωνή (η) [foni (i)] voice

ΦΩΣ φως (το) [fos (to)] light

φώτα (τα) [fota (ta)] lights (on
car)

ΦΩΤΙΑ φωτιά (η) [fotia (i)] fire
έχεις φωτιά; [ekhis fotia?] have
you got a light?

φωτογραφία (η) [fotografia (i)]
photograph

ΦΩΤΟΓΡΑΦΙΚΑ φωτογραφικά
cameras

φωτογραφική μηχανή (η)

[fotografiki mikhani (i)] camera
φωτόμετρο (το) [fotometro (to)]
light meter

X
—

χαίρετε [khereteh] hello
χαλάκι (το) [khalaki (to)] rug
χαλί (το) [khali (to)] carpet
χάλια [khalia] awful
χαμηλά φώτα (τα) [khamila fota
(ta)] sidelights
χαμηλός [khamilos] low
χαμόγελο (το) [khamoyelo (to)]
smile
χαμογελώ [khamoyelo] smile
(verb)
χάνω [khano] lose; miss
ΧΑΠΙ χάπι (το) [khapi (to)] pill
χάρηκα! [kharika!] pleased to
meet you!
ΧΑΡΠΙΚ χάρπικ (το) [kharpik
(to)] bleach (for toilet)
ΧΑΡΤΗΣ χάρτης (ο) [khartis (o)]
map
ΧΑΡΤΙ χαρτί (το) [kharti (to)]
paper
χαρτιά (τα) [khartia (ta)] playing
cards
ΧΑΡΤΙ ΑΛΛΗΛΟΓΡΑΦΙΑΣ
χαρτί αλληλογραφίας (το)
[kharti alilografias (to)] writing
paper
ΧΑΡΤΙΚΑ χαρτικά (τα)
[khartika (ta)] stationery
ΧΑΡΤΙ ΠΕΡΙΤΥΛΙΓΜΑΤΟΣ
χαρτί περιτυλίγματος [kharti
peritiligmatos] wrapping paper

ΧΑΡΤΙ ΥΓΕΙΑΣ χαρτί υγείας
[kharti iyias] toilet paper
ΧΑΡΤΟΜΑΝΤΗΛΑ
χαρτομάντηλα (τα)
[khartomandila (ta)] tissues,
Kleenex®
χαρτόνι (το) [khartoni (to)]
cardboard
χαρτονόμισμα [khartonomisma]
banknote, (US) bill
ΧΑΡΤΟΠΩΛΕΙΟ χαρτοπωλείο
(το) [khartopolio (to)] stationer's
χαρτοφύλακας (ο) [khartofilakas
(0)] briefcase
ΧΑΣΑΠΗΣ χασάπης (ο)
[khasapis (0)] butcher's
χείλι (το) [khili (to)] lip
ΧΕΙΜΕΡΙΝΟΣ χειμερινός
[khimerinos] (winter)
cinema/movie theater
χειμώνας (ο) [khimonas (0)]
winter
ΧΕΙΡΟΠΟΙΗΤΟ χειροποίητο
[khiropi-ito] handmade
χειρότερος [khiroteros] worse
χειρότερος (ο) [khiroteros (0)]
worst
ΧΕΙΡΟΤΕΧΝΙΑ χειροτεχνία
(η) crafts
χειρόφρενο (το) [khirofreno (to)]
handbrake
χέρι (το) [kheri (to)] arm; hand
χερούλι (το) [kherooli (to)]
handle
χήρα (η) [khira (i)] widow
χήρος (ο) [khiros (0)] widower
χθες [khthes] yesterday
ΧΙΛ. χιλ. thousand,
thousands

ΧΙΛΙΑ χίλια [khilia] thousand, thousands

ΧΙΛΙΑΔΕΣ χιλιάδες [khiliathes] thousand, thousands

ΧΙΛΙΑΡΙΚΟ χιλιάρικο (το) [khiliariko (to)] 1,000–drachma note/bill

χιλιόμετρο (το) [khiliometro (to)] kilometre

χιούμορ (το) [khioomor (to)] humour

χλιαρός [khliaros] lukewarm; cool

ΧΛΩΡΙΝΗ χλωρίνη (η) [khlorini (i)] bleach

χόμπυ (το) [khobi (to)] hobby

ΧΟΝΔΡΙΚΗΣ χονδρικής wholesale

χορεύω [khorevo] dance (verb)

χορός (ο) [khoros (o)] dance

χορτάρι (το) [khortari (to)] grass

χορτοφαγικός [khortofayikos] vegetarian

χορτοφάγος (ο/η) [khortofagos (o/i)] vegetarian

χρειάζομαι [khriazomeh] need (verb)

ΧΡΗΜΑΤΙΣΤΗΡΙΟ χρηματιστήριο (το) [khrimatistirio (to)] currency exchange; stock exchange

χρήση (η) [khrisi (i)] use

χρησιμοποιώ [khrisimopio] use (verb)

χρήσιμος [khrisimos] useful

Χριστούγεννα (τα) [KHristooyena (ta)] Christmas

Καλά Χριστούγεννα! [Kala KHristooyena!] Happy Christmas!

χρονιά (η) [khronia (i)] year

Χρόνια Πολλά! [khronia pola!] Happy Birthday!

του χρόνου [too khronoo] next year

πόσο χρονών είσαι; [poso khronon iseh?] how old are you?

χρόνος (ο) [khronos (o)] time; year

ΧΡΥΣΟΣ χρυσός (ο) [khrisos (o)] gold

ΧΡΥΣΟΣ ΟΔΗΓΟΣ χρυσός οδηγός (ο) [khrisos othigos (o)] yellow pages

ΧΡΥΣΟΧΟΕΙΟ χρυσοχοείο (το) [khrisokhoio (to)] jeweller's

χρώμα (το) [khroma (to)] colour

ΧΡΩΜΑΤΑ - ΣΙΔΕΡΙΚΑ χρώματα - σιδερικά paint and hardware store

χτένα (η) [khtena (i)] comb

χτυπώ [khtipo] hit (verb)

χώμα (το) [khoma (to)] earth

χώρα (η) [khora (i)] country

χωράφι (το) [khorafi (to)] field

ΧΩΡΗΤΙΚΟΤΗΤΟΣ ... ΑΤΟΜΩΝ χωρητικότητος ... ατόμων max load ... persons

χωριό (το) [khorio (to)] village

χωρίς [khoris] without

ΧΩΡΙΣ ΕΙΣΠΡΑΚΤΟΡΑ χωρίς εισπράκτορα no ticket collector

χωρισμένος [khorismenos] divorced

ΧΩΡΙΣ ΜΠΑΝΙΟ χωρίς μπάνιο [khoris banio] without

bathroom

ΧΩΡΙΣ ΝΤΟΥΣ χωρίς ντους [khoris doos] without shower

ΧΩΡΙΣ ΣΥΝΤΗΡΗΤΙΚΑ χωρίς συντηρητικά no preservatives

χωριστός [khoristos] separate

ΧΩΡΟΣ ΔΙΑ ΠΟΔΗΛΑΤΕΣ χώρος διά ποδηλάτες cycle path

χώρος φύλαξης αποσκευών (ο) [khoros filaxis aposkevon (o)] left luggage, baggage check

Ψ

ψαλίδι (το) [psalithi (to)] scissors

ΨΑΡΑΔΙΚΟ ψαράδικο (το) [psarathiko (to)] fishmonger's

ψάρεμα (το) [psarema (to)] fishing

ΨΑΡΟΤΑΒΕΡΝΑ ψαροταβέρνα (η) [psarotaverna (i)] restaurant specializing in seafood

ψάχνω [psakhno] look for

ψέματα: λέω ψέματα [leo psemata] lie (say untruth)

ψεύτικος [pseftikos] false

ψήνω [psino] bake

ΨΗΣΤΑΡΙΑ ψησταριά (η) [psistaria (i)] restaurant specializing in charcoal-grilled food

ψιλά (τα) [psila (ta)] small change

ΨΙΛΙΚΑ ψιλικά (τα) [psilika (ta)] small shop

ψυγείο (το) [psiyio (to)] fridge

ψυγείο αυτοκινήτου (το) [psiyio aftokinitoo (to)] radiator (car)

ΨΩΜΑΔΙΚΟ ψωμάδικο [psomathiko] baker's

ψωμάς (ο) [psomas (o)] baker

ψηλός [psilos] high; tall

ψώνια (τα) [psonia (ta)] shopping

πάω για ψώνια [pao ya psonia] go shopping

Ω

ΩΘΗΣΑΤΕ ωθήσατε push

ώμος (ο) [omos (o)] shoulder

ώρα (η) [ora (i)] hour

τι ώρα είναι; [ti ora ineh?] what time is it?

σε λίγη ώρα [seh liyi ora] soon

στην ώρα του [stin ora too] on time

ωραίος [oreos] beautiful; handsome; lovely

ΩΡΕΣ ΕΠΙΣΚΕΨΕΩΣ ώρες επισκέψεως visiting hours

ΩΡΕΣ ΛΕΙΤΟΥΡΓΕΙΑΣ ώρες λειτουργείας opening hours

ως [os] as, since

ΩΤΟΡΙΝΟΛΑΡΥΓΓΟΛΟΓΟΣ ωτορινολαρυγγολόγος (ο/η) ear, nose and throat specialist

ωτοστόπ (το) [otostop (to)] hitchhiking

ωτοστόπ: κάνω ωτοστόπ [kano otostop] hitchhike

Menu
Reader:
Food

Essential Terms

bread to psomi
butter to vootiro
cup to flidzani
dessert to glikisma
fish to psari
fork to pirooni
glass to potiri
knife to makheri
main course to kirio piato
meat to kreas
menu to menoo
pepper to piperi
plate to piato
salad i salata
salt to alati
set menu to tabl-dot
soup i soopa
spoon to kootali
starter to proto piato
table to trapezi

another ..., please ali mia ..., parakalo
excuse me! parakalo
could I have the bill, please? boro na ekho ton logariasmo,
parakalo?

ΑΓΓΙΝΑΡΕΣ ΑΥΓΟΛΕΜΟΝΟ
αγγινάρες αυγολέμονο
[aginares avgolemono]
artichokes in egg and
lemon sauce

ΑΓΓΟΥΡΑΚΙΑ αγγουράκια
[agoorakia] cucumbers

ΑΓΓΟΥΡΙ αγγούρι [agoori]
cucumber

ΑΓΓΟΥΡΙΑ ΚΑΙ ΝΤΟΜΑΤΕΣ
ΣΑΛΑΤΑ αγγούρια και
ντομάτες σαλάτα [agooria keh
domates salata] cucumber and
tomato salad

ΑΚΤΙΝΙΔΙΟ ακτινίδιο
[aktinithio] kiwi fruit

ΑΛΑΤΙ αλάτι [alati] salt

ΑΛΕΥΡΙ αλεύρι [alevri] flour

ΑΛΕΥΡΙ ΚΑΛΑΜΠΟΚΙΟΥ
αλεύρι καλαμποκιού [alevri
kalabokioo] cornflour

ΑΛΕΥΡΙ ΣΤΑΡΙΟΥ αλεύρι
σταριού [alevri starioo] wheat
flour

ΑΛΛΑΝΤΙΚΑ αλλαντικά
[alandika] sausages, salami,
ham etc

ΑΜΥΓΔΑΛΑ αμύγδαλα
[amigthala] almonds

ΑΜΥΓΔΑΛΩΤΑ αμυγδαλωτά
[amigthalota] macaroons;
almond pastries

ΑΝΑΝΑΣ ανανάς [ananas]
pineapple

ΑΝΘΟΤΥΡΟ ανθότυρο
[anthotiro] type of cottage
cheese

ΑΝΤΖΟΥΓΙΑ ΣΤΟ ΛΑΔΙ
αντζούγια στο λάδι [andsoo-yia
sto lathi] anchovies in oil

ΑΡΑΚΑΣ αρακάς [arakas] peas

ΑΡΑΚΑΣ ΛΑΔΕΡΟΣ αρακάς
λαδερός [arakas latheros] peas
cooked with tomato and
oil

ΑΡΑΚΑΣ ΣΩΤΕ αρακάς σωτέ
[arakas soteh] peas fried in
butter

ΑΡΝΑΚΙ αρνάκι [arnaki] lamb

ΑΡΝΑΚΙ ΕΞΟΧΙΚΟ αρνάκι
εξοχικό [arnaki exohiko] leg
of lamb baked in
greaseproof paper

ΑΡΝΑΚΙ ΜΕ ΜΠΑΜΙΕΣ
αρνάκι με μπάμιες [arnaki meh
bami-es] lamb and okra stew

ΑΡΝΑΚΙ ΜΕ ΠΑΤΑΤΕΣ ΣΤΟ
ΦΟΥΡΝΟ αρνάκι με πατάτες
στο φούρνο [arnaki meh patates
sto foorno] roast lamb and
potatoes

ΑΡΝΑΚΙ ΤΑΣ ΚΕΜΠΑΠ
αρνάκι τας κεμπάπ [arnaki tas
kebap] lamb in tomato sauce

ΑΡΝΑΚΙ ΤΗΣ ΣΟΥΒΛΑΣ
αρνάκι της σούβλας [arnaki tis
soovlas] spit-roast lamb

ΑΡΝΑΚΙ ΦΡΙΚΑΣΕ αρνάκι
φρικασέ με μαρούλια [arnaki
frikaseh meh maroolia] lamb
and lettuce in egg and
lemon sauce

ΑΡΝΙ αρνί [arni] mutton,
lamb

ΑΡΝΙ ΓΕΜΙΣΤΟ ΣΤΟ
ΦΟΥΡΝΟ αρνί γεμιστό στο
φούρνο [arni yemisto sto foorno]
oven-cooked stuffed lamb

ΑΡΝΙ ΕΞΟΧΙΚΟ αρνί
εξοχικό [arni exokhiko] lamb
cooked in greased foil with
cheese and spices
ΑΡΝΙ ΚΟΚΚΙΝΙΣΤΟ αρνί
κοκκινιστό [arni kokinisto]
lamb in tomato sauce
ΑΡΝΙ ΛΑΔΟΡΙΓΑΝΗ ΣΤΟ
ΦΟΥΡΝΟ αρνί λαδορίγανη
στο φούρνο [arni lathorigani sto
foorno] oven-cooked lamb
with oil and oregano
ΑΡΝΙ ΜΕ ΑΡΑΚΑ αρνί με
αρακά [arni meh araka] lamb
with peas
ΑΡΝΙ ΜΕ ΚΟΛΟΚΥΘΑΚΙΑ
ΑΥΓΟΛΕΜΟΝΟ αρνί με
κολοκυθάκια αυγολέμονο [arni
meh kolokiThakia avgolemono]
lamb with courgettes/
zucchini in egg and lemon
sauce
ΑΡΝΙ ΜΕ ΚΡΙΘΑΡΑΚΙ αρνί
με κριθαράκι [arni meh
kriTHaraki] lamb with pasta
ΑΡΝΙ ΜΕ ΜΑΚΑΡΟΝΙΑ
αρνί με μακαρόνια [arni meh
makaronia] lamb with
spaghetti
ΑΡΝΙ ΜΕ ΜΕΛΙΤΖΑΝΕΣ
αρνί με μελιτζάνες [arni meh
melitzanes] lamb with
aubergines/eggplants
ΑΡΝΙ ΜΕ ΜΠΑΜΙΕΣ αρνί με
μπάμιες [arni meh bami-es]
lamb with okra
ΑΡΝΙ ΜΕ ΠΑΤΑΤΕΣ ΡΑΓΟΥ
αρνί με πατάτες ραγού [arni
meh patates ragoo] lamb with

potatoes cooked in tomato
sauce
ΑΡΝΙ ΜΕ ΦΑΣΟΛΑΚΙΑ
ΦΡΕΣΚΑ αρνί με φασολάκια
φρέσκα [arni meh fasolakia
freska] lamb with runner
beans
ΑΡΝΙ ΜΕ ΧΥΛΟΠΙΤΕΣ αρνί
με χυλοπίτες [arni meh
khilopites] lamb with a type
of lasagne
ΑΡΝΙ ΜΠΟΥΤΙ ΣΤΟ
ΦΟΥΡΝΟ αρνί μπούτι στο
φούρνο [arni booti sto foorno]
oven-cooked leg of lamb
ΑΡΝΙ ΜΠΡΙΖΟΛΕΣ αρνί
μπριζόλες [arni brizoles] lamb
chops
ΑΡΝΙ ΠΑΪΔΑΚΙΑ αρνί
παϊδάκια [arni paithakia]
grilled lamb chops
ΑΡΝΙ ΤΑΣ ΚΕΜΠΑΠ αρνί
τας κεμπάπ [arni tas kebab]
chopped lamb kebab with
tomato sauce
ΑΡΝΙ ΤΗΣ ΚΑΤΣΑΡΟΛΑΣ
ΜΕ ΠΑΤΑΤΕΣ αρνί της
κατσαρόλας με πατάτες [arni tis
katsarolas meh patates]
casseroled lamb cooked
with potatoes
ΑΡΝΙ ΤΗΣ ΣΟΥΒΛΑΣ αρνί
της σούβλας [arni tis soovlas]
spit-roast lamb
ΑΡΝΙ ΦΡΙΚΑΣΕ αρνί
φρικασέ [arni frikaseh] lamb
fricassee
ΑΣΤΑΚΟΣ αστακός [astakos]
lobster

ΑΣΤΑΚΟΣ ΜΕ
ΛΑΔΟΛΕΜΟΝΟ αστακός με
λαδολέμονο [astakos meh
latholemono] lobster cooked
in lemon and oil sauce
ΑΣΤΑΚΟΣ ΜΕ ΜΑΓΙΟΝΕΖΑ
αστακός με μαγιονέζα [astakos
meh mayoneza] lobster with
mayonnaise
ΑΤΖΕΜ ΠΙΛΑΦΙ ατζέμ πιλάφι
[atzem pilafi] rice pilaf
ΑΥΓΑ αυγά [avga] eggs
ΑΥΓΑ ΒΡΑΣΤΑ αυγά βραστά
[avga vrasta] boiled eggs
ΑΥΓΑ ΒΡΑΣΤΑ ΣΦΙΧΤΑ
αυγά βραστά σφιχτά [avga
vrasta sfikhta] hard-boiled
eggs
ΑΥΓΑ ΓΕΜΙΣΤΑ αυγά
γεμιστά [avga yemista] stuffed
eggs
ΑΥΓΑ ΓΕΜΙΣΤΑ ΜΕ
ΜΑΓΙΟΝΕΖΑ αυγά γεμιστά
με μαγιονέζα [avga yemista meh
mayoneza] stuffed eggs with
mayonnaise
ΑΥΓΑ ΜΑΤΙΑ αυγά μάτια
[avga matia] fried eggs
ΑΥΓΑ ΜΕΛΑΤΑ αυγά
μελάτα [avga melata] soft-
boiled eggs
ΑΥΓΑ ΜΕ ΜΑΝΙΤΑΡΙΑ
αυγά με μανιτάρια [avga meh
manitaria] mushroom
omelette
ΑΥΓΑ ΜΕ ΜΠΕΪΚΟΝ αυγά
με μπέικον [avga meh bacon]
bacon and eggs
ΑΥΓΑ ΜΕ ΝΤΟΜΑΤΕΣ αυγά

με ντομάτες [avga meh domates]
eggs cooked in tomato
sauce
ΑΥΓΑ ΜΕ ΤΥΡΙ αυγά με τυρί
[avga meh tiri] cheese
omelette
ΑΥΓΑ ΟΜΕΛΕΤΑ αυγά
ομελέτα [avga omeleta] plain
omelette
ΑΥΓΑ ΟΜΕΛΕΤΑ ΜΕ
ΠΑΤΑΤΕΣ αυγά ομελέτα με
πατάτες [avga omeleta meh
patates] omelette with
chips/fries
ΑΥΓΑ ΠΟΣΕ αυγά ποσέ [avga
poseh] poached eggs
ΑΥΓΑ ΣΦΙΧΤΑ αυγά σφιχτά
[avga sfikhta] hard-boiled
eggs
ΑΥΓΑ ΤΗΓΑΝΗΤΑ αυγά
τηγανητά [avga tiganita] fried
eggs
ΑΥΓΑ Ω ΓΚΡΑΤΕΝ αυγά ω
γκρατέν [avga o graten] eggs
au gratin
ΑΥΓΟ αυγό [avgo] egg
ΑΥΓΟΛΕΜΟΝΟ αυγολέμονο
[avgolemono] egg and lemon
sauce
ΑΥΓΟΛΕΜΟΝΟ ΣΟΥΠΑ
αυγολέμονο σούπα [avgolemono
soopa] chicken broth with
egg and lemon
ΑΥΓΟΤΑΡΑΧΟ αυγοτάραχο
[avgotarakho] roe
ΑΧΛΑΔΙ αχλάδι [akhlathi]
pear

ΒΑΝΙΛΙΑ βανίλια [vanilia]

vanilla

ΒΑΤΟΜΟΥΡΟ βατόμουρο
[vatomooro] blackberry

ΒΕΡΙΚΟΚΟ βερίκοκο
[verikoko] apricot

ΒΟΔΙΝΟ βοδινό [vothino] beef

ΒΟΔΙΝΟ ΒΡΑΣΤΟ βοδινό
βραστό [vothino vrasto] boiled
beef

ΒΟΔΙΝΟ ΡΟΣΜΠΙΦ βοδινό
ροσμπιφ [vothino rosbif] roast
beef

ΒΟΤΑΝΑ βότανα [votana]
herbs

ΒΟΥΤΥΡΟ βούτυρο [vootiro]
butter

ΒΡΑΣΤΟ βραστό [vrasto]
boiled

ΒΥΣΣΙΝΟ βύσσινο [visino]
sour cherries

ΓΑΛΑΚΤΟΜΠΟΥΡΕΚΟ
γαλακτομπούρεκο
[galaktobooreko] cream-filled
sweet filo pastry with
honey

ΓΑΛΟΠΟΥΛΑ γαλοπούλα
[galopoola] turkey

ΓΑΛΟΠΟΥΛΑ ΓΕΜΙΣΤΗ
γαλοπούλα γεμιστή [galopoola
yemisti] stuffed turkey

ΓΑΛΟΠΟΥΛΑ
ΚΟΚΚΙΝΙΣΤΗ γαλοπούλα
κοκκινιστή [galopoola kokinisti]
turkey cooked with
tomatoes

ΓΑΛΟΠΟΥΛΑ ΨΗΤΗ ΣΤΟ
ΦΟΥΡΝΟ γαλοπούλα ψητή
στο φούρνο [galopoola psiti sto

foorno] roast turkey

ΓΑΡΔΟΥΜΠΑ γαρδούμπα
[garthoomba] spit-roast rolled
lamb offal

ΓΑΡΙΔΕΣ γαρίδες [garithes]
prawns

ΓΑΡΙΔΕΣ ΒΡΑΣΤΕΣ γαρίδες
βραστές [garithes vrastes]
boiled shrimps

ΓΑΡΙΔΕΣ ΚΟΚΤΑΙΗΛ
γαρίδες κοκταιηλ [garithes
cocktail] shrimp cocktail

ΓΑΡΙΔΕΣ ΠΙΛΑΦΙ γαρίδες
πιλάφι [garithes pilafi] shrimp
pilaf

ΓΑΡΙΔΟΠΙΛΑΦΟ
γαριδοπίλαφο [garithopilafo]
prawns with rice cooked in
butter

ΓΑΡΝΙΤΟΥΡΑ γαρνιτούρα
[garnitoora] vegetables

ΓΑΡΝΙΤΟΥΡΑ ΚΑΡΟΤΑ
ΣΩΤΕ γαρνιτούρα καρότα
σωτέ [garnitoora karota soteh]
sautéed carrots

ΓΑΡΝΙΤΟΥΡΑ
ΚΟΥΝΟΥΠΙΔΙ ΣΩΤΕ
γαρνιτούρα κουνουπίδι σωτέ
[garnitoora koonoopithi soteh]
sautéed cauliflower

ΓΑΡΝΙΤΟΥΡΑ ΠΑΤΑΤΕΣ
γαρνιτούρα πατάτες [garnitoora
patates] potatoes

ΓΑΡΝΙΤΟΥΡΑ ΣΠΑΝΑΚΙ
ΣΩΤΕ γαρνιτούρα σπανάκι
σωτέ [garnitoora spanaki soteh]
sautéed spinach

ΓΑΡΝΙΤΟΥΡΑ ΦΑΣΟΛΙΑ
ΠΡΑΣΙΝΑ ΣΩΤΕ γαρνιτούρα

φασόλια πράσινα σωτέ
[garnit**oo**ra fas**o**lia pr**a**sina sot**eh**]
sautéed runner beans

ΓΕΜΙΣΤΑ γεμιστά [yemist**a**]
stuffed, usually with rice
and/or minced meat

ΓΕΜΙΣΤΕΣ γεμιστές [yemist**es**]
stuffed vegetables

ΓΙΑΛΑΝΤΖΗ ΝΤΟΛΜΑΔΕΣ
γιαλαντζή ντολμάδες [yalantz**i**
dolm**a**thes] vine leaves stuffed
with rice

ΓΙΑΟΥΡΤΙ γιαούρτι [ya-**oo**rti]
yoghurt

ΓΙΓΑΝΤΕΣ γίγαντες [y**i**gandes]
white haricot beans; butter
beans

ΓΙΟΥΒΑΡΛΑΚΙΑ
γιουβαρλάκια [yoovarl**a**kia]
meatballs, rice and
seasoning in a sauce

ΓΙΟΥΒΑΡΛΑΚΙΑ
ΑΥΓΟΛΕΜΟΝΟ
γιουβαρλάκια αυγολέμονο
[yoovarl**a**kia avgol**e**mono]
meatballs with egg and
lemon sauce

ΓΙΟΥΒΑΡΛΑΚΙΑ ΜΕ
ΣΑΛΤΣΑ ΝΤΟΜΑΤΑΣ
γιουβαρλάκια με σάλτσα
ντομάτας [yoovarl**a**kia meh s**a**ltsa
dom**a**tas] meatballs with rice
cooked with tomatoes

ΓΙΟΥΒΕΤΣΙ γιουβέτσι
[yoov**e**tsi] oven-roasted lamb
with pasta

ΓΚΡΕΙΠΦΡΟΥΤ γκρέιπφρουτ
[grapefruit] grapefruit

ΓΛΥΚΑ γλυκά [gl**i**ka] cakes,
desserts

ΓΛΥΚΙΣΜΑ γλύκισμα
[gl**i**kisma] dessert

ΓΛΥΚΟ γλυκό [glik**o**] sweet,
dessert

ΓΛΥΚΟ ΒΥΣΣΙΝΟ γλυκό
βύσσινο [glik**o** v**i**sino] candied
cherries in syrup

ΓΛΥΚΟ ΚΑΡΥΔΑΚΙ
ΦΡΕΣΚΟ γλυκό καρυδάκι
φρέσκο [glik**o** karith**a**ki fr**e**sko]
dried fresh green walnuts
in syrup

ΓΛΥΚΟ ΜΑΣΤΙΧΑ γλυκό
μαστίχα [glik**o** mast**i**kha]
vanilla-flavoured fudge

ΓΛΥΚΟ ΜΕΛΙΤΖΑΝΑΚΙ
γλυκό μελιτζανάκι [glik**o**
melitzan**a**ki] dried small
aubergine/eggplant in
syrup

ΓΛΥΚΟ ΝΕΡΑΝΤΖΑΚΙ
γλυκό νεραντζάκι [glik**o**
nerantz**a**ki] dried bitter
orange in syrup

ΓΛΥΚΟ ΣΥΚΟ γλυκό σύκο
[glik**o** s**i**ko] candied figs in
syrup

ΓΛΥΚΟ ΣΥΚΟ ΦΡΕΣΚΟ
γλυκό σύκο φρέσκο [glik**o** s**i**ko
fr**e**sko] dried fig in syrup

ΓΛΥΚΟ ΤΡΙΑΝΤΑΦΥΛΛΟ
γλυκό τριαντάφυλλο [glik**o**
triand**a**filo] dried rose petals
in syrup

ΓΛΩΣΣΑ γλώσσα [gl**o**sa] sole;
tongue

ΓΛΩΣΣΕΣ ΤΗΓΑΝΗΤΕΣ
γλώσσες τηγανητές [gl**o**ses

tiganites] fried sole
ΓΟΥΡΟΥΝΟΠΟΥΛΟ ΣΤΟ
ΦΟΥΡΝΟ ΜΕ ΠΑΤΑΤΕΣ
γουρουνόπουλο στο φούρνο με
πατάτες [gooroonopoolo sto
foorno meh patates] oven-
cooked pork with potatoes
ΓΡΑΒΙΕΡΑ γραβιέρα [gravi-
era] hard cheese like
gruyère
ΓΡΑΝΙΤΑ γρανίτα [granita]
sorbet
ΓΡΑΝΙΤΑ ΛΕΜΟΝΙ γρανίτα
λεμόνι [granita lemoni] lemon
sorbet
ΓΡΑΝΙΤΑ ΜΠΑΝΑΝΑ
γρανίτα μπανάνα [granita
banana] banana sorbet
ΓΡΑΝΙΤΑ ΠΟΡΤΟΚΑΛΙ
γρανίτα πορτοκάλι [granita
portokali] orange sorbet
ΓΡΑΝΙΤΑ ΦΡΑΟΥΛΕΣ
γρανίτα φράουλες [granita
fraooles] strawberry sorbet

ΔΑΜΑΣΚΗΝΑ δαμάσκηνα
[thamaskina] prunes
ΔΑΜΑΣΚΗΝΟ δαμάσκηνο
[thamaskino] plum
ΔΙΠΛΕΣ δίπλες [thiples]
pancakes

ΕΛΑΙΟΛΑΔΟ ελαιόλαδο
[eleolatho] olive oil
ΕΛΙΕΣ ελιές [eli-es] olives
ΕΝΤΟΣΘΙΑ ΑΡΝΙΟΥ
ΛΑΔΟΡΙΓΑΝΗ εντόσθια
αρνιού λαδορίγανη [endosthia
arnioo lathorigani] lambs'

intestines cooked in lemon
and oil
ΕΠΙΔΟΡΠΙΟ επιδόρπιο
[epithorpio] dessert
ΕΣΚΑΛΟΠ ΜΕ ΖΑΜΠΟΝ
ΚΑΙ ΣΑΛΤΣΑ ΝΤΟΜΑΤΑΣ
εσκαλόπ με ζαμπόν και
σάλτσα ντομάτας [eskalop meh
zabon keh saltsa domatas]
escalope of veal with ham
and tomato sauce

ΖΑΜΠΟΝ ζαμπόν [zabon] ham
ΖΑΧΑΡΗ ζάχαρη [zakhari]
sugar
ΖΕΛΕ ζελέ [zeleh] jelly
ΖΥΜΑΡΙΚΑ ζυμαρικά
[zimarika] pasta and rice

ΘΑΛΑΣΣΙΝΑ θαλασσινά
[THalasina] seafood

ΚΑΒΟΥΡΙΑ καβούρια
[kavooria] crab
ΚΑΚΑΒΙΑ κακαβιά [kakavia]
mixed fish soup
ΚΑΚΑΒΙΑ ΨΑΡΟΣΟΥΠΑ
κακαβιά ψαρόσουπα [kakavia
psarosoopa] fish soup
ΚΑΛΑΜΑΡΑΚΙΑ
καλαμαράκια [kalamarakia]
baby squid
ΚΑΛΑΜΑΡΑΚΙΑ ΓΕΜΙΣΤΑ
καλαμαράκια γεμιστά
[kalamarakia yemista] stuffed
baby squid
ΚΑΛΑΜΑΡΑΚΙΑ
ΤΗΓΑΝΗΤΑ καλαμαράκια
τηγανητά [kalamarakia tiganita]

fried baby squid
ΚΑΛΑΜΑΡΙΑ καλαμάρια
⟦kalamaria⟧ squid
ΚΑΝΑΠΕ καναπέ ⟦kanapeh⟧
canapés
ΚΑΝΑΠΕ ΜΕ ΖΑΜΠΟΝ
καναπέ με ζαμπόν ⟦kanapeh
meh zabon⟧ ham canapés
ΚΑΝΑΠΕ ΜΕ ΚΡΕΑΣ ΨΗΤΟ
καναπέ με κρέας ψητό
⟦kanapeh meh kreas psito⟧ meat
canapés
**ΚΑΝΑΠΕ ΜΕ ΜΑΥΡΟ
ΧΑΒΙΑΡΙ** καναπέ με μαύρο
χαβιάρι ⟦kanapeh meh mavro
haviari⟧ black caviar canapés
**ΚΑΝΑΠΕ ΜΕ
ΤΑΡΑΜΟΣΑΛΑΤΑ** καναπέ
με ταραμοσαλάτα ⟦kanapeh meh
taramosalata⟧ taramosalata
canapés
ΚΑΝΕΛΛΑ κανέλλα ⟦kanela⟧
cinnamon
ΚΑΝΕΛΛΟΝΙΑ ΓΕΜΙΣΤΑ
κανελλόνια γεμιστά ⟦kanelonia
yemista⟧ stuffed canelloni
ΚΑΝΤΑΪΦΙ κανταϊφι ⟦kanda-
ifi⟧ shredded and rolled filo
pastry in syrup
ΚΑΠΑΜΑΣ ΑΡΝΙ καπαμάς
αρνί ⟦kapamas arni⟧ lamb
cooked in spices and
tomato sauce
ΚΑΠΝΙΣΤΟ καπνιστό
⟦kapnisto⟧ smoked
ΚΑΠΠΑΡΗ κάππαρη ⟦kapari⟧
caper
ΚΑΡΑΒΙΔΕΣ καραβίδες
⟦karavithes⟧ king prawns;

crayfish
ΚΑΡΟΤΑ καρότα ⟦karota⟧
carrots
ΚΑΡΠΟΥΖΙ καρπούζι
⟦karpoozi⟧ watermelon
ΚΑΡΥΔΙ καρύδι ⟦karithi⟧ nut
ΚΑΡΥΔΟΠΙΤΤΑ καρυδόπιττα
⟦karithopita⟧ walnut cake; cake
with nuts and syrup
ΚΑΡΧΑΡΙΑΣ καρχαρίας
⟦karkharias⟧ shark
ΚΑΣΕΡΙ κασέρι ⟦kaseri⟧
Cheddar-type cheese
ΚΑΣΤΑΝΑ κάστανα ⟦kastana⟧
chestnuts
ΚΑΣΤΑΝΑ ΓΛΑΣΕ
κάστανα γλασέ ⟦kastana glaseh⟧
glazed chestnuts, marrons
glacés
ΚΑΤΑΪΦΙ καταϊφι ⟦kata-ifi⟧
shredded filo pastry with
honey and nuts
ΚΑΤΑΛΟΓΟΣ κατάλογος
⟦katalogos⟧ menu
ΚΕΙΚ κέικ ⟦cake⟧ cake
ΚΕΙΚ ΚΑΝΕΛΛΑΣ κέικ
κανέλλας ⟦cake kanelas⟧
cinammon cake
ΚΕΙΚ ΜΕ ΑΜΥΓΔΑΛΑ κέικ
με αμύγδαλα ⟦cake meh
amigthala⟧ almond cake
**ΚΕΙΚ ΜΕ ΚΑΡΥΔΙΑ ΚΑΙ
ΣΤΑΦΙΔΕΣ** κέικ με καρύδια
και σταφίδες ⟦cake meh karithia
keh stafithes⟧ nut and sultana
cake
ΚΕΙΚ ΣΟΚΟΛΑΤΑΣ κέικ
σοκολάτας ⟦cake sokolatas⟧
chocolate cake

ΚΕΙΚ ΦΡΟΥΤΩΝ κέικ
φρούτων [cake frooton] fruit
cake

ΚΕΡΑΣΙΑ κεράσια [kerasia]
cherries

ΚΕΦΑΛΟΤΥΡΙ κεφαλοτύρι
[kefalotiri] very salty, hard
cheese

ΚΕΦΤΕΔΕΣ κεφτέδες
[keftethes] meatballs

ΚΕΦΤΕΔΕΣ ΜΕ ΣΑΛΤΣΑ
κεφτέδες με σάλτσα [keftethes
meh saltsa] meatballs in
tomato sauce

ΚΕΦΤΕΔΕΣ ΣΤΟ ΦΟΥΡΝΟ
κεφτέδες στο φούρνο [keftethes
sto foorno] oven-cooked
meatballs

ΚΕΦΤΕΔΕΣ ΤΗΓΑΝΗΤΟΙ
κεφτέδες τηγανητοί [keftethes
tiganiti] fried meatballs

ΚΙΜΑΣ κιμάς [kimas] minced
meat

ΚΛΕΦΤΙΚΟ κλέφτικο [kleftiko]
meat, potatoes and
vegetables cooked together
in a pot or foil

ΚΟΚΚΙΝΙΣΤΟ κοκκινιστό
[kokinisto] in tomato sauce

ΚΟΚΟΡΕΤΣΙ κοκορέτσι
[kokoretsi] spit-roast rolled
lamb offal

ΚΟΛΙΟΙ κολιοί [koli-i]
mackerel

ΚΟΛΙΟΙ ΨΗΤΟΙ κολιοί ψητοί
[koli-i psiti] fried mackerel

ΚΟΛΟΚΥΘΑΚΙΑ
κολοκυθάκια [kolokiThakia]
courgettes/zucchini

ΚΟΛΟΚΥΘΑΚΙΑ ΓΕΜΙΣΤΑ
ΜΕ ΚΙΜΑ κολοκυθάκια
γεμιστά με κιμά [kolokiThakia
yemista meh kima] courgettes/
zucchini stuffed with
minced meat

ΚΟΛΟΚΥΘΑΚΙΑ ΓΕΜΙΣΤΑ
ΜΕ ΡΥΖΙ κολοκυθάκια
γεμιστά με ρύζι [kolokiThakia
yemista meh rizi] courgettes/
zucchini stuffed with rice

ΚΟΛΟΚΥΘΑΚΙΑ ΓΙΑΧΝΙ
κολοκυθάκια γιαχνί
[kolokiThakia yakhni]
courgettes/zucchini and
onions in a tomato sauce

ΚΟΛΟΚΥΘΑΚΙΑ ΛΑΔΕΡΑ
κολοκυθάκια λαδερά
[kolokiThakia lathera]
courgettes/zucchini
cooked in oil

ΚΟΛΟΚΥΘΑΚΙΑ ΜΕ
ΚΡΕΑΣ κολοκυθάκια με
κρέας [kolokiThakia meh kreas]
courgette/zucchini and
beef stew

ΚΟΛΟΚΥΘΑΚΙΑ ΜΕ
ΠΑΤΑΤΕΣ κολοκυθάκια με
πατάτες [kolokiThakia meh
patates] courgettes/zucchini
with potatoes

ΚΟΛΟΚΥΘΑΚΙΑ
ΜΟΥΣΑΚΑΣ κολοκυθάκια
μουσακάς [kolokiThakia
moosakas] courgettes/
zucchini with minced meat
and béchamel

ΚΟΛΟΚΥΘΑΚΙΑ
ΠΑΠΟΥΤΣΑΚΙΑ

κολοκυθάκια παπουτσάκια [kolokiTHakia papootsakia] courgettes/zucchini with minced meat and onions

ΚΟΛΟΚΥΘΑΚΙΑ ΤΗΓΑΝΗΤΑ κολοκυθάκια τηγανητά [kolokiTHakia tiganita] fried courgettes/zucchini

ΚΟΛΟΚΥΘΟΚΕΦΤΕΔΕΣ κολοκυθοκεφτέδες [kolokiTHokeftethes] fried courgette/zucchini balls

ΚΟΛΟΚΥΘΟΤΥΡΟΠΙΤΤΑ κολοκυθοτυρόπιττα [kolokiTHotiropita] courgette/ zucchini and cheese pie

ΚΟΜΠΟΣΤΑ κομπόστα [kobosta] fruit compote

ΚΟΤΑ κότα [kota] chicken

ΚΟΤΑ ΒΡΑΣΤΗ κότα βραστή [kota vrasti] boiled chicken

ΚΟΤΑ ΨΗΤΗ ΣΤΟ ΦΟΥΡΝΟ κότα ψητή στο φούρνο [kota psiti sto foorno] roast chicken

ΚΟΤΑ ΨΗΤΗ ΤΗΣ ΚΑΤΣΑΡΟΛΑΣ κότα ψητή της κατσαρόλας [kota psiti tis katsarolas] chicken casserole

ΚΟΤΑ ΨΗΤΗ ΤΗΣ ΣΟΥΒΛΑΣ κότα ψητή της σούβλας [kota psiti tis soovlas] spit-roast chicken

ΚΟΤΟΛΕΤΕΣ ΑΡΝΙΣΙΕΣ ΠΑΝΕ κοτολέτες αρνίσιες πανέ [kotoletes arnisi-es paneh] lamb cutlets

ΚΟΤΟΛΕΤΕΣ ΜΟΣΧΑΡΙΣΙΕΣ ΠΑΝΕ κοτολέτες μοσχαρίσιες πανέ [kotoletes moskharisi-es paneh] veal cutlets

ΚΟΤΟΠΙΤΤΑ κοτόπιττα [kotopita] chicken pie

ΚΟΤΟΠΟΥΛΟ κοτόπουλο [kotopoolo] chicken

ΚΟΤΟΠΟΥΛΟ ΓΙΟΥΒΕΤΣΙ ΜΕ ΧΥΛΟΠΙΤΤΕΣ κοτόπουλο γιουβέτσι με χυλοπίττες [kotopoolo yioovetsi meh hilopites] chicken with pasta

ΚΟΤΟΠΟΥΛΟ ΚΟΚΚΙΝΙΣΤΟ κοτόπουλο κοκκινιστό [kotopoolo kokinisto] chicken in tomato sauce

ΚΟΤΟΠΟΥΛΟ ΜΕ ΜΠΑΜΙΕΣ κοτόπουλο με μπάμιες [kotopoolo meh bami-es] chicken with okra

ΚΟΤΟΠΟΥΛΟ ΜΕ ΜΠΙΖΕΛΙΑ κοτόπουλο με μπιζέλια [kotopoolo meh bizelia] chicken with peas

ΚΟΤΟΠΟΥΛΟ ΠΑΝΕ κοτόπουλο πανέ [kotopoolo paneh] breaded chicken

ΚΟΤΟΠΟΥΛΟ ΠΙΛΑΦΙ κοτόπουλο πιλάφι [kotopoolo pilafi] chicken pilaf

ΚΟΤΟΠΟΥΛΟ ΤΗΣ ΣΟΥΒΛΑΣ κοτόπουλο της σούβλας [kotopoolo tis soovlas] spit-roast chicken

ΚΟΤΟΣΟΥΠΑ κοτόσουπα [kotosoopa] chicken soup

ΚΟΥΚΙΑ ΛΑΔΕΡΑ κουκιά λαδερά [kookia lathera] broad beans in tomato sauce

ΚΟΥΝΕΛΙ κουνέλι [**koon**eli]
rabbit

ΚΟΥΝΕΛΙ ΜΕ ΣΑΛΤΣΑ
κουνέλι με σάλτσα [**koon**eli meh
saltsa] rabbit with tomato
sauce

ΚΟΥΝΕΛΙ ΣΤΙΦΑΔΟ
κουνέλι στιφάδο [**koon**eli
stifatho] rabbit with onions

ΚΟΥΝΟΥΠΙΔΙ κουνουπίδι
[koon**oopi**thi] cauliflower

ΚΟΥΝΟΥΠΙΔΙ ΒΡΑΣΤΟ
ΣΑΛΑΤΑ κουνουπίδι βραστό
σαλάτα [koon**opi**thi **vras**to **sal**ata]
boiled cauliflower salad

ΚΟΥΡΑΜΠΙΕΔΕΣ
κουραμπιέδες [**koo**rabi-ethes]
Greek shortbread

ΚΟΥΡΑΜΠΙΕΔΕΣ ΜΕ
ΑΜΥΓΔΑΛΟ κουραμπιέδες
με αμύγδαλο [**koo**rabi-ethes meh
a**mig**thalo] shortbread-type
biscuits with sesame seeds
and icing sugar

ΚΡΑΚΕΡΣ ΑΛΜΥΡΑ κράκερς
αλμυρά [**kra**kers al**mi**ra] salted
crackers

ΚΡΑΣΑΤΟ κρασάτο [kra**sa**to]
cooked in wine sauce

ΚΡΕΑΣ κρέας [**kre**as] meat,
usually beef

ΚΡΕΑΣ ΜΕ ΑΝΤΙΔΙΑ
ΑΥΓΟΛΕΜΟΝΟ κρέας με
αντίδια αυγολέμονο [**kre**as meh
an**ti**thia avgo**le**mono] beef with
endives in egg and lemon
sauce

ΚΡΕΑΣ ΜΕ ΦΑΣΟΛΙΑ ΞΕΡΑ
κρέας με φασόλια ξερά [**kre**as

meh fa**so**lia **xe**ra] beef with
butter beans

ΚΡΕΑΤΙΚΑ κρεατικά [kreh-
a**ti**ka] meat dishes

ΚΡΕΑΤΟΠΙΤΤΑ κρεατόπιττα
[kreh-a**to**pita] minced meat in
filo pastry

ΚΡΕΜΑ κρέμα [**kre**ma] cream

ΚΡΕΜΑ ΚΑΡΑΜΕΛΕ κρέμα
καραμελέ [**kre**ma karamel**eh**]
crème caramel

ΚΡΕΜΑ ΜΕ ΜΗΛΑ κρέμα
με μήλα [**kre**ma meh **mi**la]
apples with cream

ΚΡΕΜΑ ΜΕ ΜΠΑΝΑΝΕΣ
κρέμα με μπανάνες [**kre**ma meh
ba**na**nes] bananas with cream

ΚΡΕΜΜΥΔΑΚΙΑ ΦΡΕΣΚΑ
κρεμμυδάκια φρέσκα
[kremith**a**kia **fres**ka] spring
onions

ΚΡΕΜΜΥΔΙΑ κρεμμύδια
[krem**i**thia] onions

ΚΡΕΜΜΥΔΟΣΟΥΠΑ
κρεμμυδόσουπα [kremith**o**soopa]
onion soup

ΚΡΕΠΑ κρέπα [**kre**pa]
pancake

ΚΡΟΚΕΤΕΣ κροκέτες
[kro**ke**tes] croquettes

ΚΡΟΚΕΤΕΣ ΑΠΟ ΚΡΕΑΣ
κροκέτες από κρέας [kro**ke**tes
a**po kre**as] meat croquettes

ΚΡΟΚΕΤΕΣ ΜΕ ΑΥΓΑ ΚΑΙ
ΤΥΡΙ κροκέτες με αυγά και
τυρί [kro**ke**tes meh avga keh ti**ri**]
egg and cheese croquettes

ΚΡΟΚΕΤΕΣ
ΜΠΑΚΑΛΙΑΡΟΥ κροκέτες

μπακαλιάρου [kroketes bakaliaroo] cod croquettes

ΚΡΟΚΕΤΕΣ ΠΑΤΑΤΕΣ κροκέτες πατάτες [kroketes patates] potato croquettes

ΚΡΟΥΑΣΑΝ κρουασάν [croissants] croissants

ΚΥΔΩΝΙΑ κυδώνια [kithonia] quinces

ΚΥΔΩΝΟΠΑΣΤΟ κυδωνόπαστο [kithonopasto] thick jelly made from quince

ΚΥΝΗΓΙ κυνήγι [kiniyi] game

ΚΥΡΙΟ ΠΙΑΤΟ κύριο πιάτο [kirio piato] main course

ΚΩΚ κωκ [kok] cake with cream and chocolate topping

ΛΑΓΟΣ λαγός [lagos] hare

ΛΑΓΟΣ ΜΕ ΣΑΛΤΣΑ λαγός με σάλτσα [lagos meh saltsa] hare in tomato sauce

ΛΑΓΟΣ ΣΤΙΦΑΔΟ λαγός στιφάδο [lagos stifatho] hare and shallot stew

ΛΑΔΕΡΑ λαδερά [lathera] in olive oil and tomato sauce

ΛΑΔΙ λάδι [lathi] oil

ΛΑΔΟΛΕΜΟΝΟ λαδολέμονο [latholemono] olive oil and lemon dressing

ΛΑΔΟΞΥΔΟ λαδόξυδο [lathoxitho] oil and vinegar salad dressing

ΛΑΖΑΝΙΑ λαζάνια [lazania] lasagne

ΛΑΧΑΝΙΚΑ λαχανικά [lakhanika] vegetables

ΛΑΧΑΝΙΚΑ ΜΙΚΤΑ λαχανικά μικτά [lakhanika mikta] vegetables

ΛΑΧΑΝΑΚΙΑ ΒΡΥΞΕΛΛΩΝ λαχανάκια Βρυξελλών [lakhanakia vrixelon] Brussels sprouts

ΛΑΧΑΝΟ λάχανο [lakhano] cabbage

ΛΑΧΑΝΟ ΚΟΚΚΙΝΟ λάχανο κόκκινο [lakhano kokino] red cabbage

ΛΑΧΑΝΟ ΝΤΟΛΜΑΔΕΣ ΑΥΓΟΛΕΜΟΝΟ λάχανο ντολμάδες αυγολέμονο [lakhano dolmathes avgolemono] cabbage leaves stuffed with rice in egg and lemon sauce

ΛΑΧΑΝΟ ΝΤΟΛΜΑΔΕΣ λάχανο ντολμάδες [lakhano dolmathes] cabbage leaves stuffed with minced meat and rice

ΛΑΧΑΝΟ ΝΤΟΛΜΑΔΕΣ ΜΕ ΣΑΛΤΣΑ ΝΤΟΜΑΤΑΣ λάχανο ντολμάδες με σάλτσα ντομάτας [lakhano dolmathes meh saltsa domatas] vine leaves stuffed with rice in tomato sauce

ΛΑΧΑΝΟΣΑΛΑΤΑ λαχανοσαλάτα [lakhanosalata] cabbage salad

ΛΕΜΟΝΙ λεμόνι [lemoni] lemon

ΛΙΘΡΙΝΙ λιθρίνι [liTHrini] red snapper

ΛΙΘΡΙΝΙ ΨΗΤΟ λιθρίνι ψητό [liTHrini psito] grilled red snapper

ΛΟΥΚΑΝΙΚΑ λουκάνικα [lookanika] sausages

ΛΟΥΚΑΝΙΚΑ ΒΡΑΣΤΑ λουκάνικα βραστά [lookanika vrasta] boiled sausages

ΛΟΥΚΑΝΙΚΑ ΚΑΠΝΙΣΤΑ ΣΤΗ ΣΧΑΡΑ λουκάνικα καπνιστά στη σχάρα [lookanika kapnista sti skhara] grilled smoked sausages

ΛΟΥΚΑΝΙΚΑ ΤΗΓΑΝΗΤΑ λουκάνικα τηγανητά [lookanika tiganita] fried sausages

ΛΟΥΚΟΥΜΑΔΕΣ λουκουμάδες [lookoomathes] doughnuts

ΛΟΥΚΟΥΜΙΑ λουκούμια [lookoomia] Turkish delight

ΜΑΓΕΙΡΙΤΣΑ μαγειρίτσα [mayiritsa] traditional Easter soup made from lambs' intestines

ΜΑΓΙΑ μαγιά [maya] yeast

ΜΑΓΙΟΝΕΖΑ μαγιονέζα [mayoneza] mayonnaise

ΜΑΪΝΤΑΝΟΣ μαϊντανός [maindanos] parsley

ΜΑΚΑΡΟΝΑΚΙ ΚΟΦΤΟ μακαρονάκι κοφτό [makaronaki kofto] macaroni

ΜΑΚΑΡΟΝΙΑ μακαρόνια [makaronia] pasta

ΜΑΚΑΡΟΝΙΑ ΜΕ ΚΙΜΑ μακαρόνια με κιμά [makaronia meh kima] spaghetti bolognaise

ΜΑΚΑΡΟΝΙΑ ΜΕ ΦΡΕΣΚΟ ΒΟΥΤΥΡΟ ΚΑΙ ΠΑΡΜΕΖΑΝΑ μακαρόνια με φρέσκο βούτυρο και παρμεζάνα [makaronia meh fresko vootiro keh parmezana] spaghetti with butter and parmesan cheese

ΜΑΚΑΡΟΝΙΑ ΠΑΣΤΙΤΣΙΟ ΜΕ ΚΙΜΑ μακαρόνια παστίτσιο με κιμά [makaronia pastitsio meh kima] baked pasta dish with minced meat and béchamel

ΜΑΝΙΤΑΡΙΑ μανιτάρια [manitaria] mushrooms

ΜΑΝΙΤΑΡΙΑ ΤΗΓΑΝΗΤΑ μανιτάρια τηγανητά [manitaria tiganita] fried mushrooms

ΜΑΝΟΥΡΙ μανούρι [manoori] hard cheese

ΜΑΝΤΑΡΙΝΙ μανταρίνι [mandarini] satsuma, tangerine

ΜΑΡΓΑΡΙΝΗ μαργαρίνη [margarini] margarine

ΜΑΡΙΔΕΣ ΤΗΓΑΝΗΤΕΣ μαρίδες τηγανητές [marithes tiganites] small fried fish

ΜΑΡΜΕΛΑΔΑ μαρμελάδα [marmelatha] jam, marmalade

ΜΑΡΜΕΛΑΔΑ ΒΕΡΥΚΟΚΚΑ μαρμελάδα βερύκοκκα [marmelatha verikoka] apricot jam

ΜΑΡΜΕΛΑΔΑ ΠΟΡΤΟΚΑΛΙ μαρμελάδα πορτοκάλι

[marmelatha portokali] orange jam

ΜΑΡΜΕΛΑΔΑ ΡΟΔΑΚΙΝΑ μαρμελάδα ροδάκινα [marmelatha pothakina] peach jam

ΜΑΡΜΕΛΑΔΑ ΦΡΑΟΥΛΕΣ μαρμελάδα φράουλες [marmelatha fraooles] strawberry jam

ΜΑΡΟΥΛΙ μαρούλι [marooli] lettuce

ΜΑΡΟΥΛΙΑ ΣΑΛΑΤΑ μαρούλια σαλάτα [maroolia salata] green salad

ΜΕ ΛΑΔΟΛΕΜΟΝΟ με λαδολέμονο [meh latholemono] with olive oil and lemon dressing

ΜΕΛΙ μέλι [meli] honey

ΜΕΛΙΤΖΑΝΕΣ μελιτζάνες [melidzanes] aubergines/ eggplants

ΜΕΛΙΤΖΑΝΕΣ ΓΕΜΙΣΤΕΣ ΜΕ ΚΙΜΑ μελιτζάνες γεμιστές με κιμά [melitzanes yemistes meh kima] aubergines/eggplants stuffed with minced meat

ΜΕΛΙΤΖΑΝΕΣ ΓΙΑΧΝΙ μελιτζάνες γιαχνί [melitzanes yakhni] aubergines/eggplants with tomato and onions

ΜΕΛΙΤΖΑΝΕΣ ΙΜΑΜ ΜΠΑΪΛΝΤΙ μελιτζάνες ιμάμ μπαϊλντί [melitzanes imam baildi] aubergines/eggplants with garlic and tomato

ΜΕΛΙΤΖΑΝΕΣ ΜΟΥΣΑΚΑ μελιτζάνες μουσακά [melidzanes moosaka] layers of aubergine/eggplant and minced meat topped with béchamel

ΜΕΛΙΤΖΑΝΕΣ ΠΑΠΟΥΤΣΑΚΙΑ μελιτζάνες παπουτσάκια [melidzaness papootsakia] stuffed aubergines/eggplants

ΜΕΛΙΤΖΑΝΕΣ ΤΗΓΑΝΗΤΕΣ μελιτζάνες τηγανητές [melitzanes tiganites] fried aubergines/eggplants

ΜΕΛΙΤΖΑΝΟΣΑΛΑΤΑ μελιτζανοσαλάτα [melidzanosalata] puréed aubergine/eggplant dip

ΜΕΛΟΜΑΚΑΡΟΝΑ μελομακάρονα [melomakarona] sweet cakes with cinammon, nuts and syrup

ΜΕΝΟΥ μενού [menoo] menu

ΜΕ ΣΑΛΤΣΑ με σάλτσα [meh saltsa] with sauce, usually tomato sauce

ΜΗΛΑ ΓΕΜΙΣΤΑ μήλα γεμιστά [mila yemista] stuffed apples with cinammon

ΜΗΛΟ μήλο [milo] apple

ΜΗΛΟΠΙΤΤΑ μηλόπιττα [milopita] apple pie

μισοψημένο [misopsimeno] medium (steak)

ΜΟΣΧΑΡΙ μοσχάρι [moskhari] veal; tender beef

ΜΟΣΧΑΡΙ ΒΡΑΣΤΟ μοσχάρι βραστό [moskhari vrasto] veal stew

ΜΟΣΧΑΡΙ ΚΟΚΚΙΝΙΣΤΟ
μοσχάρι κοκκινιστό [moskhari kokinisto] veal in tomato sauce

ΜΟΣΧΑΡΙ ΜΕ ΑΡΑΚΑ
μοσχάρι με αρακά [moskhari meh araka] veal with peas

ΜΟΣΧΑΡΙ ΜΕ ΚΡΙΘΑΡΑΚΙ
μοσχάρι με κριθαράκι [moskhari meh kriTHaraki] veal with pasta

ΜΟΣΧΑΡΙ ΜΕ ΜΕΛΙΤΖΑΝΕΣ μοσχάρι με μελιτζάνες [moskhari meh melitzanes] veal with aubergines/eggplants

ΜΟΣΧΑΡΙ ΜΕ ΜΠΑΜΙΕΣ
μοσχάρι με μπάμιες [moskhari meh bami-es] veal with okra

ΜΟΣΧΑΡΙ ΜΕ ΠΑΤΑΤΕΣ
μοσχάρι με πατάτες [moskhari meh patates] veal with potatoes

ΜΟΣΧΑΡΙ ΜΕ ΠΑΤΑΤΕΣ ΣΤΟ ΦΟΥΡΝΟ μοσχάρι με πατάτες στο φούρνο [moskhari meh patates sto foorno] veal with potatoes cooked in the oven

ΜΟΣΧΑΡΙ ΜΕ ΠΟΥΡΕ
μοσχάρι με πουρέ [moskhari meh pooreh] veal with mashed potatoes

ΜΟΣΧΑΡΙ ΜΕ ΦΑΣΟΛΑΚΙΑ
μοσχάρι με φασολάκια [moskhari meh fasolakia] veal and green beans

ΜΟΣΧΑΡΙ ΡΟΣΜΠΙΦ
μοσχάρι ροσμπίφ [moskhari rosbif] roast beef

ΜΟΣΧΑΡΙΣΙΟΣ ΚΙΜΑΣ
μοσχαρίσιος κιμάς [moskharisios kimas] minced meat

ΜΟΣΧΑΡΙ ΣΝΙΤΖΕΛ ΜΕ ΠΑΤΑΤΕΣ ΤΗΓΑΝΗΤΕΣ
μοσχάρι σνίτζελ με πατάτες τηγανητές [moskhari schnitzel meh patates tiganites] steak and chips/fries

ΜΟΣΧΑΡΙ ΣΝΙΤΖΕΛ ΜΕ ΠΟΥΡΕ μοσχάρι σνίτζελ με πουρέ [moskhari schnitzel meh patates pooreh] steak with mashed potatoes

ΜΟΣΧΑΡΙ ΨΗΤΟ μοσχάρι ψητό [moskhari psito] veal pot roast

ΜΟΥΣΑΚΑΣ μουσακάς [moosakas] moussaka – layers of vegetables and minced meat topped with béchamel sauce

ΜΟΥΣΑΚΑΣ ΠΑΤΑΤΕΣ
μουσακάς πατάτες [moosakas patates] potatoes with minced meat and béchamel

ΜΟΥΣΤΑΡΔΑ μουστάρδα [moostartha] mustard

ΜΟΥΣΤΟΚΟΥΛΟΥΡΑ
μουστοκούλουρα [moostokooloora] Greek biscuits

ΜΠΑΚΑΛΙΑΡΟΣ
μπακαλιάρος [bakaliaros] cod; salt cod; haddock

ΜΠΑΚΑΛΙΑΡΟΣ ΚΡΟΚΕΤΕΣ μπακαλιάρος

κροκέτες [bakaliaros kroketes] haddock croquettes

ΜΠΑΚΑΛΙΑΡΟΣ ΠΛΑΚΙ μπακαλιάρος πλακί [bakaliaros plaki] salted cod cooked in tomato sauce

ΜΠΑΚΑΛΙΑΡΟΣ ΤΗΓΑΝΗΤΟΣ μπακαλιάρος τηγανητός [bakaliaros tiganitos] fried salted cod

ΜΠΑΚΛΑΒΑΔΕΣ μπακλαβάδες [baklavathes] baklava – layers of thin pastry with nuts and syrup

ΜΠΑΚΛΑΒΑΔΕΣ ΜΕ ΚΑΡΥΔΙΑ μπακλαβάδες με καρύδια [baklavathes meh karithia] baklava – layers of thin pastry with walnuts and syrup

ΜΠΑΚΛΑΒΑΣ μπακλαβάς [baklavas] baklava – filo pastry with nuts and syrup

ΜΠΑΜΙΕΣ μπάμιες [bami-es] okra

ΜΠΑΜΙΕΣ ΛΑΔΕΡΕΣ μπάμιες λαδερές [bami-es latheres] okra in olive oil and tomato sauce

ΜΠΑΝΑΝΑ μπανάνα [banana] banana

ΜΠΑΡΜΠΟΥΝΙΑ μπαρμπούνια [barboonia] red mullet

ΜΠΑΡΜΠΟΥΝΙΑ ΠΑΝΕ μπαρμπούνια πανέ [barboonia paneh] breaded red mullet

ΜΠΑΧΑΡΙΚΟ μπαχαρικό [bakhariko] spice

ΜΠΕΖΕΔΕΣ μπεζέδες [bezethes] meringues with cream

ΜΠΕΙΚΟΝ μπέικον [bacon] bacon

ΜΠΕΙΚΟΝ ΚΑΠΝΙΣΤΟ μπέικον καπνιστό [bacon kapnisto] smoked bacon

ΜΠΕΣΑΜΕΛ ΣΑΛΤΣΑ μπεσαμέλ σάλτσα [besamel saltsa] béchamel sauce

ΜΠΙΖΕΛΙΑ μπιζέλια [bizelia] peas

ΜΠΙΣΚΟΤΑ μπισκότα [biskota] biscuits

ΜΠΙΣΚΟΤΑΚΙΑ ΑΛΜΥΡΑ μπισκοτάκια αλμυρά [biskotakia almira] savoury crackers

ΜΠΙΣΚΟΤΑ ΣΟΚΟΛΑΤΑΣ μπισκότα σοκολάτας [biskota sokolatas] chocolate biscuits

ΜΠΙΦΤΕΚΙ μπιφτέκι [bifteki] hamburger; grilled meatballs

ΜΠΟΝ ΦΙΛΕ μπον φιλέ [bon fileh] fillet steak

ΜΠΟΥΓΑΤΣΑ μπουγάτσα [boogatsa] puff pastry with various fillings

ΜΠΟΥΓΑΤΣΑ ΓΛΥΚΙΑ μπουγάτσα γλυκιά [boogatsa glikia] puff pastry with cream and icing sugar

ΜΠΟΥΡΕΚΑΚΙΑ μπουρεκάκια [boorekakia] cheese or minced meat pies

ΜΠΟΥΡΕΚΙ μπουρέκι [booreki] courgette, potato and cheese pie

ΜΠΡΙΑΜΙ μπριάμι [briami]
ratatouille

ΜΠΡΙΑΜΙ ΜΕ
ΚΟΛΟΚΥΘΑΚΙΑ μπριάμι με
κολοκυθάκια [briami meh
kolokiΤΗakia] courgettes/
zucchini cooked with
potatoes in the oven

ΜΠΡΙΖΟΛΑ μπριζόλα [brizola]
chop; steak

ΜΠΡΙΖΟΛΑ ΜΟΣΧΑΡΙΣΙΑ
μπριζόλα μοσχαρίσια [brizola
moskharisia] beef steak

ΜΠΡΙΖΟΛΕΣ μπριζόλες
[brizoles] chops; steaks

ΜΠΡΙΖΟΛΕΣ ΒΟΔΙΝΕΣ ΣΤΗ
ΣΧΑΡΑ μπριζόλες βοδινές
στη σχάρα [brizoles vothines sti
skhara] grilled T-bone
steak

ΜΠΡΙΖΟΛΕΣ ΣΤΟ ΤΗΓΑΝΙ
μπριζόλες στο τηγάνι [brizoles
sto tigani] fried T-bone steak

ΜΠΡΙΖΟΛΕΣ ΧΟΙΡΙΝΕΣ
μπριζόλες χοιρινές [brizoles
khirines] pork chops

ΜΠΡΙΖΟΛΕΣ ΧΟΙΡΙΝΕΣ
ΣΤΗ ΣΧΑΡΑ μπριζόλες
χοιρινές στη σχάρα [brizoles
khirines sti skhara] charcoal-
grilled pork chops

ΜΠΡΟΚΟΛΟ μπρόκολο
[brokolo] broccoli

ΜΥΑΛΑ μυαλά [miala] brains

ΜΥΑΛΑ ΠΑΝΕ μυαλά πανέ
[miala paneh] breaded cows'
brains

ΜΥΔΙΑ μύδια [mithia] mussels

ΜΥΔΙΑ ΤΗΓΑΝΗΤΑ μύδια
τηγανητά [mithia tiganita] fried
mussels

ΝΕΦΡΑ νεφρά [nefra] kidneys

ΝΕΦΡΑ ΨΗΤΑ/ΤΗΓΑΝΗΤΑ
νεφρά ψητά/τηγανητά [nefra
psita/tiganita] grilled/fried
kidneys

ΝΤΟΛΜΑΔΑΚΙΑ
ντολμαδάκια [dolmathakia]
vine leaves stuffed with
minced meat, rice and
herbs

ΝΤΟΛΜΑΔΕΣ ντολμάδες
[dolmathes] vine or cabbage
leaves stuffed with minced
meat and/or rice

ΝΤΟΛΜΑΔΕΣ
ΑΥΓΟΛΕΜΟΝΟ ΜΕ ΚΙΜΑ
ντολμάδες αυγολέμονο με κιμά
[dolmathes avgolemono meh kima]
vine leaves with rice and
minced meat in egg and
lemon sauce

ΝΤΟΛΜΑΔΕΣ ΓΙΑΛΑΝΤΖΙ
ντολμάδες γιαλαντζί [dolmathes
yialantzi] vine leaves stuffed
with rice

ΝΤΟΜΑΤΕΣ ντομάτες
[domates] tomatoes

ΝΤΟΜΑΤΕΣ ΓΕΜΙΣΤΕΣ ΜΕ
ΚΙΜΑ ντομάτες γεμιστές με
κιμά [domates yemistes meh
kima] stuffed tomatoes with
minced meat

ΝΤΟΜΑΤΕΣ ΓΕΜΙΣΤΕΣ ΜΕ
ΡΥΖΙ ντομάτες γεμιστές με
ρύζι [domates yemistes meh rizi]
tomatoes stuffed with rice

ΝΤΟΜΑΤΕΣ ΓΕΜΙΣΤΕΣ
ντομάτες γεμιστές [domates
yemistes] stuffed tomatoes
ΝΤΟΜΑΤΟΣΑΛΑΤΑ
ντοματοσαλάτα [domatosalata]
tomato salad
ΝΤΟΜΑΤΟΣΟΥΠΑ
ντοματόσουπα [domatosoopa]
tomato soup
ΝΤΟΝΑΤΣ ντόνατς [doughnuts]
doughnuts

ΞΗΡΟΙ ΚΑΡΠΟΙ ξηροί καρποί
[xiri karpi] nuts, dried fruit
ΞΙΦΙΑΣ ξιφίας [xifias]
swordfish
ΞΥΔΙ ξύδι [xithi] vinegar

ΟΜΕΛΕΤΑ ομελέτα [omeleta]
omelette
ΟΜΕΛΕΤΑ ΛΟΥΚΑΝΙΚΑ
ομελέτα λουκάνικα [omeleta
lookanika] omelette with
sausages
ΟΡΕΚΤΙΚΑ ορεκτικά
[orektika] hors d'oeuvres,
starters
ΟΣΤΡΑΚΟΕΙΔΗ οστρακοειδή
[ostrako-ithi] shellfish

ΠΑΓΩΤΟ παγωτό [pagoto] ice
cream
ΠΑΓΩΤΟ ΒΕΡΥΚΟΚΚΟ
παγωτό βερύκοκκο [pagoto
verikoko] apricot ice cream
ΠΑΓΩΤΟ ΚΟΚΤΑΙΗΛ
παγωτό κοκταίηλ [pagoto
cocktail] ice cream cocktail
ΠΑΓΩΤΟ ΚΡΕΜΑ παγωτό

κρέμα [pagoto krema] vanilla
ice cream
ΠΑΓΩΤΟ ΜΕ ΣΑΝΤΙΓΥ
παγωτό με σαντιγύ [pagoto meh
sandiyi] ice cream with
whipped cream
ΠΑΓΩΤΟ ΜΟΚΚΑ παγωτό
μόκκα [pagoto moka] coffee-
flavoured ice cream
ΠΑΓΩΤΟ ΜΠΑΝΑΝΑ
παγωτό μπανάνα [pagoto
banana] banana ice cream
ΠΑΓΩΤΟ ΠΑΡΦΑΙ παγωτό
παρφαί [pagoto parfeh] ice
cream parfait
ΠΑΓΩΤΟ ΠΡΑΛΙΝΑ παγωτό
πραλίνα [pagoto pralina]
praline ice cream
ΠΑΓΩΤΟ ΣΟΚΟΛΑΤΑ
παγωτό σοκολάτα [pagoto
sokolata] chocolate ice cream
ΠΑΓΩΤΟ ΦΡΑΟΥΛΑ παγωτό
φράουλα [pagoto fraoola]
strawberry ice cream
ΠΑΓΩΤΟ ΦΥΣΤΙΚΙ παγωτό
φυστίκι [pagoto fistiki]
pistachio ice cream
ΠΑΞΙΜΑΔΙ παξιμάδι
[paximathi] dried, hard bread
ΠΑΝΤΖΑΡΙ παντζάρι
[pandzari] beetroot
ΠΑΠΙΑ πάπια [papia] duck
ΠΑΠΡΙΚΑ πάπρικα [paprika]
paprika
ΠΑΡΜΕΖΑΝΑ παρμεζάνα
[parmezana] parmesan
ΠΑΣΤΑ πάστα [pasta] cake
ΠΑΣΤΑ ΑΜΥΓΔΑΛΟΥ
πάστα αμυγδάλου [pasta

amigthaloo] almond gâteau
ΠΑΣΤΑ ΚΟΡΜΟΣ πάστα
κορμός [pasta kormos]
chocolate log
ΠΑΣΤΑ ΝΟΥΓΚΑΤΙΝΑ
πάστα νουγκατίνα [pasta
noogatin] cream gâteau
ΠΑΣΤΑ ΣΟΚΟΛΑΤΙΝΑ
πάστα σοκολατίνα [pasta
sokolatina] chocolate gâteau
ΠΑΣΤΑ ΦΡΑΟΥΛΑ πάστα
φράουλα [pasta fraoola]
strawberry gâteau
ΠΑΣΤΙΤΣΙΟ παστίτσιο
[pastitsio] macaroni cheese
or lasagne-type dish, with
minced meat and white
sauce
ΠΑΣΤΙΤΣΙΟ ΛΑΖΑΝΙΑ
παστίτσιο λαζάνια [pastitsio
lazania] lasagne
ΠΑΣΤΙΤΣΙΟ ΜΑΚΑΡΟΝΙΑ
ΜΕ ΚΙΜΑ παστίτσιο
μακαρόνια με κιμά [pastitsio
makaronia meh kima] baked
pasta dish with minced
meat and béchamel
ΠΑΣΤΟ παστό [pasto] salted
ΠΑΤΑΤΕΣ πατάτες [patates]
potatoes
ΠΑΤΑΤΕΣ ΓΑΡΝΙΤΟΥΡΑ
πατάτες γαρνιτούρα [patates
garnitoora] potatoes
ΠΑΤΑΤΕΣ ΓΙΑΧΝΙ πατάτες
γιαχνί [patates yakhni]
potatoes cooked with
onion and tomato
ΠΑΤΑΤΕΣ ΚΑΙ
ΚΟΛΟΚΥΘΑΚΙΑ ΣΤΟ

ΦΟΥΡΝΟ πατάτες και
κολοκυθάκια στο φούρνο
[patates keh kolokiтнakia sto
foorno] potatoes, courgettes/
zucchini and tomatoes
baked in the oven
ΠΑΤΑΤΕΣ ΚΟΛΟΚΥΘΙΑ
ΜΟΥΣΑΚΑΣ πατάτες
κολοκύθια μουσακάς [patates
kolokiтнia moosakas] potatoes
with courgettes/zucchini,
minced meat and cheese
sauce
ΠΑΤΑΤΕΣ ΠΟΥΡΕ πατάτες
πουρέ [patates pooreh] mashed
potatoes
ΠΑΤΑΤΕΣ ΡΙΓΑΝΑΤΕΣ
πατάτες ριγανάτες στο φούρνο
[patates riganates sto foorno]
oven-cooked potatoes with
oregano
ΠΑΤΑΤΕΣ ΣΟΥΦΛΕ πατάτες
σουφλέ [patates soofleh]
potato soufflé
ΠΑΤΑΤΕΣ ΣΤΟ ΦΟΥΡΝΟ
ΡΙΓΑΝΑΤΕΣ πατάτες στο
φούρνο ριγανάτες [patates sto
foorno riganates] potatoes
baked in the oven with
oregano, lemon and olive
oil
ΠΑΤΑΤΕΣ ΤΗΓΑΝΙΤΕΣ
πατάτες τηγανιτές [patates
tiganites] chips, French fries
ΠΑΤΑΤΕΣ ΤΣΙΠΣ πατάτες
τσιπς [patates tsips] chips,
French fries
ΠΑΤΑΤΟΣΑΛΑΤΑ
πατατοσαλάτα [patatosalata]

potato salad

ΠΑΤΖΑΡΙΑ πατζάρια [patzaria] beetroot

ΠΑΤΣΑΣ πατσάς [patsas] tripe; soup made from lambs' intestines

ΠΑΤΣΑΣ ΣΟΥΠΑ πατσάς σούπα [patsas soopa] tripe soup

ΠΕΠΟΝΙ πεπόνι [peponi] melon

ΠΕΣΤΡΟΦΑ πέστροφα [pestrofa] trout

ΠΕΣΤΡΟΦΑ ΨΗΤΗ πέστροφα ψητή [pestrofa psiti] grilled trout

ΠΗΧΤΗ πηχτή [pikhti] potted meat

ΠΙΛΑΦΙ πιλάφι [pilafi] rice

ΠΙΛΑΦΙ ΜΕ ΓΑΡΙΔΕΣ πιλάφι με γαρίδες [pilafi meh garithes] shrimp pilaf

ΠΙΛΑΦΙ ΜΕ ΜΥΔΙΑ πιλάφι με μύδια [pilafi meh mithia] pilaf with mussels

ΠΙΛΑΦΙ ΜΕ ΣΑΛΤΣΑ ΝΤΟΜΑΤΑ πιλάφι με σάλτσα ντομάτα [pilafi meh saltsa domata] pilaf with tomato sauce

ΠΙΛΑΦΙ ΤΑΣ-ΚΕΜΠΑΠ πιλάφι τας-κεμπάπ [pilafi tas kebab] rice with cubes of beef in tomato sauce

ΠΙΠΕΡΙ πιπέρι [piperi] pepper (spice)

ΠΙΠΕΡΙΕΣ πιπεριές [piperi-es] peppers

ΠΙΠΕΡΙΕΣ ΓΕΜΙΣΤΕΣ ΜΕ

ΚΙΜΑ πιπεριές γεμιστές με κιμά [piperi-es yemistes meh kima] peppers stuffed with minced meat

ΠΙΠΕΡΙΕΣ ΓΕΜΙΣΤΕΣ ΜΕ ΡΥΖΙ πιπεριές γεμιστές με ρύζι [piperi-es yemistes meh rizi] peppers stuffed with rice

ΠΙΠΕΡΙΕΣ ΓΕΜΙΣΤΕΣ πιπεριές γεμιστές [piperi-es yemistes] stuffed peppers

ΠΙΠΕΡΙΕΣ ΚΟΚΚΙΝΕΣ πιπεριές κόκκινες [piperi-es kokines] red peppers

ΠΙΠΕΡΙΕΣ ΠΡΑΣΙΝΕΣ πιπεριές πράσινες [piperi-es prasines] green peppers

ΠΙΡΟΣΚΙ πιροσκί [piroski] minced meat or sausage rolls

ΠΙΤΣΑ πίτσα [pizza] pizza

ΠΙΤΣΑ ΜΕ ΖΑΜΠΟΝ πίτσα με ζαμπόν [pizza meh zabon] ham pizza

ΠΙΤΣΑ ΜΕ ΜΑΝΙΤΑΡΙΑ πίτσα με μανιτάρια [pizza meh manitaria] mushroom pizza

ΠΙΤΣΑ ΜΕ ΝΤΟΜΑΤΑ ΤΥΡΙ πίτσα με ντομάτα τυρί [pizza meh domata tiri] cheese and tomato pizza

ΠΙΤΣΑ ΣΠΕΣΙΑΛ πίτσα σπέσιαλ [pizza special] special pizza

ΠΙΤΤΑ πίττα [pita] pie

ΠΙΤΤΑ ΜΕ ΚΙΜΑ πίττα με κιμά [pita meh kima] minced meat pie

ΠΛΑΚΙ πλακί [plaki] baked in

the oven in a tomato sauce
πολύ ψημένο [poli psimeno]
overdone
ΠΟΡΤΟΚΑΛΙ πορτοκάλι
[portokali] orange
ΠΟΥΛΕΡΙΚΑ πουλερικά
[poulerika] poultry
ΠΟΥΤΙΓΚΑ πουτίγκα [pootiga]
pudding
ΠΟΥΤΙΓΚΑ ΜΕ ΑΝΑΝΑ
πουτίγκα με ανανά [pootiga meh
anana] pineapple pudding
ΠΟΥΤΙΓΚΑ ΜΕ ΚΑΡΥΔΙΑ
πουτίγκα με καρύδια [pootiga
meh karithia] walnut pudding
ΠΟΥΤΙΓΚΑ ΜΕ ΣΤΑΦΙΔΕΣ
πουτίγκα με σταφίδες [pootiga
meh stafithes] sultana pudding
ΠΡΑΣΑ πράσα [prasa] leeks
ΠΡΑΣΟΠΙΤΤΑ πρασόπιττα
[prasopita] leek pie
ΠΡΩΤΟ ΠΙΑΤΟ πρώτο πιάτο
[proto piato] starter

ΡΑΒΑΝΙ ραβανί [ravani] very
sweet sponge cake
ΡΑΒΙΟΛΙΑ ραβιόλια [raviolia]
ravioli
ΡΙΓΑΝΗ ρίγανη [rigani]
oregano
ΡΟΔΑΚΙΝΟ ροδάκινο
[rothakino] peaches
ΡΟΣΜΠΙΦ ΑΡΝΙ ΜΟΣΧΑΡΙ
ροσμπίφ αρνί μοσχάρι [rozbif
arni moskhari] roast beef, veal
or lamb
ΡΥΖΙ ρύζι [rizi] rice
ΡΥΖΟΓΑΛΟ ρυζόγαλο
[rizogalo] rice pudding

ΡΩΣΙΚΗ ΣΑΛΑΤΑ ρώσικη
σαλάτα [rosiki salata] Russian
salad

ΣΑΛΑΜΙ σαλάμι [salami]
salami
ΣΑΛΑΤΑ σαλάτα [salata] salad
ΣΑΛΑΤΑ
ΑΜΠΕΛΟΦΑΣΟΥΛΑ σαλάτα
αμπελοφάσουλα [salata
abelofasoola] runner bean
salad
ΣΑΛΑΤΑ ΚΟΥΝΟΥΠΙΔΙ
ΒΡΑΣΤΟ σαλάτα κουνουπίδι
βραστό [salata koonoopithi
vrasto] boiled cauliflower
salad
ΣΑΛΑΤΑ ΜΑΡΟΥΛΙΑ
σαλάτα μαρούλια [salata
maroolia] lettuce salad
ΣΑΛΑΤΑ ΝΤΟΜΑΤΕΣ ΚΑΙ
ΑΓΓΟΥΡΙΑ σαλάτα ντομάτες
και αγγούρια [salata domates
keh agooria] tomato and
cucumber salad
ΣΑΛΑΤΑ ΝΤΟΜΑΤΕΣ-
ΠΙΠΕΡΙΕΣ σαλάτα ντομάτες-
πιπεριές [salata domates piperi-
es] tomato and green
pepper salad
ΣΑΛΑΤΑ ΣΠΑΡΑΓΓΙΑ
σαλάτα σπαράγγια [salata
sparagia] asparagus salad
ΣΑΛΑΤΑ ΦΑΣΟΛΙΑ ΞΗΡΑ
σαλάτα φασόλια ξηρά [salata
fasolia xira] butter bean salad
ΣΑΛΑΤΑ ΧΟΡΤΑ
ΒΡΑΣΜΕΝΑ σαλάτα χόρτα
βρασμένα [salata khorta

vrasmena] chicory salad

ΣΑΛΑΤΑ ΧΩΡΙΑΤΙΚΗ
σαλάτα χωριάτικη [salata
khoriatiki] Greek salad –
tomatoes, cucumber,
peppers, feta, olives and
boiled eggs with olive oil
and vinegar dressing

ΣΑΛΙΓΚΑΡΙΑ σαλιγκάρια
[saligaria] snails

ΣΑΛΤΣΑ σάλτσα [saltsa]
sauce

ΣΑΛΤΣΑ ΜΠΕΣΑΜΕΛ
σάλτσα μπεσαμέλ [saltsa
besamel] béchamel sauce

ΣΑΛΤΣΑ ΝΤΟΜΑΤΑ σάλτσα
ντομάτα [saltsa domata]
tomato sauce

ΣΑΜΑΛΙ σάμαλι [samali]
semolina cake with honey

ΣΑΝΤΙΓΥ σαντιγύ [sandiyi]
whipped cream

ΣΑΝΤΟΥΙΤΣ σάντουιτς
[sandwich] sandwich

ΣΑΡΔΕΛΛΕΣ σαρδέλλες
[sartheles] sardines

ΣΑΡΔΕΛΛΕΣ ΛΑΔΙΟΥ
σαρδέλλες λαδιού [sartheles
lathioo] sardines in oil

ΣΕΛΙΝΟ σέλινο [selino]
celery

ΣΙΜΙΓΔΑΛΙ σιμιγδάλι
[simigthali] semolina

ΣΙΡΟΠΙ σιρόπι [siropi] syrup

ΣΚΟΡΔΑΛΙΑ σκορδαλιά
[skorthalia] thick garlic sauce

ΣΚΟΡΔΑΛΙΑ ΜΕ ΨΩΜΙ
σκορδαλιά με ψωμί [skorthalia
meh psomi] thick garlic sauce

made with bread

ΣΚΟΡΔΟ σκόρδο [skortho]
garlic

ΣΟΚΟΛΑΤΑΚΙΑ
σοκολατάκια [sokolatakia] little
chocolate cakes; milk
chocolates

ΣΟΛΟΜΟΣ σολομός [solomos]
salmon

ΣΟΛΟΜΟΣ ΚΑΠΝΙΣΤΟΣ
σολομός καπνιστός [solomos
kapnistos] smoked salmon

ΣΟΥΒΛΑΚΙΑ σουβλάκια
[soovlakia] meat grilled on a
skewer, served in pitta
bread

ΣΟΥΒΛΑΚΙΑ ΑΠΟ ΚΡΕΑΣ
ΑΡΝΙΣΙΟ σουβλάκια από
κρέας αρνίσιο [soovlakia apo
kreas arnisio] lamb
souvlaki/kebab

ΣΟΥΒΛΑΚΙΑ ΑΠΟ ΚΡΕΑΣ
ΜΟΣΧΑΡΙΣΙΟ σουβλάκια
από κρέας μοσχαρίσιο
[soovlakia apo kreas moskharisio]
veal souvlaki/kebab

ΣΟΥΒΛΑΚΙΑ ΑΠΟ ΚΡΕΑΣ
ΧΟΙΡΙΝΟ σουβλάκια από
κρέας χοιρινό [soovlakia apo
kreas khirino] pork souvlaki/
kebab

ΣΟΥΒΛΑΚΙΑ ΝΤΟΝΕΡ ΜΕ
ΠΙΤΤΑ σουβλάκια ντονέρ με
πίττα [soovlaki doner meh pita]
donner kebab with pitta
bread

ΣΟΥΒΛΑΚΙ ΚΑΛΑΜΑΚΙ
σουβλάκι καλαμάκι [soovlaki
kalamaki] shish kebab

ΣΟΥΠΑ σούπα [**soo**pa] soup

ΣΟΥΠΑ ΠΑΤΣΑΣ σούπα πατσάς [**soo**pa pat**sas**] tripe soup

ΣΟΥΠΑ ΡΕΒΥΘΙΑ σούπα ρεβύθια [**soo**pa re**vi**THia] chickpea soup

ΣΟΥΠΑ ΤΡΑΧΑΝΑΣ σούπα τραχανάς [**soo**pa trakha**nas**] milk broth with flour

ΣΟΥΠΑ ΦΑΚΕΣ σούπα φακές [**soo**pa fa**kes**] lentil soup

ΣΟΥΠΑ ΦΑΣΟΛΙΑ σούπα φασόλια [**soo**pa fa**so**lia] bean soup

ΣΟΥΠΑ ΨΑΡΙ σούπα ψάρι [**soo**pa p**sari**] fish soup

ΣΟΥΠΑ ΨΑΡΙ ΑΥΓΟΛΕΜΟΝΟ σούπα ψάρι αυγολέμονο [**soo**pa psari avgo**lemo**no] fish soup with egg and lemon

ΣΟΥΠΕΣ σούπες [**soo**pes] soups

ΣΟΥΠΙΕΣ σουπιές [soopi-**es**] cuttlefish

ΣΟΥΠΙΕΣ ΜΕ ΣΠΑΝΑΚΙ σουπιές με σπανάκι [soopi-**es** meh spa**naki**] cuttlefish and spinach stew

ΣΟΥΠΙΕΣ ΤΗΓΑΝΗΤΕΣ σουπιές τηγανητές [soopi-**es** tigani**tes**] fried cuttlefish

ΣΟΥΣΑΜΙ σουσάμι [soo**sami**] sesame

ΣΟΥΤΖΟΥΚΑΚΙΑ σουτζουκάκια [sootzoo**kaki**a] spicy meatballs in red sauce

ΣΟΥΦΛΕ σουφλέ [soofl**eh**] soufflé

ΣΠΑΓΓΕΤΟ ΜΕ ΦΡΕΣΚΟ ΒΟΥΤΥΡΟ ΚΑΙ ΠΑΡΜΕΖΑΝΑ σπαγγέτο με φρέσκο βούτυρο και παρμεζάνα [spa**ge**to meh fr**esk**o v**oo**tiro keh parme**zana**] spaghetti with butter and parmesan cheese

ΣΠΑΝΑΚΙ σπανάκι [spa**naki**] spinach

ΣΠΑΝΑΚΟΠΙΤΤΑ σπανακόπιττα [spanak**o**pita] spinach (and sometimes feta) in filo pastry

σπάνιος [**spanios**] rare (steak)

ΣΠΑΡΑΓΓΙΑ ΣΑΛΑΤΑ σπαράγγια σαλάτα [spa**rag**ia sa**lata**] asparagus salad

ΣΠΕΣΙΑΛΙΤΕ σπεσιαλιτέ [spesialit**eh**] speciality

ΣΠΛΗΝΑΝΤΕΡΟ σπληνάντερο [splin**ande**ro] intestines stuffed with spleen

ΣΤΑΦΙΔΕΣ σταφίδες [sta**fithes**] dried fruit

ΣΤΑΦΙΔΟΨΩΜΟ σταφιδόψωμο [stafith**opso**mo] bread with raisins

ΣΤΑΦΥΛΙΑ σταφύλια [sta**filia**] grapes

ΣΤΙΦΑΔΟ στιφάδο [sti**fatho**] chopped meat with onions; hare or rabbit stew with onions

ΣΤΟ ΦΟΥΡΝΟ στο φούρνο

[sto **foorno**] baked in the oven

ΣΤΡΕΙΔΙΑ στρείδια [**strithia**] oysters

ΣΥΚΑ σύκα [**sika**] figs

ΣΥΚΩΤΑΚΙΑ συκωτάκια [**sikotakia**] liver

ΣΥΚΩΤΑΚΙΑ ΜΑΡΙΝΑΤΑ συκωτάκια μαρινάτα [**sikotakia marinata**] liver cooked in rosemary

ΣΥΚΩΤΑΚΙΑ ΠΙΛΑΦΙ συκωτάκια πιλάφι [**sikotakia pilafi**] liver pilaf

ΣΥΚΩΤΑΚΙΑ ΣΤΗ ΣΧΑΡΑ συκωτάκια στη σχάρα [**sikotakia sti skhara**] grilled liver

ΣΥΚΩΤΑΚΙΑ ΤΗΓΑΝΗΤΑ συκωτάκια τηγανητά [**sikotakia tiganita**] fried liver

ΣΥΚΩΤΙ ΨΗΤΟ συκώτι ψητό [**sikoti psito**] charcoal-grilled liver

ΣΥΝΑΓΡΙΔΑ ΨΗΤΗ συναγρίδα ψητή [**sinagritha psiti**] grilled sea bream

ΣΦΥΡΙΔΑ ΒΡΑΣΤΗ σφυρίδα βραστή [**sriritha vrasti**] boiled pike

ΣΩΤΕ σωτέ [**soteh**] lightly fried, sautéed

ΤΑΡΑΜΑΣ ταραμάς [**taramas**] cod roe

ΤΑΡΑΜΟΚΕΦΤΕΔΕΣ ταραμοκεφτέδες [**taramokeftethes**] roe pâté balls with spices

ΤΑΡΑΜΟΣΑΛΑΤΑ ταραμοσαλάτα [**taramosalata**] cod roe dip

ΤΑΡΤΑ τάρτα [**tarta**] tart

ΤΑΡΤΑ ΜΕ ΚΕΡΑΣΙΑ τάρτα με κεράσια [**tarta meh kerasia**] cherry tart

ΤΑΡΤΑ ΜΕ ΚΡΕΜΑ ΚΑΙ ΑΜΥΓΔΑΛΑ τάρτα με κρέμα και αμύγδαλα [**tarta meh krema keh amigthala**] cream and almond tart

ΤΑΡΤΑ ΜΕ ΚΡΕΜΑ ΚΑΙ ΚΑΡΥΔΙΑ τάρτα με κρέμα και καρύδια [**tarta meh krema keh karithia**] walnut and cream tart

ΤΑΡΤΑ ΜΕ ΦΡΑΟΥΛΕΣ τάρτα με φράουλες [**tarta meh fraooles**] strawberry tart

ΤΑΡΤΑ ΜΗΛΟΥ τάρτα μήλου [**tarta miloo**] apple tart

ΤΑΣ-ΚΕΜΠΑΠ τας-κεμπάπ [**tas kebab**] spicy lamb cutlets

ΤΑΣ-ΚΕΜΠΑΠ ΠΙΛΑΦΙ τας-κεμπάπ πιλάφι [**tas kebab pilafi**] spicy lamb cutlets pilaf

ΤΖΑΤΖΙΚΙ τζατζίκι [**dzadziki**] yoghurt, cucumber and garlic dip

ΤΗΓΑΝΗΤΟΣ τηγανητός [**tiganitos**] fried

ΤΗΓΑΝΙΤΕΣ τηγανίτες [**tiganites**] pancakes

ΤΗΣ ΚΑΤΣΑΡΟΛΑΣ της κατσαρόλας [**tis katsarolas**] casseroled

ΤΗΣ ΣΟΥΒΛΑΣ της σούβλας [**tis soovlas**] roast on a spit

ΤΗΣ ΣΧΑΡΑΣ της σχάρας [tis skharas] grilled over charcoal

ΤΟΝΝΟΣ τόννος [tonos] tuna

ΤΟΝΝΟΣΑΛΑΤΑ τοννοσαλάτα [tonosalata] tuna salad

ΤΟΣΤ τοστ [tost] toasted sandwich

ΤΟΣΤ ΚΛΑΜΠ τοστ κλαμπ [tost club] toasted club sandwich

ΤΟΣΤ ΜΕ ΑΥΓΟ τοστ με αυγό [tost meh avgo] egg sandwich

ΤΟΣΤ ΜΕ ΖΑΜΠΟΝ τοστ με ζαμπόν [tost meh zabon] toasted ham sandwich

ΤΟΣΤ ΜΕ ΚΟΤΟΠΟΥΛΟ τοστ με κοτόπουλο [tost meh kotopoolo] toasted chicken sandwich

ΤΟΣΤ ΜΕ ΚΡΕΑΣ τοστ με κρέας [tost meh kreas] toasted meat sandwich

ΤΟΣΤ ΜΕ ΜΠΙΦΤΕΚΙ τοστ με μπιφτέκι [tost meh bifteki] toasted hamburger

ΤΟΣΤ ΜΕ ΤΥΡΙ τοστ με τυρί [tost meh tiri] toasted cheese sandwich

ΤΟΥ ΑΤΜΟΥ του ατμού [too atmoo] steamed

ΤΟΥΡΣΙ τουρσί [toorsi] pickled

ΤΟΥΡΤΑ τούρτα [toorta] gâteau

ΤΟΥΡΤΑ ΑΜΥΓΔΑΛΟΥ τούρτα αμυγδάλου [toorta amigthaloo] almond gâteau

ΤΟΥΡΤΑ ΚΡΕΜΑ ΜΕ ΦΡΑΟΥΛΕΣ τούρτα κρέμα με φράουλες [toorta krema meh fraooles] strawberry cream gâteau

ΤΟΥΡΤΑ ΜΟΚΚΑ τούρτα μόκκα [toorta moka] coffee gâteau

ΤΟΥΡΤΑ ΝΟΥΓΚΑΤΙΝΑ τούρτα νουγκατίνα [toorta noogatina] nougat gâteau

ΤΟΥΡΤΑ ΣΑΝΤΙΓΥ τούρτα σαντιγύ [toorta sandiyi] whipped cream gâteau

ΤΟΥΡΤΑ ΣΟΚΟΛΑΤΑΣ τούρτα σοκολάτας [toorta sokolatas] chocolate gâteau

ΤΡΟΥΦΑΚΙΑ τρουφάκια [troofakia] small chocolate fudge cake

ΤΣΙΠΟΥΡΕΣ τσιπούρες [tsipoores] sea bream

ΤΣΙΠΟΥΡΕΣ ΨΗΤΕΣ τσιπούρες ψητές [tsipoores psites] roast sea bream

ΤΣΙΠΣ τσιπς [tsips] crisps, (US) potato chips

ΤΣΟΥΡΕΚΙ τσουρέκι [tsooreki] light sponge

ΤΣΟΥΡΕΚΙΑ τσουρέκια [tsoorekia] sweet bread with fresh butter (Christmas/Easter dish)

ΤΥΡΙ τυρί [tiri] cheese

ΤΥΡΙΑ τυριά [tiria] cheese

ΤΥΡΟΠΙΤΤΑ τυρόπιττα [tiropita] cheese and egg in filo pastry

ΤΥΡΟΠΙΤΤΑΚΙΑ
τυροπιττάκια [tiropitakia] small
cheese pies

ΦΑΒΑ φάβα [fava] chick pea
soup
ΦΑΚΕΣ φακές [fakes] lentil
soup
ΦΑΣΟΛΑΔΑ φασολάδα
[fasolatha] bean soup with
celery, carrots and tomatoes
ΦΑΣΟΛΑΚΙΑ φασολάκια
[fasolakia] green beans
ΦΑΣΟΛΑΚΙΑ ΛΑΔΕΡΑ
φασολάκια λαδερά [fasolakia
lathera] green beans in olive
oil and tomato sauce
ΦΑΣΟΛΑΚΙΑ ΦΡΕΣΚΑ
ΓΙΑΧΝΙ φασολάκια φρέσκα
γιαχνί [fasolakia freska yakhni]
runner beans with onion
and tomato
ΦΑΣΟΛΑΚΙΑ ΦΡΕΣΚΑ
ΣΑΛΑΤΑ φασολάκια φρέσκα
σαλάτα [fasolakia freska salata]
runner bean salad
ΦΑΣΟΛΙΑ φασόλια [fasolia]
beans
ΦΑΣΟΛΙΑ ΓΙΓΑΝΤΕΣ
ΓΙΑΧΝΙ φασόλια γίγαντες
γιαχνί [fasolia yigandes yakhni]
butter beans with onion
and tomato
ΦΑΣΟΛΙΑ ΓΙΓΑΝΤΕΣ ΣΤΟ
ΦΟΥΡΝΟ φασόλια γίγαντες
στο φούρνο [fasolia yigandes sto
foorno] oven-cooked butter
beans
ΦΑΣΟΛΙΑ ΓΙΓΑΝΤΕΣ

φασόλια γίγαντες [fasolia
yigandes] large dried beans
in tomato sauce
ΦΑΣΟΛΙΑ ΣΟΥΠΑ φασόλια
σούπα [fasolia soopa] bean
soup
ΦΕΤΑ φέτα [feta] feta cheese
ΦΙΛΕ ΜΙΝΙΟΝ φιλέ μινιόν
[fileh minion] thin fillet steak
ΦΙΛΕΤΟ φιλέτο [fileto] fillet
steak
ΦΛΟΓΕΡΕΣ ΜΕ ΚΡΕΜΑ
φλογέρες με κρέμα [floyeres
meh krema] round sweets
filled with cream
ΦΟΝΤΑΝ φοντάν [fondan]
sweets
ΦΟΝΤΑΝ ΑΜΥΓΔΑΛΟΥ
φοντάν αμυγδάλου [fondan
amigthaloo] almond sweets
ΦΟΝΤΑΝ ΑΠΟ ΚΑΡΥΔΑ
φοντάν από καρύδα [fondan apo
karitha] coconut sweets
ΦΟΝΤΑΝ ΑΠΟ ΚΑΡΥΔΙΑ
φοντάν από καρύδια [fondan
apo karithia] walnut sweets
ΦΟΝΤΑΝ ΙΝΔΙΚΗΣ
ΚΑΡΥΔΑΣ φοντάν ινδικής
καρύδας [fondan inthikis karithas]
coconut sweets
ΦΟΝΤΑΝ ΠΟΡΤΟΚΑΛΙΟΥ
φοντάν πορτοκαλιού [fondan
portokali-oo] orange sweets
ΦΟΥΝΤΟΥΚΙΑ φουντούκια
[foondookia] hazelnuts
ΦΡΑΟΥΛΕΣ φράουλες [fra-
ooles] strawberries
ΦΡΑΟΥΛΕΣ ΜΕ ΣΑΝΤΙΓΥ
φράουλες με σαντιγύ [fra-ooles

meh sandiyi] strawberries
with whipped cream

ΦΡΙΚΑΣΕ ΑΡΝΙ φρικασέ αρνί
[frikaseh arni] lamb cooked in
lettuce with cream sauce

ΦΡΟΥΙ-ΓΚΛΑΣΕ φρουί-
γκλασέ [frooi-glaseh] dried
assorted fruits with sugar

ΦΡΟΥΤΑ φρούτα [froota]
fruit

ΦΡΟΥΤΟΣΑΛΑΤΑ
φρουτοσαλάτα [frootosalata]
fruit salad

ΦΡΥΓΑΝΙΑ φρυγανιά [frigania]
toast

ΦΡΥΓΑΝΙΕΣ φρυγανιές
[frigani-es] French toast

ΦΥΛΛΟ ΠΙΤΤΑΣ φύλλο
πίττας [filo pitas] filo pastry

ΦΥΣΤΙΚΙΑ φυστίκια [fistikia]
peanuts

ΦΥΣΤΙΚΙΑ ΑΙΓΙΝΗΣ
φυστίκια Αιγίνης [fistikia Eyinis]
pistachios

ΧΑΒΙΑΡΙ χαβιάρι [khaviari]
caviar

ΧΑΛΒΑΣ χαλβάς [khalvas]
halva, sweet made from
semolina, sesame seeds, nuts
and honey

ΧΑΜΠΟΥΡΓΚΕΡ
χάμπουργκερ [khamburger]
hamburger

ΧΗΝΑ χήνα [khina] goose

ΧΟΙΡΙΝΟ χοιρινό [khirino]
pork

ΧΟΙΡΙΝΟ ΜΕ ΣΕΛΙΝΟ
χοιρινό με σέλινο [khirino meh

selino] pork casserole with
celery

ΧΟΙΡΙΝΟ ΠΑΣΤΟ χοιρινό
παστό [khirino pasto] salted
pork

ΧΟΙΡΙΝΟ ΣΟΥΒΛΑΣ χοιρινό
σούβλας [khirino soovlas] pork
on the spit

ΧΟΙΡΙΝΟ ΣΤΗ ΣΧΑΡΑ
χοιρινό στη σχάρα [khirino sti
skhara] grilled pork

ΧΟΙΡΙΝΟ ΦΟΥΡΝΟΥ ΜΕ
ΠΑΤΑΤΕΣ χοιρινό φούρνου
με πατάτες [khirino foornoo meh
patates] roast pork with
potatoes

ΧΟΡΤΑ ΒΡΑΣΜΕΝΑ
ΣΑΛΑΤΑ χόρτα βρασμένα
σαλάτα [khorta vrasmena salata]
boiled chicory salad

ΧΟΡΤΑΡΙΚΑ χορταρικά
[khortarika] vegetables

ΧΟΡΤΟΣΟΥΠΑ χορτόσουπα
[khortosoopa] vegetable
soup

ΧΤΑΠΟΔΑΚΙ ΞΥΔΑΤΟ
χταποδάκι ξυδάτο [khtapothaki
xithato] pickled octopus

ΧΤΑΠΟΔΙ χταπόδι [khtapothi]
octopus

ΧΤΑΠΟΔΙ ΒΡΑΣΤΟ χταπόδι
βραστό [khtapothi vrasto]
boiled octopus

ΧΤΑΠΟΔΙ ΚΡΑΣΑΤΟ
χταπόδι κρασάτο [khtapothi
krasato] octopus in wine

ΧΤΑΠΟΔΙ ΜΕ
ΜΑΚΑΡΟΝΑΚΙ χταπόδι με
μακαρονάκι [khtapothi meh

makaron**aki**] octopus with macaroni

ΧΤΑΠΟΔΙ ΠΙΛΑΦΙ χταπόδι πιλάφι [khtap**o**thi pil**a**fi] octopus pilaf

ΧΤΑΠΟΔΙ ΣΤΙΦΑΔΟ χταπόδι στιφάδο [khtap**o**thi stif**a**tho] octopus with small onions

ΧΥΛΟΠΙΤΕΣ χυλοπίτες [khilop**i**tes] tagliatelle

ΧΥΛΟΠΙΤΕΣ ΜΕ ΒΟΥΤΥΡΟ ΚΑΙ ΤΥΡΙ χυλοπίτες με βούτυρο και τυρί [khilop**i**tes meh v**oo**tiro keh tir**i**] tagliatelle with butter and cheese

ΧΥΛΟΠΙΤΕΣ ΜΕ ΚΙΜΑ χυλοπίτες με κιμά [khilop**i**tes meh kim**a**] tagliatelle with minced meat sauce

ΧΥΛΟΠΙΤΕΣ ΜΕ ΚΟΤΟΠΟΥΛΟ χυλοπίτες με κοτόπουλο [khilop**i**tes meh kot**o**poolo] tagliatelle with chicken

ΧΩΡΙΑΤΙΚΗ ΣΑΛΑΤΑ χωριάτικη σαλάτα [khori**a**tiki sal**a**ta] Greek salad – tomatoes, cucumber, peppers, feta, olives and boiled eggs with olive oil and vinegar dressing

ΨΑΡΙ ψάρι [ps**a**ri] fish

ΨΑΡΙ ΒΡΑΣΤΟ ΜΑΓΙΟΝΕΖΑ ψάρι βραστό μαγιονέζα [ps**a**ri vrast**o** mayon**e**za] steamed fish with mayonnaise

ΨΑΡΙΑ ψάρια [ps**a**ria] fish

ΨΑΡΙΑ ΓΛΩΣΣΕΣ ΒΡΑΣΤΕΣ ΜΕ ΑΥΓΟΛΕΜΟΝΟ ψάρια γλώσσες βραστές με αυγολέμονο [ps**a**ria gl**o**ses vrast**e**s meh avgol**e**mono] steamed sole with oil and lemon

ΨΑΡΙΑ ΜΑΡΙΝΑΤΑ ψάρια μαρινάτα [ps**a**ria marin**a**ta] marinated fish

ΨΑΡΙΑ ΤΗΓΑΝΗΤΑ ψάρια τηγανητά [ps**a**ria tigan**i**ta] fried fish

ΨΑΡΙΑ ΨΗΤΑ ΣΤΗ ΣΧΑΡΑ ψάρια ψητά στη σχάρα [ps**a**ria psit**a** sti skh**a**ra] charcoal-grilled fish

ΨΑΡΟΣΟΥΠΑ ψαρόσουπα [psar**o**soopa] fish soup

ΨΗΤΟ ψητό [ps**i**to] grilled over charcoal; oven-roasted

ΨΗΤΟ ΣΤΗ ΣΧΑΡΑ ψητό στη σχάρα [ps**i**to sti skh**a**ra] grilled

ΨΩΜΑΚΙ ψωμάκι [psom**a**ki] roll

ΨΩΜΙ ψωμί [psom**i**] bread

ΨΩΜΙ ΑΣΠΡΟ ψωμί άσπρο [psom**i** aspro] white bread

ΨΩΜΙ ΓΙΑ ΤΟΣΤ ψωμί γιά τοστ [psom**i** ya tost] sliced bread

ΨΩΜΙ ΜΑΥΡΟ ψωμί μαύρο [psom**i** mavro] brown bread

ΩΜΟΣ ωμός [om**os**] raw

Menu
Reader:
Drink

Essential Terms

beer i bira
bottle to bookali
brandy to koniak
coffee o kafes
cup: a cup of ... ena flidzani ...
fruit juice o khimos frooton
gin to tzin
 a gin and tonic ena tzin meh tonik
glass: a glass of ... ena potiri ...
milk to gala
mineral water to emfialomeno nero
orange juice i portokalatha
red wine to kokino krasi
rosé to rozeh
soda (water) i sotha
soft drink to anapsiktiko
sugar i zakhari
tea to tsa-i
tonic (water) to tonik
vodka i votka
water to nero
whisky to whisky
white wine to aspro krasi
wine to kras
wine list o katalogos ton krasion

another ..., please ali mia ..., parakalo

ΑΕΡΙΟΥΧΟ αεριούχο
[aeriookho] fizzy
ΑΛΚΟΟΛ αλκοόλ [alko-ol]
alcohol
ΑΝΑΝΑΣ ΧΥΜΟΣ ανανάς
χυμός [ananas khimos]
pineapple juice
ΑΝΑΨΥΚΤΙΚΟ αναψυκτικό
[anapsiktiko] soft drink
ΑΠΕΡΙΤΙΦ απεριτίφ [aperitif]
aperitif
ΑΣΠΡΟ ΚΡΑΣΙ άσπρο κρασί
[aspro krasi] white wine

ΒΟΤΚΑ βότκα [votka] vodka
ΒΥΣΣΙΝΑΔΑ βυσσινάδα
[visinatha] black cherry juice

ΓΑΛΑ γάλα [gala] milk
ΓΑΛΑ ΚΑΚΑΟ γάλα κακάο
[gala kakao] chocolate milk
ΓΑΛΛΙΚΟΣ ΚΑΦΕΣ γαλλικός
καφές [galikos kafes] filter
coffee; French coffee
ΓΛΥΚΟ ΚΡΑΣΙ γλυκό κρασί
[gliko krasi] sweet wine

ΕΛΛΗΝΙΚΟΣ ΚΑΦΕΣ
ελληνικός καφές [elinikos
kafes] Greek coffee

ΖΕΣΤΗ ΣΟΚΟΛΑΤΑ ζεστή
σοκολάτα [zesti sokolata] hot
chocolate

ΚΑΚΑΟ κακάο [kakao] cocoa
ΚΑΤΑΛΟΓΟΣ ΚΡΑΣΙΩΝ
κατάλογος κρασιών [katalogos
krasion] wine list

ΚΑΦΕΣ καφές [kafes] coffee
ΚΑΦΕΣ ΜΕΤΡΙΟΣ καφές
μέτριος [kafes metrios]
medium-sweet Greek
coffee
ΚΑΦΕΣ ΒΑΡΥΣ ΓΛΥΚΟΣ
καφές βαρύς γλυκός [kafes
varis glikos] sweet Greek
coffee
ΚΑΦΕΣ ΜΕ ΓΑΛΑ καφές με
γάλα [kafes meh gala] coffee
with milk
ΚΟΚΑ ΚΟΛΑ κόκα κόλα
[koka kola] Coca-Cola®
ΚΟΚΚΙΝΟ ΚΡΑΣΙ κόκκινο
κρασί [kokino krasi] red wine
ΚΟΚΤΕΗΛ κοκτέηλ [kokteil]
cocktail
ΚΟΝΙΑΚ κονιάκ [koniak]
brandy
ΚΡΑΣΙ κρασί [krasi] wine
ΚΡΑΣΙ ΑΣΠΡΟ κρασί άσπρο
[krasi aspro] white wine
ΚΡΑΣΙ ΚΟΚΚΙΝΟ κρασί
κόκκινο [krasi kokino] red
wine
ΚΡΑΣΙ ΜΑΥΡΟΔΑΦΝΗ
κρασί μαυροδάφνη [krasi
mavrothafni] sweet red wine
ΚΡΑΣΙ ΡΕΤΣΙΝΑ κρασί
ρετσίνα [krasi rotsina] retsina
ΚΡΑΣΙ ΡΟΖΕ κρασί ροζέ
[krasi rozeh] rosé wine
ΚΡΑΣΙ ΤΟΥ ΜΑΓΑΖΙΟΥ
κρασί του μαγαζιού [krasi too
magazi-oo] house wine

ΛΕΜΟΝΑΔΑ λεμονάδα
[lemonatha] lemonade

ΛΙΚΕΡ λικέρ [liker] liqueur

ΜΕΤΑΛΛΙΚΟ ΝΕΡΟ
μεταλλικό νερό [metaliko nero]
mineral water

ΜΗΛΟΧΥΜΟΣ μηλοχυμός
[milokhimos] apple juice

ΜΠΥΡΑ μπύρα [bira] beer,
lager

ΝΕΣΚΑΦΕ νέσκαφέ [neskafeh]
Nescafé®, instant coffee

ΝΕΣΚΑΦΕ ΦΡΑΠΕ νέσκαφέ
φραπέ [neskafeh frapeh] iced
coffee

ΝΕΡΟ νερό [nero] water

ΝΤΟΜΑΤΑ ΧΥΜΟΣ ντομάτα
χυμός [domata khimos] tomato
juice

ΟΥΖΟ ούζο [oozo] ouzo

ΟΥΙΣΚΥ ουίσκυ whisky,
scotch

ΠΑΓΑΚΙ παγάκι [pagaki] ice
cube

ΠΑΓΟΣ πάγος [pagos] ice

ΠΟΡΤΟΚΑΛΑΔΑ
πορτοκαλάδα [portokalatha]
orange juice

ΠΟΡΤΟΚΑΛΙ ΧΥΜΟΣ
πορτοκάλι χυμός [portokali
khimos] orange juice

ΠΟΤΑ ποτά [pota] drinks

ΡΑΚΗ ρακή [raki] strong
spirit, eau-de-vie

ΡΕΤΣΙΝΑ ρετσίνα [retsina]
retsina

ΡΟΖΕ ΚΡΑΣΙ ροζέ κρασί
[rozeh krasi] rosé wine

ΡΟΥΜΙ ρούμι [roomi] rum

ΣΤΑΦΥΛΙ ΧΥΜΟΣ σταφύλι
χυμός [stafili khimos] grape
juice

ΤΖΙΝ τζιν [tzin] gin

ΤΖΙΝ ΜΕ ΤΟΝΙΚ τζιν με
τόνικ [tzin meh tonik] gin and
tonic

ΤΣΑΙ τσάι [tsa-i] tea

ΤΣΑΙ ΜΕ ΛΕΜΟΝΙ τσάι με
λεμόνι [tsa-i meh lemoni]
lemon tea

ΤΣΙΠΟΥΡΟ τσίπουρο [tsipooro]
type of ouzo

ΦΡΑΠΕ φραπέ [frapeh] iced
coffee

ΧΥΜΟΣ χυμός [khimos] juice

ΧΩΡΙΣ ΚΑΦΕΪΝΗ χωρίς
καφεΐνη [khoris kafeini]
decaffeinated